MARCEL PROUST

Marcel Proust

ROGER SHATTUCK

Princeton University Press
Princeton, New Jersey

Published by Princeton University Press,
41 William Street, Princeton, New Jersey 08540
Copyright © 1974 by Roger Shattuck

First Princeton Paperback printing, 1982
LCC 81-47990
ISBN 0-691-06513-6
ISBN 0-691-01391-8 pbk.

Printed in the United States of America by Princeton
University Press, Princeton, New Jersey

Reprinted by arrangement with the Viking Press

CONTENTS

DIAGRAMS

NOTE ON TEXTS
AND TRANSLATIONS

Five different English-language editions of Proust's novel are in circulation carrying the unsatisfactory title, *Remembrance of Things Past*. In all editions except the last, the first six volumes are translated by C. K. Scott Moncrieff:

Modern Library, 7 volumes, 1924-32: final volume translated by Frederick A. Blossom

Random House, 7 volumes in 2, 1932: final volume translated by Frederick A. Blossom

Chatto & Windus, 7 volumes, 1922-70: final volume translated by Andreas Mayor

Vintage Books, 7 volumes, 1971: final volume translated by Andreas Mayor

Random House, 7 volumes in 3, 1981: translated by C. K. Scott Moncrieff and Terence Kilmartin, last volume translated by Andreas Mayor

Any of the five editions is satisfactory. Presumably the latest Moncrieff-Kilmartin-Mayor version will appear in paperback and gradually become standard. This revised edition offers numerous improvements (including synopses) along with remaining flaws. I deal at length with the translations in "Kilmartin's Way," *New York Review of Books*, June 25, 1981.

Because of the multiplicity of English-language editions, and because the original French text of quotations has not been included here, all page references given in parentheses are to the standard French editions of Proust's works. (There is also a seven-volume edition of the novel in Livre de Poche.) The following abbreviations are used:

JS: Jean Santeuil précédé de *Les Plaisirs et les jours*. Paris: Gallimard, Bibliothèque de la Pléiade, 1971.

CSB: Contre Sainte-Beuve précédé de *Pastiches et mélanges* et suivi de *Essais et articles*. Paris: Gallimard, Bibliothèque de la Pléiade, 1971.

I: *A la recherche du temps perdu*. Paris: Gallimard, Bibliothèque de la Pléiade, 1954, tome I.
II: ———, tome II.
III: ———, tome III.

Translations from Proust quoted in the text are by Roger Shattuck.

BIOGRAPHICAL NOTE

1871	Proust born July 10. Brother born two years later.
1880	First asthma attack.
1882–90	Studies at Lycée Condorcet. Military service. Brief university study.
1890–1907	Social climbing. Publishes stories and essays in literary reviews and newspapers. Influence of Robert de Montesquiou. *Les Plaisirs et les jours* published in 1896. Discovers Ruskin's work and translates two of his books. Two versions of a novel remain unpublished. Father and mother die (1903, 1905).
1908–13	Intense work on a new draft of his novel; "finished" in 1912. First volume published in 1913. Second in preparation.
1914–22	Constant writing and poor health. World acclaim after the Goncourt Prize is awarded to second volume in 1919. Two more volumes published before Proust dies on November 18, 1922.
1923–27	Appearance of remaining three volumes.

The Work and Its Author

i

Among the handful of genuine classics produced in this century, Marcel Proust's *In Search of Lost Time* is the most oceanic—and the least read. Publishers' sales figures in all countries confirm the latter observation. Let us begin on this bleak terrain and work back gradually to what is compelling and often entertaining in Proust. To ignore what impedes easy access to his work would be foolish. Proust's substantial reputation as an extreme case of something—longwindedness, psychological vivisection, the snobbery of letters, salvation by memory—rests not on wide readership but on a myth of uniqueness defended by a dedicated few. In an era when the significance and the privileged status of the work of art are being cast into doubt, this ultimate monument to the artistic vocation, banked high on all sides by interpretation and biography, refuses to sink back into the sands of time.

OBSTACLES AND INDUCEMENTS

The inordinate length of Proust's novel (3000 pages) goes a long way toward explaining the scarcity of readers. Even Russian novelists usually limit themselves to half that length. Balzac's one-hundred-volume print-out of all French society comes in separate packages; the links between the volumes serve as a special reward for the perservering. The first two sections of Proust's novel, "Combray" and "Swann in Love," can stand separately and have earned many admirers. Yet true believers insist that there is no substitute for the cumulative effect of the whole work. Understandably, many readers hesitate to make the investment of time and attention required to assimilate even a fraction of the whole.

Compounding the challenge of sheer magnitude, there is Proust's style. His transcontinental sentences contribute to the appearance of a motionless plot. The original French is no easier than the translations. How can one follow a story line (if there really is one) through such labyrinthine prose? Furthermore, Proust originally planned to publish his novel in two compact volumes in rapid succession. The five-year interval of war that occurred after the appearance of the first volume and the tremendous expansion of the text it led to, forced him to change his plans. Published between 1913 and 1927 in multiple installments, the *Search* is basically divided into seven volumes of very unequal length. For a decade and a half critics tried to judge the whole from a few parts. As a result, Proust had to serve as the sole qualified guide to his own uncompleted work. Endless letters, several newspaper interviews, and over a hundred pages in his last volume are devoted to rebutting his critics and explaining how he was constructing the vast edifice. The opening sections, he insists, give a distorted impression of the whole. Everything hangs on the conclusion. Gradually, Proust's description of his work has been validated by three generations of critics. But for fifteen years his work appeared piecemeal in the face of enormous odds against comprehension. It looks almost like a conspiracy against readers.

These basic circumstances surrounding Proust's work have spawned a set of secondary misunderstandings. Many of them can be traced to remarks by early critics, some of whom were sympathetic. Edmund Wilson, the earliest and most perceptive of American critics, admired Proust's work; yet he called the *Search* "one of the gloomiest books ever written." In this instance his critical acumen failed him. Proust's novel earns its place in literature as a great comic tale, punctuated with smiles and guffaws. Henry James produced a formula that has been well received: "inconceivable boredom associated with the most extreme ecstasy which it is possible to imagine." It is hard to read the sentence as anything but dispraise. The volume of "tributes" a dozen English writers devoted to Proust in 1923 sows even more confusion. Joseph Conrad finds intellectual analysis at its most creative, but "no reverie, no emotion. . . ." Three pages later, George Saintsbury insists on a "constant relapse upon—and sometimes self-restriction to—a sort of dream element." Had they read the same author? Arnold Bennett wrote more in outrage than in tribute and could not excuse "the clumsy centipedalian crawling of the interminable sentences." Then there is Aldous Huxley's description (though not in this same volume) of Proust as a hermaphrodite, toadlike creature spooning his own tepid juice over his face and body. On the centenary of Proust's birth in 1971 *The New York Times Book Review* assigned its front page to the novelist William H. Gass for a discussion of Proust's work. Gass's rancorous article adds little to Bennet's comments.

> . . . there is no special truth in him. . . . Proust writes a careless self-indulgent prose, doesn't he? . . . Epithet follows epithet like tea cakes in flutes of paper. . . .

It is a style that endangers the identity of the self in its reckless expressions of it.   —*July 11, 1971*

The fact that many of these critics contradict one another does not discredit them collectively or individually. But it does mean that we must beware of incomprehension and prejudice. The most persistent negative judgments of Proust can be reduced to two. First, Proust's work is boring because of slackness in both style and construction. Second, the moral universe of Proust's work never breaks free from the attitude of a spoiled, sickly, adolescent snob born to wealth on the fringes of high culture and high society. To these criticisms I shall add two more that are less frequently voiced.

Clausewitz describes war as the continuation of policy by other means. Like many authors, Proust often treated writing as a continuation of life by other means. The word can conquer where the flesh is weak. Having discovered this path, Proust became one of the great megalomaniacs of literature, unwilling (in part because of his semi-invalid condition in later years) to relinquish any small hold he could gain over other people by writing. In his letters he often mixed honey with acid. He dominated his mother with inter-bedroom memoranda and his friends with pitiful pleas for help. He sought to hypnotize his readers and to command the world from his sickbed. This sensitive weakling sought power and won it.

The last stricture is closely related. From Proust's writings, as from an electric generator, flows a powerful current always ready to shock not only our morality but our very sense of humanity. He undermines individual character as the source of anything coherent or reliable in our behavior. Love and friendship, honesty and sexuality crumble into mockeries of human relationships. Except for Marcel's immediate family, no one in the *Search* escapes the curses of selfishness, self-contempt, and snobbery. Few grounds for human dignity survive Proust's touch. The inhumanity of artistic creation seems to triumph over everything.

Quite deliberately I have begun with a harsh and seriously distorted version of Proust's stature. Each of the charges could be rebutted and probably disproved. But I feel it is wise not to affirm his innocence but to ask for a far more illuminating verdict: *guilty—but not as charged*. For Proust had the power to modify, as he went along, the laws under which he wrote and under which he asks us to read. Neither the novel form nor "human nature" remains unchanged after he has passed. The problem is to detect and measure the shifts. Snobbery, megalomania, and instability of character do indeed loom large in the world Proust creates. The first task of the critic is to prevent the uninitiated reader from reacting against these elements before he understands how they fit together to make a remarkably coherent work of art.

No single theory or approach will make Proust easily and quickly available to all inquiring minds. The very resistance of his work to simplification and analysis constitutes its most evident general characteristic. Beyond this feature, however, we discover endless contradictions in the *Search*. Walt Whitman lived at peace with the fact that he contradicted himself. He said that he contained multitudes. Proust asks the next question. How much of his multitudinous self can a person be or embody at one time? The first answer is plain common sense: it all depends. It depends on many things, from chance and volition to memory and forgetting. The second answer is categorical. No matter how we go about it, *we cannot be all of ourselves all at once*. Narrow light beams of perception and of recollection illuminate the present and the past in vivid fragments. The clarity of those fragments is sometimes very great. They may even overlap and reinforce one another. However, to summon our entire self into simultaneous existence lies beyond our powers. We live by synechdoche, by cycles of being. More profoundly than any other novelist, Proust perceived this state of things and worked as an economist of the personality. In himself and in others he observed its fluctuations and partial realizations. Through habit and convention we may find security in "the immobility of the things around us" (I, 6). Yet it affords only temporary refuge. We yield with excitement, apprehension, and a deeper sense of existence to the great wheeling motion of experience. On a single page Proust refers to that endless shifting process as both "the secret of the future" and "the darkness we can never penetrate" (II, 67). He also has a word for it: our lot is "intermittence," the only steady state we know.

As in life itself, the scope of action and reflection encountered in the *Search* exceeds the capacity of one mind to hold it all together at one time. Thus the novel embodies and manifests the principle of intermittence: to live means to perceive different and often conflicting aspects of reality. This iridescence never resolves itself completely into a unitive point of view. Accordingly, it is possible to project out of the *Search* itself a series of putative and intermittent authors. Precisely that has happened. The portraitist of an expiring society, the artist of romantic reminiscence, the narrator of the laminated "I," the classicist of formal structure—all these figures are to be found in Proust, approximately in that order of historical occurrence. All are present as discernible components of his vision and his creation. His principle of intermittence anticipates such veerings of critical emphasis. It is in the middle of a literary discussion that his Narrator observes, *"On ne se réalise que successivement"* (III, 380). It really means: one finds, not oneself, but a succession of selves. Similarly, Proust's work is still going on in our gradual discovery of it.[1]

[1] Critical attention to Proust shows no sign of flagging and has begun to dispel the misconceptions and to probe the

THE LIFE OF AN *Enfant Nerveux*

If forced to make the distinction, most of us would indicate a deeper and more lasting interest in people than in works. We ascribe greatness or goodness more readily to an individual person, accountable for the actions of his whole life, than to a deed detached from its context of individual agency and motivation in a person's life. One could with good reason interpret the history of Western civilization as a sustained attempt to divert us toward a concern with good works, both ethical and artistic. Religion and esthetics have developed along curiously parallel paths. Yet fundamentally our attention directs itself toward men and women, their temperaments and their lives. Only a lifetime provides an adequate unit of significance and value. (We have also cultivated a powerful materialist doctrine: the tendency to judge a man not by what he is or does, but by what he *owns*.)

It is not surprising, therefore, that the biography of so curious a figure as Proust should exert a fascination equal to that of his literary work. I suspect that more readers have read through George D. Painter's biography of Proust than have reached the end of the *Search*. Furthermore, Proust's work lies in very close proximity to his life. On two occasions toward the end of the novel, when he supplied a first name for his Narrator-hero, Proust used his own, Marcel (III, 75, 157). Writers' lives are neither holy ground nor useless appendages. Without some knowledge of Proust's biography, we would remain blind to a whole section of countryside surrounding his work and lending meaning to it.

Proust's life began with the Paris Commune of 1871

---

paradoxes I have mentioned. Among recent critics Gilles Deleuze, Gérard Genette, René Girard, and J.-F. Revel have produced fine studies in French. The books by Leo Bersani and George Stambolian in English maintain a comparable level of discourse. See Short Bibliography, p. 177.

and ended in fame and exhaustion four years after World War I. In those fifty-one years he lived two closely interlocking careers. Beginning very early, this sensitive, gifted young man with something slightly Middle Eastern about his soft manner and dark look, carried out a brilliant escape from his bourgeois background and from the professional career expected of the eldest son of a prominent Paris doctor. He accomplished this feat by ingratiating himself with the wealthy and sometimes aristocratic families of his schoolmates at the Lycée Condorcet. By the age of seventeen, exploiting his talents as a mimic and conversationalist, he was visiting literary salons and learning his way in society. In his mid-thirties, soon after the death of both his parents, his first career as a somewhat eccentric man of the world gave way to another activity: literature. Up to that point Proust's writing had served his social ambitions or had been kept hidden. He now reversed the poles of his existence. For the last fifteen years of his life, his social connections and his worldliness furnished the raw material of his writing.

It was a shift, never a clean break. Proust claimed that he wrote parts of his first book at the age of fourteen (*JS*, 902), and there is little reason to doubt him. Just a month before he died, suffering terribly and aware of how much remained to be done on the final volumes of his novel, he got out of bed to go to a party given by the Comte and Comtesse de Beaumont. The overlap of careers was extensive. Nevertheless, the general movement of Proust's life pivots on an obscure point, somewhere between 1905 and 1909, in which north and south changed places. He became a convert—a convert to true faith in himself as the novelist of his own conversion.

Such a schematic version of Proust's life keeps things simple and clear. It glosses over minor conflicts of fact and major conflicts of interpretation. There are good reasons for us to seek a closer knowledge of how Proust became a convert to his own calling. The most systematic and the least satisfactory explanations of Proust's life are pseudomedical. Son and brother of prominent doctors, Proust was himself a contributor to this line of thought. Inevitably he had heard that the terrors and upheavals of the Commune (his father was almost shot by accident) had affected his mother's pregnancy. Sickly at birth, he nevertheless survived. Nine years later came his first serious attack of asthma; he received all the attention he could want, and his condition stabilized during youth and early manhood. The attacks recurred in his mid-twenties, at about the time he was coming to terms with his homosexuality. Mostly from his own testimony we know that he was prone to hypochondria, voyeurism, and certain forms of sadomasochism. Psychoanalysts have produced resounding terms to apply to the roots of his condition. When Serge Béhar speaks of "infantile neurosis developing into coenesthopathy in the adult," he is affirming a diseased condition of the organic sensation of existence and well-being. Perhaps: but this ground is as treacherous as it is fascinating. And I wonder if the technical vocabulary really improves on the term Proust's family applied to him very early and which he cites frequently in *Jean Santeuil: un enfant nerveux*.

It is significant that all psychological studies of Proust accept his designation of the determining childhood scene: the goodnight kiss described near the opening of the *Search*. But to what extent is it part of Proust's biography? To what extent is it fiction? In the earlier *Jean Santeuil* version of the scene, the little boy revels in the power and freedom he finds when he finally triumphs over his mother's refusal to leave her guests and come to his room to kiss him goodnight. The same scene in the *Search* emphasizes a strong aftertaste of disappointment over the fact that his mother and father give in to his importunings. Their capitulation, the Narrator states, undermines what little will power the boy has to control his moods. No one has gone further than Proust himself in probing the complete significance of this scene. But we cannot for that reason read it unquestioningly as autobiography.[2]

Heredity provides another way of explaining Proust's temperament and behavior. George Painter seems to accept the "fact" of Proust's "hereditary neurasthenia" and calls attention to a similar condition in a paternal aunt who became a recluse. André Maurois lays great emphasis on the mingling of two parental strains: French-Catholic and Jewish. One cannot readily attribute contrasting character traits to these two races or religions as true genetic strains. On the other hand, the marriage did combine two contrasting cultures. In Proust's sensibility one soon detects the jostling opposition between city and country, between cosmopolitan Paris and provincial, semipastoral Illiers/Combray. His father never lost the brusque manners of a village candlemaker's son. Dr. Proust was the first of a long line of farmers and tradesman to leave Illiers. Mme. Proust,

[2] In a volume of provocative psychoanalytic studies, *L'Arbre jusqu'aux racines*, Dominique Fernandez interprets the whole of the *Search*, and this sequence in particular, as an elaborate feint on Proust's part to distract our attention from his jealousy of his younger brother and disappointment in his father, and from the overpowering domination of his mother. Thus, according to Fernandez, Proust masks the true origins of his homosexuality and protects the myth of the happy family. Many of Fernandez' points are persuasive, but he has a distressingly narrow belief in "precise psychological causes" from which all human behavior will "necessarily flow." Those causes reduce a novel to an excrescence of a psychological case history. I cannot acept this tight determinism on any level of life or literature. Proust's novel makes revelations that transcend his particular case and cannot be read back into it. There, in fact, lies the principal justification for calling it a novel. Fernandez also argues that *Jean Santeuil* is a better and more courageous book than the *Search* because it reveals more about Proust's neurosis than the final novel. Though Fernandez argues his premise very resourcefully, his conclusion does not follow.

fifteen years younger than her husband, was the highly educated, art-loving daughter of a wealthy stockbroker. Her brother was a bachelor and ladies' man; her mother had connections in elegant society and in the world of literature and the arts. The tidal movement of the *Search* arises not from a contrast of races or religions but from a geographic and intellectual exchange between city culture and country culture. We glimpse it first in the "two ways" that polarize the child's world of Combray, and later in the contrast between Combray itself and Paris.

Whatever Proust's medical and psychological condition may have been, and whatever his heredity, he found his own path into the Parisian life of *la belle époque*. He had a quick mind, a prodigious memory (especially for poetry), and a hypersensitive discernment of other people's feelings and reactions. Despite frequent illnesses during his teens, he was healthy enough to excel in school, especially in philosophy. The philosophy teacher Darlu, who tutored him privately for a year, made a profound impression on him and introduced him to the idealist analysis of the contrast between appearance and reality. Very early, Proust fixed on reading and literature as the locus of his interests. He apparently experienced puppy love a number of times. In the most intense instance, his parents thwarted his desires for Marie de Benardaky by insisting that she was socially too far beyond his reach. Taking advantage of a law discriminating in favor of the rich and educated, Proust volunteered at eighteen for one year of military service. Though he did not distinguish himself as a soldier, he made several good friends among the other privileged young men and later called that year the happiest of his life.

One of the favorite pastimes in that self-conscious society was a modified game of truth or consequences played by filling in an elegantly printed questionnaire. Some families kept albums containing these questionnaires along with other mementos of their friends and relatives. In Proust's case we have two such documents, one written at thirteen and the other at twenty. Despite the artificial circumstances, Proust's answers furnish two unmatchable probes of these early years of the slow bloomer. Where possible, I quote both sets of answers.

What is for you the greatest unhappiness? To be separated from maman (13). Not to have known my mother and grandmother (20).

In what place would you like to live? In the land of the Ideal, or rather of my ideal (13). In the place where certain things I want would come to pass as if by enchantment—and where tender feelings would always be shared (20).

Your ideal of earthly happiness? To live near all my loved ones, with the charms of nature, lots of books and musical scores, and, not far away, a French theater (13). I'm afraid it isn't high enough, and I'm afraid of destroying it by telling it (20).

For what faults do you have the greatest indulgence? For the private life of geniuses (13). For those I understand (20).

Your principal fault? Not to know how, not to be able, to will something [*vouloir*] (20).

What would you like to be? Myself, as people I admire would like me to be (20).

Your favorite quality in a man? Intelligence, the moral sense (13).

Your favorite quality in a woman? Tenderness [*douceur*], naturalness, intelligence (13).

Your favorite occupation? Reading; daydreaming; poetry (13). Loving (20).

Your present state of mind? Annoyance [*ennui*] over having thought about myself to answer all these questions (20).

Even for the era these are precocious answers, steeped in literary attitudes, and displaying the capacity to speak the truth within certain limits of coyness and insecurity. No bumbler wrote these apothegmatic lines.

At twenty this young sensitive had to face the painful

question of what he would do with himself. For close to fifteen years he temporized and spent his days and nights essentially in the provinces of his mind looking for the capital. He entered the university and took a degree in law and another in literature. He also qualified by competitive examination for an unsalaried library position, and then never started work. For several years his best efforts went into two complementary activities: writing short stories and literary sketches for the newspapers and symbolist reviews, and cultivating the elegant families of the friends he had made at school and during military service. He memorialized his success in both lines with the publication of his first collection, *Pleasures and Days* (1896). It was an overly elegant edition illustrated by a salon hostess, Madeleine Lemaire, with a preface extorted from Anatole France. It looked like the work of a dilettante with powerful connections, even though it does not read that way.

The strongest presence in Proust's life at this juncture was Comte Robert de Montesquiou-Fezensac. Fifteen years older, he had everything Proust thought he wanted. The Count was descended from the model for D'Artagnan of *The Three Musketeers* and could claim most of European nobility as relatives by blood or marriage. Immense wealth enabled him to cultivate an esthetic manner and way of life remarkable enough to have already inspired one notorious book, Huysmans' *A rebours*. He was also a published poet of some note and flaunted his homosexuality with enormous style. Proust fawned on him for several years before he could pull away, and the fascination never disappeared entirely. When Montesquiou mentioned his young friend once in print, Proust had to fight a pistol duel with a critic who seized the occasion to ridicule him as "one of those small-time fops in literary heat." No one was hurt.

The Dreyfus Affair exploded in November 1897. Proust, aged twenty-six, was intensely committed to the Dreyfus cause from the start. He helped get Anatole

France's signature for the Petition of the Intellectuals, attended every session of Zola's trial, and was active in support of Colonel Picquart, the second hero of the affair. This public behavior placed Proust in the opposite camp from both his family (his father knew practically every minister) and most of his society hostesses. He recorded the harrowing tension and the human consequences of these events in sections of a novel he had been working on in spurts and fragments for some four years. *Jean Santeuil* provides scenes from the sad yet charmed life of a young man who can never pull himself together and is forever protected from above. After some eight-hundred pages without form or continuity, Proust abandoned the manuscript in apparent dissatisfaction.

He was still in the provinces. His next discovery was John Ruskin, the English art critic and social thinker. Between 1899 and 1905 Proust spent much of his time reading him and making "pilgrimages" to the sites in France and Italy about which Ruskin had written. He went on to translate two of Ruskin's books (with the help of his mother and an English girl friend), and to write prefaces that grew until they almost swallowed the texts they were intended to present. Proust performed a dance with Ruskin similar to the one he had performed with Montesquiou. For a time Ruskin's combination of esthetic sensitivity, scholarship, and social thought won his deep admiration. Later he found Ruskin guilty of a false idolatry of art and of a masked moralism. This long encounter with Ruskin was deeply profitable for Proust. He was able to clarify his own ideas on art and to acknowledge to himself that fiction was still his goal. In 1902, at the peak of his Ruskin absorption, he wrote to Prince Antoine Bibesco:

> . . . a hundred characters for novels, a thousand ideas keep asking me to give them substance, like those shades that keep asking Ulysses in the *Odyssey* to give

them blood to drink and bring them to life, and that the hero pushes aside with his sword.

At thirty, Proust was already a deeply eccentric man, and still living at home on an allowance. His preferred schedule of rising in the late afternoon and going to bed at dawn estranged him from his own family. The events of the next few years came perilously close to paralyzing him. His younger brother, a doctor following in their father's footsteps, married in 1903 and set up on his own. At the wedding Marcel was a grotesque, semi-invalid figure in several overcoats and mufflers. A few months later their father died, and Mme Proust devoted herself for two years to caring for Proust's asthma and hay fever, and helping him translate Ruskin. She also organized dinners for his friends in their apartment. Then, after a short illness, Mme Proust died in 1905. Her son lay for almost two months in sleepless seclusion in the apartment, and then spent six weeks in a private clinic. After this, his nocturnal and neurotic behavior became more pronounced than ever.

The shift I have mentioned in Proust's career took place over the next four years—not a single event or development, but a gradual convergence of forces already at work. He began to withdraw slowly from his salon life and saw his friends in restaurants late at night. He could now have homosexual affairs by hiring young men as chauffeurs or secretaries. Writing a series of literary pastiches increased his conviction that he must find his own style and his own form. Meanwhile, his writing was becoming more and more autobiographical. In 1908 his drafts of a projected critical essay, *Against Sainte-Beuve*, kept turning into personal narrative whenever he let them take their course. If Proust had any revelation, it must have been the discovery that he could accommodate his irresistible autobiographical impulse in the novel form. During a lull in his writing in January 1909, he apparently had an unexpected and compelling surge of memory over a cup of tea into which he dipped some dry toast. When he described the incident in the preface he was writing for *Against Sainte-Beuve*, a number of similar reminiscences came to mind. Some missing element had fallen into place, and now it seemed as if he were at work on a wholly new book. Yet it was really the same one—the book begun in *Pleasures and Days*, tried again and laid aside in *Jean Santeuil*, tried once more in the anecdotal pages that open the preface to Ruskin's *Sesame and Lilies*, carried on in *Against Sainte-Beuve*. Endowed with a new plan but no firm title, this transmuted work took possession of him during the spring of 1909 and filled the rest of his life. By August, he wrote proudly and optimistically to Mme Emile Strauss, one of his hostesses: "I have begun—and finished—a whole long book." About the same time he gave a few details to Alfred Vallette, a possible publisher for it.

> I'm finishing a book which, in spite of its provisional title, *Against Sainte-Beuve: Recollection of a Morning*, is a genuine novel and an indecent novel in some of its sections. The book ends with a long conversation on Sainte-Beuve and aesthetics.

We should probably be grateful that Vallette refused Proust's novel then, for it was many years and hundreds of pages away from being finished. But at least it was begun, and already getting out of control.

These developments were the signal for Proust to modify his life of indecision and distraction. In the fall of 1909 he announced to his friends a kind of withdrawal and retreat, referring mysteriously yet resolutely to the long work ahead of him. His caginess about the title and plan of his novel made it sound like a scientific discovery or a military secret. In 1910 he sealed himself into the bedroom of his new apartment by lining it with cork, and sent out irregular reports on the page count he had reached. A few close friends like Georges de Lauris and Reynaldo Hahn, sworn to confidence, were allowed to read the oilcloth covered notebooks. They gave him the encouragement he needed. Of course, Proust did not retire completely from Parisian life as he had known it. He kept up with his friends and, at intervals, muffled in outlandish clothes, dropped in on an elegant hostess just as her party was breaking up. He even went occasionally to a music hall or an art gallery, and he listened to concerts and plays by subscribing to a service that allowed members to hear live performances over the telephone. But from now until his death in 1922, his novel took precedence over everything else. The tide had turned. His forays into the outer world and the bulk of his letters were either means of obtaining information for his writings or attempts to arrange the proper publication and reception for his work. For the latter purpose he pulled every string, used every connection, and called in every outstanding debt available to him. Yet four publishing houses refused his book. After a cursory look, André Gide turned it down for Gallimard as too snobbish and amateurish. He later changed his mind. Grasset, a new house, finally published it, at the author's expense, in 1913. All Proust's advance work was barely sufficient to launch this first of two projected volumes. By the time Gallimard published the second volume after the war, the manuscript had grown unsuppressibly, frighteningly, like a carnivorous vine that would finally entwine and devour its owner.

The remainder of Proust's life takes on a mythological quality. His nocturnal, bedridden, disorderly work habits seem heroic. In his private life he mixed low-grade hedonism with deliberate psychological and moral experiment. What looks degraded to some of us may be edifying to others. This man of shrewd medical insight mercilessly punished his frail body and refused proper advice, even from his brother. He followed what he told Louis de Robert was his "only rule": "to yield to one's demon, to one's thought, to write on everything to the point of exhaustion." When he was awarded the prestigious Goncourt prize in 1919 for the second volume of the novel, *A l'ombre des jeunes filles en fleurs*, the event barely ruffled the waters in his special universe of nurture and devotion. His work had become a living being, making demands of its own. "For me it had turned into a son. The dying mother must still submit to the fatigue of taking care of him" (III, 1941–42). He knew he had given birth.

The last decade of Proust's life displays an outward life gradually abdicated in favor of a work—both the inward process and the material product. Yet there is nothing reluctant or tragic about his abdication. It does not resemble the two great royal departures of the era, when a Spanish king bowed to republicanism and an English king chose love of a commoner over royalty. With surprising confidence Proust simply decided in favor of the dense tropical growth he felt within him. For he discovered that it was at last assuming a shape it had not exhibited earlier. Throughout his life, Proust composed in a discontinuous fashion. Except possibly in the earliest short stories, he did not start at the beginning of a narrative and follow it through to the end. Observations and incidents and characters came to him in disparate fragments directly based on his day-to-day experience. His notebooks seem to be in total disarray in spite of the dazzling insights they carry. In reading *Jean Santeuil*, still virtually a notebook, one rarely receives the sense of a direction in which events are moving. It drifts to a standstill. The prose pieces Proust wrote for the abandoned essay-novel, *Against Sainte-Beuve*, display this desultory quality to an even greater extent. He seems totally at sea.

But after 1909 he has a chart and a course. The "very exacting composition" Proust lays claim to in a letter to Louis de Robert in 1912 was the major new element that had entered his work and claimed his energies. In the *Search* he holds his characters and his story in an

iron grasp. Lengthy digressions and hernia-like extensions of a single scene or sentiment do not mean that
he has lost track of where his characters are going and
what they have already been through. Considering its
length, unfinished condition, and the handicapped circumstances in which he wrote the novel, it contains
extraordinarily few repetitions and inconsistencies. The
over-all design and the narrative links rarely waver, a
difficult feat in view of the complex strategies of divul-
gence and development he set for himself. Yet Proust
never relished the final stage of assembling and fitting.
"Writing is easy for me," he wrote Gallimard. "But to
patch things together, to set all the bones, that's more
than I can face. For some time I've realized that I leave
out the best pieces, because I would have to fit this
detail to that one, and so on." Even so, beneath all that
flesh Proust did set the bones of his narrative and created strong joints to carry the sustained movements of
its development.

The other major shift in Proust's writing after 1909
concerns the narrative voice in which he wrote. With a
few revealing exceptions, *Jean Santeuil* employs the
third person to designate a "hero" very close to Proust
in biographical and psychological terms. The opening
pages of *On Reading*, and the preface to *Against Sainte-
Beuve* use the *I* without feint or dissembling to represent
Proust as a real person and signatory. In none of these
texts has he found his true discursive pitch and pace.
Somewhere in the early stages of the *Search*, however,
when he still thought it was *Against Sainte-Beuve*, a
double reaction occurs. It is both a fusion and a fission
attacking the *I*. First of all Proust calls in both the
scantily veiled third-person of *Jean Santeuil* and his
various uses of the first person. He combines them into
the *je* of the *Search*—both narrator and character, a
double personage in one pronoun. At the same time
Proust takes himself, his life, and his character, and
divides them up among a number of characters in the

novel: Charlus, Bloch, Swann, as well as Marcel and the Narrator.

This fission-fusion process explains why it is so unsatisfactory to keep asking if Marcel or the Narrator represents Proust. There can be no doubt that the *Search* embodies a version—both revelation and disguise—of Proust's life. The links are too evident to discount, from the setting and action to details like the Narrator having translated Ruskin's *Sesame and Lilies*. But Proust's disclaimers are equally powerful. He insists that his book be read as a self-contained story and not as autobiography masquerading as fiction. It would be foolish to insist on one of these approaches to the exclusion of the other. Toward the end of the novel one comes upon an odd passage which makes a tiny step toward reconciliation. There is nothing like it elsewhere in the *Search*.

> In this book, in which every fact is fictional and in which not a single character is based on a living person, in which everything has been invented by me according to the needs of my demonstration, I must state to the credit of my country that only Françoise's millionaire relatives, who interrupted their retirement in order to help their needy niece, are real people, existing in the world (III, 846).

Here, I believe, Proust is pointing out to us a kind of vestigial navel cord, a detail which proves that his vast work does not coincide with actuality but was born from it. Ideas of slow gestation and final parturition do greater justice to the novel's origins than concepts of literal imitation or of complete autonomy.

In Proust's final years the autobiographical nature of the *Search* seems less significant than the literary nature of its author's life. He prepares us for this perspective with the much quoted line in which he attacks the failure of Sainte-Beuve's critical method to take into account what true wisdom should have told him: ". . . that a book is the product of a different self from the

one we display in our habits, in society, in our vices"
(*CSB*, 221–22). This may be as close as we can come
to gospel. But there is a further question. Need we
assume that the authorial self has been formed prior
to the composition of the work? Valéry liked to point
out that, as the criminal may be the product of
his crime, so the author may be the product of his
literary work. What I have said about Proust's "abdication" points to a sense in which, *as author*, he was the
product of his work in progress. In the cases most crucial
to literature, writing is less a record of what has actually
happened to someone than a discovery-creation of what
might potentially happen to people, "author" included.
The symbiotic relationship between man and book grows
as much out of aesthetic as out of biographical factors.
The development of "the other self" who wrote the
Search can be traced within the novel itself, but not in
terms of finding keys to characters and identifying incidents transposed from Proust's life. They are incidentals.
Mysteriously and steadily, the *Search* secreted its true
author, the literary creature we call Marcel Proust.

The biographical Proust spent his last three years in
bed, in great part in order to escape the demands of
literary celebrity. Surrounded by galley proofs, manuscripts, and strange potions, he lived his unfinished book
as totally and exclusively as an author can without
losing his sense of reality. What kept him sane and
even practical was the desire to assure his work an
enlightened readership. He answered most letters (but
not one from an American girl who had read his novel
steadily for three years and then rebuked him: "Don't
be a *poseur*. . . . Tell me in two lines what you wished
to say"), contributed to newspaper surveys on trends
and styles, and took time to write two superb essays on
his masters: Flaubert and Baudelaire. His remarks about
the tonality of tenses and the place of metaphor in their
work apply also to his own. An occasional Lazarus-like
sortie formed part of the pattern. Shot up with adren-

alin and caffeine, he submitted to a ceremonial mid-
night meeting with James Joyce at a large supper party
for Diaghilev, Picasso, and Stravinsky. Neither author
had read the other's work. They talked about the only
other subject that mattered to them: their health. Another time, Proust let himself be taken to the fashionable
1920s nightspot, le Boeuf sur le toît. He never shed his
heavy overcoat and was almost swept into a drunken
brawl. Meanwhile the work never stopped, even during
the final months. Most of all Proust feared the affliction
that had tortured Baudelaire at the end: aphasia. Yet,
beneath the complaints, Proust found a wonderful excitement in the tension between his mission to finish
his work and his simple mortality. Three months before
the end, he answered "a little question" submitted to
various prominent persons by the newspaper, *l'Intransi-
geant*: "If the world were coming to an end, what would
it mean to you?"

> I believe that life would suddenly appear wonderful
> to us, if we were suddenly threatened with death as
> you propose.

Death had long since become his faith, his inspiration.
The final complication was pneumonia. He died on
November 18, 1922.

AN OVERDETERMINED UNIVERSE

At intervals throughout the *Search*, Marcel goes to
stay in a strange place. Each time it is as if he has to
reconstitute from scratch all his perceptions and habits,
the whole orientation of his life. Toward the middle of
the novel, he visits his close friend Saint-Loup in Don-
cières, a town where Saint-Loup is doing his military
service in the cavalry. What strikes Marcel first on
arriving is the "perpetual, musical, and warlike vibra-
tility" (II, 70) that hangs in the air. For several pages
after that the whole narrative texture is woven out of

unfamiliar sounds. He notices Saint-Loup's modified accent. The crackling fire in his friend's barracks room makes Marcel think that someone must be in there while he stands listening in the hall outside the closed door. Once he enters the empty room, the ticking of an unseen clock seems to come from all directions until Marcel has spotted it and given the object and the sound a specific location. And then this acoustical disorientation infects everything, even Marcel's friendship for Saint-Loup and his sense of his own identity in the world. In other words, when his impressions are most vivid, he loses his bearings. Marcel's "auditory hyperesthesia" (II, 72), which Saint-Loup specifically mentions here as making life difficult for his visitor, serves not to fix the world more clearly in place for Marcel but to send it skittering off toward new patterns and multiple vanishing points. The disconcerting effect of strange sounds throws every element of life into play again, and thus into jeopardy. Even familiar sensations recover significance and urgency.

This dense network of perpetually reconstituted connections between impressions, feelings, meanings, and words constitutes one of the fundamental qualities of Proust's work. He conveys it in the resonance of the prose and in the over-all architecture of the action. The superb opening "scene," in which the Narrator puts himself together like Humpty-Dumpty out of fragmentary impressions of waking and dreaming, is baffling at first. Nothing created out of so many elements could be simple. Even when the Narrator fails to achieve this self-creation *ex omnibus* (dialectically the equivalent of *ex nihilo*), the writing itself emits a powerful sense of the links among the things around us and our experiences of them. Proust writes from deep inside the world of Baudelaire's *correspondances*, close to Leonardo's universe where the painter said he saw actual lines connecting objects in a kind of visible geometry.

In one respect this sense of the plenitude of relations

between things runs counter to a human temper often treated in modern literature. In writers like Kafka and Camus we discern a quality of emptiness which it is hard to describe. For K and Meursault, experience generates very little motivation to undertake anything, to oppose the world or to affirm oneself. They act out of gratuitous impulse or yield to mere circumstance. In Proust the opposite is true. Multiple desires and motivations converge on every action and often impede its execution. Marcel goes to unbelievable lengths to explain to himself the behavior of the women in his life. For them as for him potential motives are often spelled out in a series of either/or propositions. But one motive will never prove to be the correct one and eliminate the others. After two pages of speculation on the character and behavior of one of his oldest friends, Gilberte Swann, Marcel throws up his hands. "None of these hypotheses was absurd" (III, 708). The mystery of Proust's world arises not from gratuitousness or from the absence of motivation but from the conflictingly overdetermined quality of most actions, and from the adaptability of most actions to a great number of attributions. Until Marcel reaches a wider wisdom, what happens around him is not indifferent but overwhelming.

How to Read a Roman-fleuve[1]

ii

PRACTICAL MATTERS

Prospective Proust readers have to. make a series of decisions that can be best expressed as questions with tentative answers.

In what language should one read Proust? Anyone who can comfortably read Balzac or Tocqueville or Camus in the original should tackle the *Search* in French. The translation will not turn out to be much easier for him, and he should at least make the attempt. Because of the résumés and indices it contains, the three-volume Pléiade edition in French has great advantages over the inexpensive seven-volume pocket edition. To the reader restricted to English, I can

---

[1] This chapter is addressed to those seeking guidance for a first reading of Proust. Readers already familiar with the *Search* and looking for commentary on its shape and significance should skip to Chapter III.

state that the Moncrieff translation is a sustained piece of craftsmanship with a recognizable style in English that echoes the original. But Moncrieff is not infallible. Occasionally he Bowdlerizes. It is hard to excuse some of his clumsy errors.[2]

The Kilmartin revision of Moncrieff's six volumes plus Mayor's translation of the last volume has made some of the necessary repairs (see "Note on Texts and Translations," page vii). The ragged state of Proust's own text in the later volumes cannot be rectified. Considering the immense labor of translating Proust, we are well served in English.[3]

A reader whose French is shaky should probably use a translation. Yet I know several enterprising individuals who have laid out the French and English texts

[2] One example should suffice. Moncrieff's confusion over pronouns shifts the hesitations of Swann's sensibility into Odette's mind. Nothing could be more out of character.

Et ce fut Swann qui, avant qu'elle laissât tomber [son visage], comme malgré elle, sur ses lèvres, le retint un instant, à quelque distance, entre ses deux mains. Il avait voulu laisser à sa pensée le temps d'accourir, de reconnaître le rêve qu'elle avait si longtemps caressé et d'assister à sa réalisation, comme une parente qu'on appelle pour prendre sa part du succès d'un enfant qu'elle a beaucoup aimé (I, 233).

And Swann it was who, before she allowed her face, as though despite her efforts, to fall upon his lips, held it back for a moment longer, at a little distance between his hands. He had intended to leave time for her mind to overtake her body's movements, to recognize the dream which she had so long cherished and to assist at its realisation, like a mother invited as a spectator when a prize is given to the child she has reared and loved. (Moncrieff's translation.)

With the minimum of correction, the second sentence should read: "He had intended to leave time for his mind to overtake his body's movements, to recognize the dream which it had so long cherished. . . ." In the next sentence, *parente* means "relative."

[3] The *Search* has also been translated in full into fifteen other languages.

side by side and developed their own gymnastic method for straddling these two platforms.

In either language one has to read with a kind of patient faith that Proust is not leading us down the garden path and that he will bring the sentence, the scene, and the book to a clear conclusion. And so he does. He tells us himself that he is forever tacking against the wind, and describes a mind "following its habitual course, which moves foward by digressions, going off obliquely in one direction and then in the other" (II, 816). In order to follow this course of advance by indirection, I believe it is best to approach the reading of Proust as if it were a kind of long-term cure, or an initiation to unfamiliar mental and physical movements evolved by another culture. A steady, leisurely pace, without the tension of fixed deadlines, serves best. Certain habits of thought can thus be laid aside as others are slowly acquired. It may take months, even years. The *Search* creates a season of the mind outside temporal limits.

How many of the 3000 pages should one read? How much food or drink is enough? The reader should probably not decide the question in advance and should let his appetite guide him. Some will stop short, scoffing, in the opening pages. Others will continue in absorption to the last page and then start over again. Many more will ask for a middle way, and they should be shown one. We have Frazer and Gibbon in one-volume editions. With great profit as a boy I read *Don Quijote* and *Robinson Crusoe*, *Arabian Nights*, and *Gulliver's Travels* in truncated children's editions. When copyright expires, will we be offered a pocket Proust? *In Search of Lost Time* in three-hundred pages? The prospect is not utterly unthinkable. As in the classics mentioned above, there is in Proust a deep universal element, an esthetic consciousness, that may one day reach many more people than can read his novel. A film might open the way, though it seems unlikely. Several ambitious projects have already collapsed. Pinter's screenplay still awaits a producer. A Frenchman wrote a novel a few years ago which describes at length the effect of a reading of Proust's novel on his central character. Yet such surrogates seem inadequate. Even a sensitive anthology of set pieces and self-contained reflections cannot represent Proust, for it conveys no sense of the whole or of the underlying movement. The resourceful independent reader will thread his own way through the text and take sensible short cuts. On the other hand, reading Proust in an organized course with a competent teacher to set the level of understanding and interpretation and with perceptive students willing to participate in class discussions can develop into a very rewarding collective experience. But a term or semester course is too short and often leads to intense frustration at the end.

Though few have ever been proposed in print, there are various ways of reading approximately a third of the *Search* and supplying the missing sections through summaries.[4] Proust's other writings, though they have various merits, can wait until one has fully assimilated the *Search*.

Are there devices or approaches that can facilitate one's reading? Both in translation and in the original, Proust slows most readers down. His sentences move through long spirals that will not be hastened. He offers few paragraph breaks to declare the steps and stages of his thought. Unlike most nineteenth-century novelists

[4] The following is one suggestion, which any Proustian could criticize: *Swann's Way* (the first three quarters: "Combray" and "Swann in Love"); *Within a Budding Grove* (Part Two: "Balbec"); *Guermantes's Way* (II, Chapter One: "The Grandmother's Death"); *Sodom and Gomorrah* (first thirty pages and the last thirty: "Charlus and Albertine"); *The Captive* (first thirty pages and two hundred pages on the concert at the Verdurins arranged by Charlus); *The Sweet Cheat Gone* (omit); *Time Regained* (first thirty pages and the last two hundred: "Combray" again, and the last reception and reflections on writing). . . .

he does not construct out of short chapters that divide the story into convenient mental mouthfuls. One simply cannot force one's speed and hope to register the prose. Gradually, however, it can come to sound appropriate and effective.

When you look at it closely, no passage in Proust seems typical. The patterns he makes are numerous and contrasting. But it may be helpful to consider one medium-long sentence in order to pick out a few stylistic features that are recognizably his. The sentence quoted below appears in an important juncture at the beginning of *Swann's Way.* Swann is an elegant, wealthy Jew, much sought after in the best Parisian society. His worldly milieu has made him both sensitive and blasé. He devotes most of his life to a series of love affairs with women from all classes who happen to catch his eye. His story begins against this background.

> But, *whereas* each of these liaisons, or each of these flirtations, had been the more or less complete realization of a dream inspired by the sight of a face or body that Swann had, spontaneously, without effort, found attractive, on the contrary, *when* one day at the theater he was introduced to Odette de Crécy by one of his former friends, who spoke of her as a charming woman with whom he might get along, but painted her as more difficult than she really was in order to seem to have done him a bigger favor in introducing him, *she appeared to Swann not unattractive certainly but to have a kind of beauty that was indifferent to him,* that did not stir his desire, even inspired a kind of physical repulsion in him, to be the sort of woman, as happens to all of us in different ways, who is the opposite of what our senses ask for (I, 195–96) [Italics added].

By linking more than a dozen subordinate clauses to the ends of one principal clause, Proust has composed a difficult sentence. But the fully articulated syntax and the rhythm it enforces firmly direct the reading. The emphatic initial *But*, commands attention. Immediately following, *whereas* projects far out ahead an organizing power that lasts until it is picked up by *when* and carried on to the central statement. The construction here is more sturdy than subtle. Why does Proust write one sentence instead of three or four? What is the effect?

Had he used several sentences, he would have had to rely on modifiers and rhetorical devices to bring out the central proposition. Or he would have had to delete details. In the sentence as written, subordination serves to arrange a large amount of material around the clause: "she appeared . . . indifferent to him. . . ." The facts that the introduction took place in the theater, and that she was not presented as a woman of easy virtue, are minor yet revealing details. Proust uses the nuances and hierarchies of syntax to hold these details in perspective. Furthermore, the very relationships expressed by the connectives (*whereas, when, who;* in other contexts he concentrates on causative, concessive, or conditional relations) form an essential part of Proust's subject. This sentence contrives to tell us not only the circumstances under which Swann first met Odette but also to suggest the whole sinuous course of their love affair. Before that interlude his life followed a recognizable pattern; during it that pattern is so disrupted as to leave a deep mark on Swann; and at its close (I, 382) he looks back at its surprising beginning (and in effect at this very sentence) to wonder bemusedly how it ever happened. A great number of complex, half-understood circumstances converge on any significant event, and then diverge toward a future of undivulged possibilities. The passage just quoted is one example of how Proust's prose tends to reproduce that plenitude. He wants to make us see that intersection of lines. Compare the similar yet distinctly more serpentine movement of the sentence that begins, "Then, like a city . . .," in the document reproduced in the Appendix (page 170). One could, of course, go much further. Mallarmé wrote his most ambitious poem "Un coup de dés" in the form of a single, repeatedly proliferating, meticulously articulated sentence. If a novelist begins to experience both time and meaning as fundamentally continuous, he might well aspire to write one unbroken sentence, paralleling consciousness itself, shadowing or even overshadowing reality. Though tempted by such a course, Proust pulled back before he abandoned syntax and readability. He shaped the world of his fiction by forming it into high relief in his prose, not by flattening it out endlessly or by cutting it up into little pieces. This same principle of fullness explains his effective use, at long intervals, of a contrasting device: the tersest possible form of declaration, a staccato phrase, an abrupt question. "It was himself." "Dead forever?" "My whole being capsized." The flowing periods of his prose create extended stretches of lived time. They also set the scene for unexpected and devastating reversals which occur in very few words. We notice the lengthiness more than the brevity, and, indeed, there is more of the former. Both belong to the fullness of his style.

The best way to discover and respond to Proust's expressive voice, as well as the deliberate pacing of his narrative, is to hear the prose, to read it aloud. For he often works by a kind of mimicry at one remove, echoing and aping his characters without abandoning the steady flow of his own thought. The unnamed Norwegian philosopher speaks a totally different French from that of Dr. Cottard or of Odette, and we are allowed to hear each of them. Without an auditory sense of the text, even in its most reflective and interior passages, the visual field of urelieved print tends to become oppressive. Translations cannot convey the original texture, yet on this score Moncrieff performs remarkably well. He will bear reading aloud.

Apart from the speech rhythm and inflections stirred up by the text, there are two other items a reader can watch for to help him find his way. Proust frequently employs a recurrent narrative detail or incident as a kind of refrain to orient the course of action. In the "Combray" section, fifty pages of pure description are pinned together by the minute mystery of whether or not Mme Goupil got to mass on time. For Swann, the question of who was with Odette the afternoon she did not answer her doorbell becomes the very axis of his life. Marcel develops an imaginary passion for Baronne de Putbus's reputedly sexy maid, whom he has never laid eyes on. He keeps trying to trace her, always without success, in a series of maneuvers that span the latter half of the novel. These colored strands surface just often enough in the narrative fabric to help reveal its pattern.

The other feature a reader would do well to remain on the alert for carries more significance than the narrative refrains. It reveals the plastic quality of the action. From time to time in the story Marcel is told or discovers a small item of information which, when fully grasped and fitted into place, changes his entire perspective on the relationship between important characters or on the nature of human conduct. The aging down-to-earth Marquise de Villeparisis, a girlhood friend of Marcel's grandmother, turns out to be closely related to the aristocratic and inaccessible Guermantes, whom he intensely desires to know. The eminent painter, Elstir, turns out to be the same person as Biche, or Tiche, the ridiculous and vulgar young man in Mme Verdurin's first "little clan." The battle of Méséglise in World War I makes that village famous in world history; yet the Combray church, the incarnation of Marcel's childhood and of French history, is destroyed. A hint is passed in the closing pages that the virtuous Duchesse de Guermantes may not, after all, have always been the most faithful of wives. These tiny shocks profoundly modify the great web of relations and reactions that constitute the substance of the book. One must read Proust as carefully as a detective story in which any detail may become a clue to everything else. Every page tends toward the accumulation of the familiar, the security of habit, in order to establish the sense of location and identity we all need. At the same time every page glows with a blend of excitement and anxiety over the possible introduction of a new element. We half anticipate a break in routine which will disrupt the pattern and launch the whole setting into unpredictable motion. This ambivalent mood, which seems to posit boredom as the inevitable background for excitement, emerges beautifully in "Combray." The *train-train* or unvarying daily round of events that characterizes life in Aunt Léonie's house is both tested and reinforced by the "asymetrical Saturday" (I, 110). On that day each week lunch is served a full hour early to allow Françoise to go to market. The variation, astonishing to everyone, is itself assimilated into the routine. Yet the risk of that established departure from schedule prepares the way for all the dismay and despair to come when this tight little life falls apart.

THE ELEMENTS OF THE STORY

The biggest help in reading Proust is to have the persons and places of the story clear in one's mind. For this purpose I have arranged the elements in tables and diagrams to accompany the prose exposition that follows.

The *Search* has five major settings (see Diagram I). I mention places before persons because so much of the action consists of Marcel's gradual and painful accommodation to new settings, and of the association of character with particularities of place. Albertine *is* essentially Balbec incarnate and carries always within her the sensuousness of flowers and the mutability of the sea. Furthermore, all geography in Proust, from ocean to bed to church steeple, is symbolic, even animistic. "The various places of the earth are also beings, whose per-

I. PLACES

Combray	Paris	Balbec	Doncières	Venice
Church of St-Hilaire	Champs-Elysées Gardens	Grand Hôtel	Cavalry Barracks	(Trip planned and canceled)
Aunt Léonie's House	Guermantes's Town House	Beach	Hotel de Flandre	Visit with Mother
Swann's Way (Méséglise) (Tansonville)	Marcel's Family's Apartment	Elstir's Studio	Pension	
Guermantes's Way	Salons	Rivebelle		
Martinville Steeples	Houses of Prostitution	La Raspelière		

sonality is so strong that some people die of being separated from them" (*JS*, 96, 534).

The first setting is the village of COMBRAY, presumably near Chartres. (Proust later shifts it eastward into the World War I combat zone.) Marcel and his parents spend vacations there. Aunt Léonie's house and the village church are described as if one would never seek to appeal from their simple reality to a higher realm. Combray embodies the solidarity of family origins as well as the roots of French civilization—Church, people, royalty. The two "ways" along which Marcel and his family take their walks divide the countryside, and the universe, into two irreconcilable and seemingly inaccessible worlds. Marcel will eventually penetrate into both: the Guermantes's way, or the aristocracy with all its remote mysteries; and Swann's way, a worldly, artistic domain tinged with evil and scandal. After the opening two-hundred pages, Combray does not again become the setting of the story except for a brief section in the last volume. Yet it is never out of mind.

PARIS, where most of the novel takes place, is reduced to a few elements. At first everything revolves around the Champs-Elysées gardens where Marcel meets Gilberte Swann as a playmate. Later Marcel and his family move to a new apartment attached to the town house of the Duc and Duchesse de Guermantes. Around this complex of rooms, courtyards, and shops, the streets lead away to two further regions: the various salons to which Marcel is invited, and the houses of ill repute he later stumbles into or visits.

BALBEC is an imaginary seaside resort town in Normandy or Brittany, closely modeled on Cabourg, whose beaches attracted great numbers of French and English summer visitors at the turn of the century. (The Grand Hôtel still stands next to the beach in Cabourg, a massive building with long corridors and a slow-moving, open-cage elevator.) Marcel drives occasionally to Rivebelle, where there is a good restaurant. Elstir's studio is on the beach at Balbec. It is out of this very seascape that "the young girls in bloom" seem to materialize; they arouse Marcel's most enduring desires. A short train ride along the coast brings one to La Raspelière, the estate rented during the summer by the Verdurins.

Inland from Balbec lies the military town of DON-CIÈRES, where Saint-Loup is doing his service in the cavalry. Marcel here makes his first long stay away from his family. On returning to Paris he suddenly perceives his grandmother as a complete stranger, an old lady approaching death.

Early in the novel Marcel's father decides that the family will make a trip to VENICE. Marcel becomes so overwrought with anticipation that the trip has to be canceled. The image of Venice haunts him all his life until he finally makes the journey with his mother long after the desire to do so has passed.

Through these five settings several hundred named characters circulate. Most of them are minor, and their number includes many historical figures who flit by, barely glimpsed on the outer edges of the events. About twenty-five characters carry the central action (see Diagram II).

From start to finish there is someone in the novel saying *I*. Like the single Martinville spire on the horizon, which separates into two and then three steeples as one approaches it, different voices and different beings step out from behind that first-person singular. Yet the linguistic and semidramatic illusion of their unity inside a single pronoun is one of the principal devices used in the book to weld together the disparate levels of identity and narrative, and to permit rapid shifts among different modes of discourse. The *I* in Proust is an eternal pivot chord. Marcel Muller, the most careful analyst of this aspect of Proust's work, distinguishes seven distinct *I*'s. Let us here be content with two, plus a self-effacing third.

II. CHARACTERS

I	Family	Early Friends	Guermantes	Artists	Others
Marcel	Mother	Françoise	Marquise de Villeparisis	Bergotte	M. and Mme Verdurin
Narrator	Grandmother	Swann	Saint-Loup	Elstir	Albertine
(Author)	Aunt Léonie	Odette	Charlus	Vinteuil	Cottard
	Father	Gilberte	Duc and Duchesse	La Berma	Jupien
	Uncle Adolphe	Bloch	Prince and Princesse	Rachel	Norpois
		Legrandin	Mlle de Saint-Loup	Morel	

MARCEL, the boy who grows up in the course of the novel and who does not know at any given point what the future holds for him, says *I*. Though the given name, "Marcel" (with no family name to complete it), is mentioned only twice in 3000 pages—and even then skittishly and not for direct attribution—I feel that no other designation will serve for the "hero" as he develops in the narrative. Secondly, the NARRATOR says *I*; he is Marcel grown old and become a writer who, as he tells his own story in roughly chronological order, both reflects on it and refers to events that violate the chronology. Thirdly, on the rare occasions when he materializes beside the two others, the AUTHOR says *I*. He is not the biographical Proust but his literary persona, commenting on his novel and its relation to truth and reality. Within and around the essentially double *I* of the story sparks a constant arc of irony, sympathy, and regret. Marcel and the Narrator move slowly toward one another across the long reaches of the book, constantly signaling, sometimes lost, until they finally meet in the closing pages. That reunited *I*, like Plato's lovers, produces a whole which is the book itself.

Along the way, this linguistically single yet ontologically double *I* produces several curious effects. In spite of his constant efforts to do so, Marcel never adequately beholds himself and cannot really believe in his identity or his role. As a result, it is as if a segment of negative space occupies the center of the action, a hole in the fabric. Marcel eludes himself and eludes us. We never learn what he really looks like. He seems as much of an absence as a presence. Understandably, the reader has difficulty identifying with this inchoate creature and spends a portion of his time sifting the evidence and supplying appearances and character traits to square with the reported events. The Narrator collaborates by presenting Marcel as piteous, weak-willed, egotistical, and sometimes downright deceitful. Yet somehow Marcel makes his way in the world and seems to have more friends than enemies. This wayward and uncertain nature of the principal character gives the reader an active part to play. He cannot coast through the incidents by stepping into the shoes of the hero. Identification does not function. The reader must seek out the Marcel almost crouching behind the events and reluctant to be brought forward as a person with a name and a recognizable character.

These fluctuations in the first person of Proust's novel also mean that the question of omniscience is never settled. There are only conflicting claims. Marcel observes everything yet cannot trust his perceptions. What he learns from experience is that appearances deceive us. The Narrator commands wide knowledge and often speaks with a wisdom that seems to rise above the transitory. For he has learned that general laws and character types inlay our experience with many striking regularities. The shadowy figure of the Author lurks behind them both, barely whispering that knowledge comes of having truly lived one's life and belongs therefore to death. These approaches to wisdom vie with one another throughout the *Search*. The simplest aspect of the novel, the presence of an *I* speaking, leads into unforeseen complexities and subtleties held together primarily by that speaking *I*. In the pages that follow I shall try to distinguish carefully between "Marcel" and "the Narrator," but that terminology will not do full justice to their counterpoint in the text.

In the course of his life Marcel moves among several recognizable groups of characters. The members of his family form the most compact group. In fact his MOTHER and GRANDMOTHER virtually fuse into a single maternal presence that hovers over Marcel until close to the end. AUNT LÉONIE is an eccentric imaginary-invalid, who keeps track of every living thing in Combray from her top-floor observation post. As he ages, Marcel comes to resemble her in many respects. The FATHER's undefined professional eminence and official connections inspire awe and respect. UNCLE ADOLPHE, the black sheep of the family who keeps mistresses and lives high, leaves an indelible impression on Marcel.

Second, there are the various people Marcel knows from his childhood in Combray and who for that reason alone form a class apart. FRANÇOISE, the eternal and ever-present servant, embodies the durability of the peasantry and the stern demands of a muse. SWANN, a wealthy Jewish neighbor with unassuming manners and an entree to the most elegant Parisian society, is the first person to trouble Marcel's secure world. Swann's earlier love affair and eventual marriage with the cocotte ODETTE sets the motifs of Marcel's own career. Their daughter, GILBERTE, is his first love. LEGRANDIN, the local snob, and BLOCH, a precocious ill-mannered comrade, also enter the story in Combray. The Swann family preoccupies Marcel until he becomes obsessed by the noble family of Guermantes.

Long after the apparition of the DUCHESSE DE GUERMANTES in the Combray church, Marcel meets the members of this group in strict order of ascending social rank: The MARQUISE DE VILLEPARISIS, a school friend of Marcel's grandmother; her nephew, the MARQUIS DE SAINT-LOUP; his uncle the BARON DE CHARLUS, the most haughty and the most debased personage of the entire clan; the DUC AND DUCHESSE DE GUERMANTES, neighbors both in Combray and in Paris; and the PRINCE AND PRINCESSE DE GUERMANTES, who occupy the pinnacle of Paris aristocracy and whose "world" Marcel finally enters. MLLE DE SAINT-LOUP, daughter of Robert de Saint-Loup and Gilberte Swann, appears briefly at the end of the novel. Swann's way and the Guermantes's way unite in her youthful form.

Beyond these clearly defined groupings there are several looser sets of characters. The three major artists—BERGOTTE, a writer; VINTEUIL, a composer; and ELSTIR, a painter—exert a profound intellectual influence on the action and, through their works, on three of the principal love affairs. They do not know each other, and they stand apart from the three performing artists: MOREL, a violinist; and LA BERMA and RACHEL, both actresses. Morel becomes deeply entangled in the story through sexual intrigue.

The remaining personages do not really form a category. MONSIEUR and MADAME VERDURIN belong to the wealthy bourgeoisie and have immense (and successful) social ambitions. DR. COTTARD lends his medical renown and preposterous conversation to their little group of friends. ALBERTINE, captured and kept but never fully possessed, occupies more of Marcel's attention than any other single character. The MARQUIS DE NORPOIS is the perfect ambassador; JUPIEN, his counterpart at the other end of the spectrum, is the ultimate functionary of vice.

Approximately eight great love affairs establish powerful and lasting links between certain of these characters (see Diagram III). Five involve Marcel, and three introduce other couples. The two sets alternate so that the first-person account of one of Marcel's loves is usually followed by the third-person account of another couple. The passionate yet never sullied love between Marcel and his mother and grandmother is fully introduced before the long arabesque-like curve of the affair between Swann and Odette. Then, like a juvenile echo of "Swann in Love," we are immersed in Marcel's adolescent love for Gilberte. Later he shyly and fruitlessly follows the Duchesse de Guermantes through the streets. (For the sake of simplicity I omit Marcel's general infatuation with the band of young girls on the beach at Balbec. A season later his sentiments converge on one of them: Albertine.) The next love to appear is Saint-Loup's prodigal passion for the actress Rachel, whose talent is almost equal to her ambition. Marcel's jealous attachment to Albertine, the girl who came up out of the sands of Balbec, lasts through four volumes. Meanwhile, Charlus has pawned what remains of his reputation for the handsome, philandering violinist Morel. To these six one

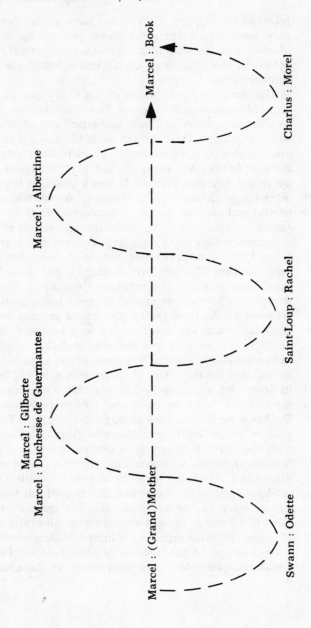

III. COUPLES

Marcel : Book

Charlus : Morel

Marcel : Albertine

Saint-Loup : Rachel

Marcel : Gilberte
Marcel : Duchesse de Guermantes

Marcel : (Grand) Mother

Swann : Odette

must add a seventh case, which is really double. During the long central sections of the novel Marcel seems to be in love with his own social success, even though he is aware of the vanity and superficiality of his surroundings. Then in the final volume his narcissism gives way to the urgency of a literary calling—his last and true love.

The society scenes with their ritualized pomp and gossip complement the exasperated intensity of the love affairs (see Diagram IV). These dinners and receptions and parties make up about a third of the book and lie along a gradually ascending social curve that finally turns back on itself. In the first volume Swann attends both a pretentious bourgeois dinner party at the Verdurins, at which the hostess directs her guests like performing animals, and an elegant musical soirée given by the Marquise de Saint-Euverte. Marcel's social progress begins humbly on the evening ex-Ambassador Norpois dines with his parents. Later, sitting in the orchestra during a charity evening at the Opéra, he watches the godlike Guermantes assembled in their box. Two receptions given by the Marquise de Villeparisis, a dinner with the Duc and Duchesse de Guermantes, and finally a soirée given by the Prince and Princesse de Guermantes, carry him to the pinnacle of aristocratic society in Paris and of his social ambitions. After this, social elevation becomes blurred by the intermingling of characters and castes. Twice Marcel attends major events at the Verdurins'. As time goes on their social chic and their wealth rival the status of the Guermantes. The most rewarding musical performance in the entire book takes place in their salon. Ultimately the astounding remarriage between the Prince de Guermantes and Mme Verdurin *veuve* transforms the social terrain to prepare for the last great reception, the novel's finale where all opposites meet.

Another third of the *Search* consists of passages of solitary meditation on perennial themes: childhood and

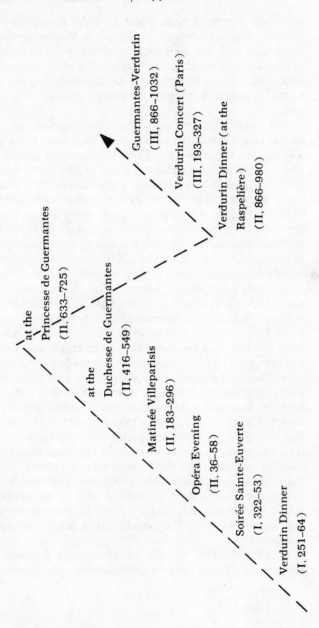

IV. SOCIETY SCENES

Verdurin Dinner
(I, 251–64)

Soirée Sainte-Euverte
(I, 322–53)

Opéra Evening
(II, 36–58)

Matinée Villeparisis
(II, 183–296)

at the
Duchesse de Guermantes
(II, 416–549)

at the
Princesse de Guermantes
(II, 633–725)

Verdurin Dinner (at the
Raspelière)
(II, 866–980)

Verdurin Concert (Paris)
(III, 193–327)

Guermantes-Verdurin
(III, 866–1032)

sleep; love, death, and time; art and morality. These psychological and philosophical thoughts cannot be described as detachable or extraneous. They enter the action as subtly and vitally as dreams shadow our waking life. It is essential to the mood and movement of the novel that it should open and close as its does with a sustained reflective passage by the undivided *I*. Marcel's thoughts on sleep, for example, are acts of mind which affect his development as much as any acts of love or social behavior.

THE PLOT

Proust's story does not emerge steadily from his text like news on a ticker tape. The narrative current is highly intermittent. Incidents collect in a series of great pools, like the social scenes just discussed. These pools engulf the landscape and give the impression of near motionlessness while we plumb the depths. Then, usually with little transition, we are carried to another wide basin of incident. Each of these pools has a geographical setting and, with the exception of "Swann in Love," covers a surprisingly short time interval. Usually it is a single season represented by a few crucial days. They are really pools of imperceptibly flowing time. The Narrator means more than mere topography when he refers to "the Combray basin" (III, 968), for that quiet body of time turns out to be an expanding universe that encroaches on all others.

Three significant sections stand outside these pools. The seven pages that open the book and the fifteen that close it frame the story by presenting it first as dream and last as art. Spanning the center of the novel is located a third sequence split into two parts that form an internal frame: the grandmother's death and (many months and four hundred pages later) Marcel's delayed realization of his loss (II, 314–15, 755–63). He experiences the full force of "intermittence of heart." The maturity Marcel attains after this rite of passage is incomplete and transitory, for it occurs in the midst of powerful distractions. Yet it reintroduces the almost forgotten forces of death and memory. This double incident holds the action in place from within, a recall to mortality in the middle of a story that is turning strongly toward frivolity.

In summarizing the plot now, I shall try above all to sketch the large movement of the action as it flows from pool to pool. It seems practical not to follow all Proust's divisions, which are makeshift or misleading at a few points, but to deal with large-scale, coherent bodies of event. Parts two and eight in the scheme followed below serve as intervals or intermissions. Though essential for spacing and timing, they fall outside the main action.

1. COMBRAY (I, 3–187). An unnamed Narrator of uncertain age is writing about himself in the first person. Yet he seems to be cut off from himself and from his past, out of which he can genuinely remember as his own only one vivid scene. One night during the Narrator's childhood (we shall call the boy Marcel), Monsieur Swann's company at dinner led Marcel's mother to refuse to come upstairs to kiss him goodnight. In protest, he kept himself awake until Swann had gone. She then relented, read to him, and spent the night in his room. Surprised, Marcel almost regretted her decision, which the Narrator calls "a first abdication" (I, 38). But this is all the Narrator can recall until, suddenly and unexpectedly, stimulated one day by the savor of a *madeleine* cake dipped in tea, he recovers the whole panorama of his childhood summers in the village of Combray. There, Marcel lived surrounded by older members of his family, according to the established routines of village and domestic life, discovering the pleasures of walking and eating and reading. Gradually his idyllic security is undermined by experiences that lead beyond "the drama of going to bed." People show unexpected and even contradictory sides. He sees they have no adequate way to

express their feelings. Meanwhile, Marcel becomes deeply aware of "the two ways" or paths that divide the village: one goes to the distant estate of the aristocratic Guermantes family, the other to Swann's house. Both ways whisper alluringly to the boy, drawing him away from his own lowly path. He feels the first stirrings of a literary vocation, along with an even stronger despair of ever becoming a writer.

2. SWANN IN LOVE (I, 188–382). Dropping back almost a generation, the Narrator relates in the third person the love affair between the Jewish man of the world, Swann, and the cocotte, Odette. She is really not his type of woman at all, yet his esthetic imagination propels him slowly through a powerful cycle of attraction toward this ordinary and enigmatic woman. Though he usually travels in the highest society, Swann begins to frequent the bourgeois Verdurin circle, where Odette is welcome and where he is finally humiliated in punishment for his lofty connections. His jealousy of Odette grows to pathological proportions before he begins a slow recovery. One assumes they will drift apart. Yet when they reappear in the narrative, they have married and had a daughter.

3. PARIS: GILBERTE SWANN (I, 383–641). As a boy playing in the Champs-Elysées gardens Marcel falls in love with Gilberte, the daughter of Swann and Odette. He also feels a strong fascination for the society of the father and mother. His love goes through an evolution similar to that of Swann's love for Odette and finally fades. Meanwhile, he is introduced to the charm of the theater, to sexual satisfaction, to the restraints imposed by his own poor health, and to literary eminence as embodied in the successful author, Bergotte. Marcel becomes increasingly aware of the difficulty of attaining happiness and of the unpredictable nature of human character.

4. BALBEC AND THE YOUNG GIRLS (I, 642–955). Now in his teens, Marcel goes with his grandmother for the

summer to Balbec, a fashionable resort on the English Channel. The Marquise de Villeparisis is staying in the same hotel. This former schoolmate of the grandmother's is a lady of high birth and scandalous past. Through her Marcel now meets the Baron de Charlus, as changeable as he is haughty, and her nephew, Robert de Saint-Loup. This elegant and intelligent young man is about Marcel's age; against all expectations they become the best of friends. Both Charlus and Saint-Loup belong to the Guermantes family. Yet for Marcel these summer days beside the beach focus increasingly on a somewhat rowdy band of young girls with bicycles, and then on one of them in particular, Albertine, apparently their leader. Her free behavior carries a hint of license and even of vice. After observing her for weeks, Marcel meets her in the studio of the painter Elstir, whose work he begins to understand and admire. When, at the end of his stay, Marcel tries to kiss Albertine in his hotel room, he fails ignominiously. Her true nature seems impenetrable, and he cannot even ascertain his own feelings toward her.

5. ENTERING THE GUERMANTES'S WORLD (II, 9–750). Back in Paris, Marcel and his family move into an apartment that belongs to the Duc and Duchesse de Guermantes and overlooks their town house. He has seen the Duchess once in Combray during a church service. She struck him at first as ugly. Yet, as he watched her across the church, she seemed to assume the symbolic beauty of her name. He now falls awkwardly in love and schemes shamelessly to meet her. For this purpose he goes to visit her nephew, Saint-Loup, who is doing his military service in Doncières. Robert is very friendly, yet remains guarded about his Guermantes relatives. He takes Marcel to lunch in Paris with his mistress, Rachel, and to one of her rehersals. They go on to a reception at Mme de Villeparisis's, where Marcel finally does meet the Duchess. He also again sees the Baron de Charlus, who takes a curiously personal interest in him.

After this first glimpse of the Guermantes's world, Marcel's grandmother dies at the end of an exhausting ten-day agony.

Marcel's initiation into society continues, but along two complementary paths he had not foreseen: elegance and vice. Attending a dinner given by the Duke and Duchess, Marcel is first dazzled by the aristocratic guests, including the Princesse de Parme, then disappointed by the mediocrity of their conversation and behavior, and finally re-enchanted by the historical and genealogical patina of their mere names. Late that night Marcel visits Charlus, as invited, and is received in an ambiguous, almost violent manner. He cannot fathom the reasons. However, a few months later he watches from a window while Charlus picks up another man in the courtyard of their house. Marcel finally realizes that the Baron is a homosexual.

Marcel's ultimate advance into the Guermantes's society associates elegance and vice even more dramatically. At a huge evening reception at the Prince and Princesse de Guermantes', the eminences of Parisian aristocracy are laid out for Marcel's inspection in a crowded ceremonial portrait. Beneath the resounding titles, the magnificent surroundings, and the polite conversation, Marcel soon detects not only snobbery and political depravity (the Dreyfus Case is at its height), but also rampant homosexuality that taints some of the most honorable names. After this hollow realization of his social ambitions, Marcel finds that what he really wants more than anything is to have Albertine to himself.

6. BALBEC: ALBERTINE AND THE VERDURIN CLAN (II, 751–1131). The first night of his second visit to Balbec, Marcel is overwhelmed by the recollection of his grandmother and the meaning of her death. He sees Albertine regularly, and at the same time begins to suspect her of Lesbian inclinations. His jealousy makes increasing demands on her. The young couple attends the weekly dinner parties given by the Verdurins at the country

place they rent for the summer. Their circle of bourgeois friends has its own quaint customs and its own snobbery. The presence among them of the Baron de Charlus and of his protégé, the violinist Morel, adds a now familiar note of elegance and vice to these dinners. But as the summer goes on, Marcel finds that both Balbec and Albertine have lost their charm. Just at this point, he is appalled to discover that Albertine is a close friend of a notorious lesbian. He decides that he wants to marry her.

7. ALBERTINE IN PARIS: CAPTIVITY AND ESCAPE (III, 9–677). There is no marriage. That winter Albertine comes to live with Marcel in his apartment. Françoise and his mother hover disapprovingly in the background. He establishes a tyrannical routine in which he barely lets Albertine out of his sight without careful supervision. Spying and lying become their way of life, from which neither can escape. In order to pursue his suspicions about Albertine, Marcel goes to a reception at the Verdurins' Paris apartment. Charlus has arranged for Morel to give a concert that evening and has invited a small number of his aristocratic friends and relatives to attend this bourgeois affair. For Marcel the evening brings a great and lasting revelation of the pleasures of music. For most of the others, the evening devolves into a shameful public struggle over the dubious loyalty and real talent of Morel. Both the Guermantes and the Verdurins behave like boors. Unable to control either his homosexuality or his snobbery, Charlus is finally humiliated by his own protégé.

More than ever obsessed by jealousy and driven to deceit by a feeling of being himself a caged bird, Marcel hypocritically suggests separation to Albertine. He hopes that the prospect will strengthen her attachment to him. Instead, he wakes up one morning to find her packed and gone.

Marcel cannot bribe her to come back, nor can he

resolve his own contradictory feelings. A telegram announces that Albertine has been killed in a fall from a horse. Immediately afterward two letters from her arrive. In the one she wrote last, she asks—apparently sincerely —to come back to him. In Marcel's mind all sentiments and motives seem to crumble at this touch. Yet a jealous curiosity to know the "truth" about Albertine's private life continues to absorb him for some time. Slowly he gains a little distance, helped by the publication of one of his articles in the *Figaro* and by seeing Gilberte again. She has a new name and a new social being. Marcel also visits Venice with his mother. Certain earlier portions of the action now begin to drift back toward the surface of the story.

8. INTERMISSION (III, 677–854). Robert de Saint-Loup and Gilberte marry and are unhappy. Robert turns out to be a homosexual and neglects his wife. Marcel goes to visit Gilberte at Tansonville, the estate where Swann had lived near Combray. The village and its surroundings have lost their magic. One night he reads a passage in the Goncourt brothers' journal about the Verdurin salon in days past. The aura of their prose convinces him once again that he will never become a writer. While at Tansonville, Marcel discovers that the two "ways" which seem to lie in totally opposed directions do in fact join farther out in the countryside, just as the marriage of Gilberte and Robert has united two alien elements of society.

The war now interrupts the story. Marcel makes several long stays in a rest home outside Paris. During his rare visits to the city he learns how wartime conditions are transforming everyday life and the social hierarchy. Saint-Loup dies a hero at the front. Charlus descends further than ever into vice and self-degradation. Only Françoise survives, barely changed by age, the eternal attendant.

9. TIME RECAPTURED (III, 854–1048). Many years

later, Marcel returns to Paris resigned to a life of boredom and indifference. An engraved invitation to a reception given by the Prince and Princesse de Guermantes
reawakens a little of the original spell of that name.
Marcel finds no reason to deprive himself of the frivolous pleasure of seeing all those people again. When he
arrives at the Guermantes's house and while he waits
in the study for a musical interlude to finish, an upsurge
of familiar sensations washes over him. These sensations, resembling the *madeleine* incident of the opening
pages, set off a great sunburst of memory reaching all
the way back to his earliest childhood and his mother
reading to him in Combray. Alone in the study, he
meditates on the nature of art and literature and re-
encounters what he has believed utterly lost: the vocation to write. His subject will be this very loss of his
calling—and the rediscovery of it. Having found the
shape of his book in his own erring life, he feels ready
to begin work.

However, when he enters the salon and meets his
acquaintances, his new optimism crumbles into dust,
for he cannot recognize any of these people who are, in
effect, the substance of his past and the subject of his
book. Age has transformed them all into grotesque pup-
pets of their former selves. At the same time the very
poles of society have reversed themselves through marriage, money, and natural evolution. The Princesse de
Guermantes is no one else but—in her third marriage—
Mme Verdurin. Stunned, Marcel recovers himself only
when he meets Mlle de Saint-Loup, Gilberte's daughter,
who fuses in her flesh the two ways of his childhood
and renders visible the intervening years. Reconciled to
time and to his own place both in it and outside it,
Marcel at last resolves to write the book he has carried
within him, and avoided, for so long. It will embody his
response to time. He sets to work, troubled only by the
realization that he has little time left in which to complete his task.

After a long life of false starts and distractions, a man discovers that he can after all reach a goal he gave up while still a boy: to write a novel. For the purpose he renounces the vanities of life and society, but only after having experienced them and learned from them. On the threshold of death he chooses art.

It is not a complicated plot in spite of its length. Marcel attains true mortality by assuming both its greatness and its puniness and by becoming his own Narrator. The story does not arrange the world into opposed forces vying for victory. For Marcel, all creatures, including those he loves most, are at the same time antagonists and accomplices. He struggles to see and to be—himself. When he holds his mother or Albertine captive, he has won no victory. There is only the long search, whose reward is the discovery that it all makes a story worth telling.

Do we believe such a story enough to respond to it? Though much modern criticism dismisses such considerations as entirely alien to literature, we can appropriately raise the question of verisimilitude. Proust's "rule" of writing to the point of exhaustion led to obvious extravagance. Some operatic or analytic passages overwhelm us. And how could any reader accept the coincidences on which the plot often turns? At the perfect moment Marcel moves into an apartment right in the Guermantes's back yard. Is it a fairy story? Charlus's great passion turns out to be for Morel, the son of Uncle Adolphe's valet and an acquaintance of Marcel's. Marcel is even on the scene and watching through the train window when Charlus picks up Morel on the platform. Yet Proust's universe, including Paris, is so small, so provincial even, that such events seem to belong. They were bound to happen. There is a similar inevitability about the characters as well. Like Goya and Daumier, Proust created devastating caricatures without sacrificing the complexity and humanity of his personages. Few of us have known people so distinguished and so depraved as Charlus, or so alluringly evasive as Albertine. Psychologically one of the most extravagant situations is Marcel's obsessive fascination with the name and nature of the Guermantes. He has a veritable love affair with a noble family. Yet in context, these portrayals achieve the unforgettable truth of fiction.

Homosexuality poses a more serious problem. It motivates Charlus, Saint-Loup, Mlle Vinteuil, Albertine (probably), Gilberte (possibly), the Prince de Guermantes, Morel (who is bisexual), and a large number of people in all strata of society. Proust would seem to be working with a set of characters so prone to homosexuality as to compromise the value and appeal of the novel. Not all of Charlus's harangues on the subject deserve the space they occupy. But it is worth noting that Proust, unlike Gide, never treated homosexuality as a higher form of love. He portrays it either as a condition determined by natural biological forces or as a taint, an unfortunate flaw in the distribution of human traits. And he sometimes acknowledges his obsession by releasing it in a scene of Rabelaisian exaggeration, like the first reception at the Prince and Princesse de Guermantes's.

Despite its extravagances, the *Search* remains a convincing portrait of an era. Certain details are priceless. When he begins going to exclusive parties, Marcel is utterly confused by the fad among the chic men of leaving their hats on the floor instead of consigning them to a footman. The descriptions of the telephone, automobile, and airplane in their early days have astonishing freshness, both documentary and poetic. More important is the fact that Proust inherited from Stendhal and Balzac a sensitivity to the process of social change. One gets the feeling that he takes time to paint the mores of Combray and of the Guermantes and Verdurin clans—three contrasting spheres of life—in order to be able to display the revolving motion that will gradually shift everyone's relative position. Yet the change does not obliterate all continuity. Though an era may be closing, the generations come and go in a cyclic movement that re-creates as much as it destroys. The wheel of fortune remains.

In living through the incidents I have summarized, Marcel reacts to more than society at large. He enacts a three-way conflict. We see him first shaped and defined by his family, who surround him with love yet never fully understand him. We see him reaching out yearningly toward society—society both in the form of an aristocratic caste which for a time he admires and envies, and in the form of men and women he seeks to know as individuals and possibly to love and possess. And we see him retreating increasingly within himself to find a quiet domain from which to observe others covertly yet understandingly. A great steady eye, he watches, trying never to condemn family or society, but letting us behold all the ways in which they fail him. In the end he does not fail us, or himself. For he tells his story in full.

The Comic Vision

By one of the essential conventions in the
Search, Marcel remains innocent for a long time.
"Innocent" is of course a relative term. This
tender young boy catches on very early to what
makes the world go round. Not unlike his invalid
Aunt Léonie, he learns to bend his mother and
his grandmother to his will. Françoise, the family
cook and retainer, shows him that even a stern
code of conduct compromises with reality. And
Marcel contrives to spy on some juicy goings-on
in Combray and to pick up all available scandal
and gossip about the guests at the Grand Hôtel
in Balbec. Yet the way the story is told implies
that all worldly wisdom belongs to the Narrator
and that Marcel drifts wide-eyed through the
wicked world as a kind of cultivated cherub. Even
though Marcel's age is not made clear, the scenes
where he supposedly fails to comprehend the

Baron de Charlus's homosexual signaling in Balbec are disingenuous. But innocence has its limits. With a dramatic sense of timing not easily discernible behind the slow-moving narrative, Proust finally stages the great reversal. Approximately halfway through the novel he places four pivotal scenes in which Marcel loses his youth, his innocence, and his illusions.[1]

The first of these four scenes, probably the most moving one in the entire book, is the week-long agony and death of the grandmother. The kindest, truest person in the story metamorphoses into a series of human and bestial figures before death lays her to sleep, restored to herself as a little girl. The event has a strong though delayed effect on Marcel. Henceforward, in spite of his mother's continuing solicitude, Marcel senses that he is alone and unprotected. Immediately following this death sequence, and almost without transition. Albertine visits him in his apartment and yields to his desire, thus confirming his earliest sexual experience. A long society scene intervenes before the third climactic sequence: Marcel happens to observe the startling encounter between the Baron de Charlus and Jupien and comprehends at last that they are homosexuals. This recognition scene reveals a whole new world to Marcel; the Narrator compares him to Ulysses, who at first did not recognize Pallas Athena. That same evening, Marcel achieves the ultimate social honor of being received at one of the elegant evening receptions given by the Prince and Princesse de Guermantes. The account of that event—a one hundred fifty-page novella in itself—describes Marcel's loss of any last shred of belief that these "aristocrats" have something special or godlike about their persons and their lives. Despite their prestigious names,

---

[1] His virginity slipped away earlier, first in a clumsy encounter with an anonymous cousin, then in a *maison de passe* with Bloch (I, 575–78). Though these incidents "opened a new era" in his life (I, 711), the narrative does not fully register them until later.

they are as stupid, as self-centered, and as unhappy as the rest of the world. Furthermore, they are even more racked than others by the vice of snobbery, from which one might think they could free themselves.

Thus Marcel's eyes are finally opened. This succession of scenes turns Marcel away from his social climbing and back toward his highly unsatisfactory yet absorbing relationship with Albertine. The respective themes of these four passages—death, love, vice, and social behavior—give them a distinctness that is reinforced by the settings and the characters. Yet they share a common attitude toward experience, an understanding of which I consider crucial to a responsive reading of the novel. In order to bring out this aspect of Proust's work, I shall examine all four scenes, beginning with the shortest, Albertine's visit.

Late one afternoon in Paris as Marcel lies moping on his bed, Albertine walks in unannounced. He finds her changed since the previous summer, more sophisticated. She responds to his advances, letting him kiss her. The copious yet discreet narrative implies that their caresses lead to further satisfactions, though apparently not coitus. After a long, banal conversation about mutual acquaintances and a fond good-by, Albertine leaves. Summarized in this bare form, the incident promises very little more than the commonplaces of sex. Let's see what Proust has done with it.

When Albertine walks in on him, Marcel is thinking quite lascivious thoughts, not about Albertine but about another attractive girl from Balbec from whom he expects a message that evening. Two hours later when Albertine leaves, Marcel will not commit himself to a time to see her again. The other girl is still very much on his mind, and he wants to keep his time open. Thus the scene is framed in carnal desire, but carefully deflected so that Albertine's entrance comes both as a total surprise and as perfectly appropriate to the mood.

We are reminded, however, that when Marcel first tried to make a pass at Albertine the previous summer in what looked like a perfect setup in his hotel room, she literally pulled the cord on him and rang for help. Will she respond now? The real question, the old refrain of every unexpected or long-delayed encounter with her, is: who is Albertine? Marcel stumbles about among sensual memories of Albertine in Balbec and present realities. "I don't know whether what took possession of me at that moment was a desire for Balbec or for her" (II, 351). He decides in any case that he is not in love with Albertine and wants no more than a simple, peaceful satisfaction from her presence.

But now he notices her language, the expressions she calmly produces from the new "social treasure" she has accumulated since the previous summer. Marcel makes a number of "philological discoveries" about her vocabulary. They provide the "evidence of certain upheavals, the nature of which was unknown to me, but sufficient to justify me in all my hopes" (II, 356). Marcel is indeed reading Albertine like a book.

> "*To my mind* [Albertine said], that's the best thing that could possibly happen. I regard it as the perfect solution, the stylish way out."
>
> All this was so novel, so manifestly an alluvial deposit leading one to suspect such capricious wanderings over terrain hitherto unknown to her, that, on hearing the words "to my mind," I drew her down on the bed beside me (II, 356).

Marcel has interpreted the signs correctly. If one is familiar with the way Proust moves calmly away from such moments and continues as if from another planet, the next sentences will come naturally.

> No doubt it does happen that women of moderate culture, on marrying well-read men, receive such expressions as part of their dowry. And shortly after

the metamorphosis which follows the wedding night, when they start paying calls. . . .

The sentence goes on for twenty lines. Having succeeded in maneuvering Albertine onto the bed. Marcel has wits enough about him only to try the "I'm not ticklish" approach. Albertine cooperates and, as they shift into position, asks considerately if she isn't too heavy. Then it happens.

As she uttered these words, the door opened and Françoise, carrying a lamp, walked in.

Albertine scrambles back to a chair. It is not clear whether Françoise has been following every move from outside the door or is simply bringing in the lamp at the usual hour. In the two-page examination of this interruption, we learn that Françoise's smallest actions constitute a moral language inflicting her code of values on everyone around her. She emerges convincingly from the analysis as the mythological figure of "Justice Shedding Light on Crime." Caught practically *in flagrante delicto*, Marcel tries to carry it off.

"What? the lamp already? Heavens, how bright it is." My object, as may be imagined, was by the second of these exclamations to account for my confusion, and by the first to excuse my slow reactions. Françoise replied with cruel ambiguity, "Do you want me to sniff it out?"

". . . snuff?" Albertine murmured in my ear, leaving me charmed by the lively familiarity with which, taking me at once for master and accomplice, she insinuated this psychological affirmation in the form of a grammatical question (II, 360).[2]

When Françoise leaves, Albertine is ready for action again. But not so Marcel. There is a precedent. Swann,

[2] Moncrieff translated Françoise's faulty subjunctive, *"Faut-il que j'éteinde?"* as "Do you want me to extinglish it?" Albertine supplies, "—guish!"

about to kiss Odette, tries to delay things in order to take full cognizance of what is happening. (See the passage quoted in the note on p. 26.) He senses something momentous and final in the act they are about to perform. Marcel holds off for similar reasons, about which we learn in some detail. Unhurriedly he rehearses the successive stages of their acquaintance and tries to reconstruct "this little girl's novel"—that is, her life beyond his ken. Knowing that it is now possible to kiss Albertine means more to Marcel than acting on the opportunity; his principal concern seems to be to breathe back into her person all the "mystery" she once carried so that, in kissing her cheeks, he will be kissing "the whole Balbec beach" (II, 363). Next comes a short disquisition on kissing and the dubious prospect of knowing anything by lip contact. We are now fifteen pages and probably an hour's reading time into the scene, and there would seem to be no way of spinning things out much longer. Marcel has her where he wants her, except that the old refrain never ceases: who is Albertine? I quote with only a few cuts.

> To begin with, as my mouth began gradually to approach the cheeks which my eyes had tempted it to kiss, my eyes, in changing position saw a different pair of cheeks; the throat, studied at closer range and as though through a magnifying glass, showed a coarser grain and a robustness which modified the character of the face.
>
> Apart from the most recent applications of the art of photography—which can set crouching at the foot of a cathedral all the houses, which time and time again, when we stood near them, appeared to reach almost the height of towers. . . . [ten more lines on photography] I can think of nothing that can so effectively as a kiss evoke out of what we believed to be a thing with one definite appearance, the hundred other things which it may equally well be, since each is related to a no less legitimate view of it. In short,

just as at Balbec Albertine had often appeared different to me, so now . . . [here seven lines to say that
such slow motion really serves to pass very rapidly
in review all the different impressions one has had
of a person] . . . during this brief passage of my lips
toward her cheek, it was ten Albertines that I saw;
she was like a goddess with several heads, and whenever I sought to approach one of them, it was
replaced by another. At least so long as I had not
touched her head, I could still see it, and a faint
perfume reached me from it. But alas—for in this
business of kissing our nostrils and eyes are as ill-
placed as our lips are ill-shaped—suddenly my eyes
ceased to see; next, my nose, crushed by the colli-
sion, no longer perceived any fragrance, and, without thereby gaining any clearer idea of the taste of
the rose of my desire, I learned from these unpleasant
signs, that at last I was in the act of kissing Albertine's cheek (II, 364–65).

Notice, among other things, that it is never directly
recorded in the testimony given here that Marcel kisses
Albertine. At the crucial moment, he literally loses his
senses. She vanishes. Consciousness cannot track experience to its lair. It must wait outside while another being,
blind but active, performs a deed that the consciousness
then reconstructs *ex post facto* from flimsy evidence.
The question "Who is Albertine?" pales to triviality
beside its counterpart: "Who am *I*?" But here Proust
has done two things simultaneously. He has shown how
sheer awareness, self-reflexiveness, erodes the reality of
any action, even, or rather particularly, when we attach
great significance to it; and he has written a superb
pastiche of his own style, a savage-sympathetic blow-up
of all the gestures with which he usually introduces us
to reality and its bitter disappointments. The relaxed
reader can be amused both by Marcel's resounding defeat of his own purposes *as he achieves them*, and the
Narrator's detachment from his own involuted narrative.

This "Kissing Albertine" sequence will bear sustained scrutiny. Most obviously, it dramatizes the dissociation of love, an idealized sentiment created by the imagination, from desire, focused on a material object. The passage also hints at Marcel's great yearning, in the midst of jealousies and disappointments, for the peaceable kingdom. He hopes Albertine will calm his life as his mother and grandmother were able to do. But few moments of serenity will in fact come from this budding affair. The action here echoes several other themes: the power of language to influence thought, the intermittent quality of character and identity, and the ironic timing of important events in our lives. But more important than this disparate content is the fact that all of it fuses not into a romantic or erotic scene but into a primarily comic incident. There is no element in the scene that fails to contribute to the mood of self-mockery leading to open laughter.

This is the shortest of the four sequences that turn Marcel's life toward the long plateau of maturity. It will be revealing to look at the other three in reverse order.

At the evening reception at the Prince and Princesse de Guermantes's sumptuous *hôtel particulier*, Marcel attains his social ambitions and, through one hundred fifty pages, observes the inflated emptiness and corruption of that society. The description of the characters recalls Daumier and even George Grosz. The Duc de Guermantes's crinkly hair, when he is angry, "seems to come out of a crater" (II, 683). The Marquise de Citry is "still beautiful, but barely suppressing a death rattle" (*"encore belle, mais presque l'écume aux dents"*) (II, 687). The comic element here is no mere matter of applied detail. From the start Marcel suspects that the invitation he has received to this chic affair is a hoax, and that he will be turned away at the door. His attempts to track down the origin of his invitation lead nowhere. Yet he cannot stay away. It gradually builds up to one

of the great drolleries in Proust. The scene begins with
an elaborate preparatory sequence about the head footman having been picked up the night before by an
anonymous and generous gentleman who was in fact
the Duc de Châtellerault. As it happens the Duke is
just ahead of Marcel in line as they wait to have their
names belted out to the guests by this same, now impos-
ing footman. When the footman learns, from the man's
own lips, his anonymous lover's identity, he "shouts [it]
out with truly professional gusto tinged with intimate
tenderness." Marcel now totters forward. His fears about
the spuriousness of his invitation to this prestigious
event have been built up for pages. I can only quote.

But now it was my turn to be announced. Absorbed in
contemplation of my hostess, who had not yet seen
me, I had not thought of the function—terrible to me,
although not in the same sense as to M. de Châtellerault—of this footman garbed in black like a execu-
tioner, surrounded by a group of lackeys in the most
cheerful livery, stout fellows ready to seize hold of an
intruder and cast him out. The footman asked me
my name, I told it to him as mechanically as the con-
demned man allows himself to be strapped to the
block. Straightening up he lifted his majestic head
and, before I could beg him to announce me in a
lowered tone so as to spare my own feelings if I were
not invited and those of the Princesse de Guermantes
if I were, shouted the disturbing syllables with a force
capable of shaking the very vaulting in the ceiling.
    The famous Huxley (whose grandson occupies an
unassailable position in the English literary world of
today) relates that one of his patients stopped going
out socially because often, on the actual chair that
was pointed out to her with a courteous gesture, she
saw an old gentleman already seated. She could be
quite certain that either the gesture of invitation or
the old gentleman's presence was a hallucination, for
her hostess would not have offered her a chair that
was already occupied. And when Huxley, to cure her,

forced her to reappear in society, she felt a moment of painful hesitation when she asked herself if the friendly sign that was being made to her was the real thing, or if, in obedience to a nonexistent vision, she was about to sit down in public upon the knees of a flesh-and-blood gentleman. Her brief uncertainty was agonizing. Less so perhaps than mine. After the sound of my name, like the rumble that warns us of a possible cataclysm, I was bound, at least in order to plead my own good faith, and as though I were not tormented by any doubts, to advance toward the Princess with a resolute air.

She caught sight of me when I was still a few feet away and (in an action that left no further doubt about my being the victim of a conspiracy) instead of remaining seated, as she had done for her other guests, rose and came toward me. A moment later I was able to heave the sigh of relief of Huxley's patient, who, having made up her mind to sit down in the chair, found it vacant and realized that it was the old gentleman who was the hallucination. The Princess had just held out her hand to me with a smile (II, 637–38).

Proust narrates the incident with a precision of timing and flourish worthy of an acrobat balanced on top of a thirty-foot stack of tables. Twice he lets us think he is going to fall, first when he allows the Duke's subplot to take over, and later when he interrupts the story at the climax with the tantalizing Huxley digression. But he never loses control, and the story inches on. Basically Proust draws his effects here out of the double *I*. The enigmatic appearance of all unfamiliar things fills Marcel with anxiety and the Narrator with amusement. The resultant text shows us hallucination playing chase with perception, danger with detachment. We smile or chuckle each time the acrobat comes close to falling, though we remain apprehensive. After this opening, it is hard not to look for comedy in the rest of the scene.

We are not disappointed. Another comic motif helps

to bind together these one hundred fifty pages. After this reception at their brother's house, the Duc and Duchesse de Guermantes plan to go on to a costume ball where the Duke, an incorrigible ladies' man, will see his latest mistress. One of his cousins, we learn, is at death's door. The rules of decorum would normally keep them home, but they find an excuse to go to the Prince's reception anyway. When they return home between parties to change into their costumes, they learn that the cousin has finally died. All is lost. They can no longer ignore the proprieties. But the Duke, intent on his rendezvous, will not accept defeat. He girds himself to brush aside this obstacle with barely a nod toward decorum. "You're exaggerating!" he says resolutely to the two ancient ladies who have brought the news. He and the Duchess sally forth. The little motif of whether or not they will finally attend the costume ball winds through the entire episode. It is the same narrative device I mentioned earlier, a kind of refrain to lead the reader through a prolonged development. Yet this induced suspense over a triviality and its mechanical repetition has a comic effect that Proust exploits to the full. Other instances carry a similar effect. Aunt Léonie's whole day hangs on finding out from Eulalie whether Mme Goupil made it to mass on time, yet when Eulalie finally visits her, she forgets to ask. Likewise, the elaborate leads about the Baronne de Putbus's sexy chambermaid are finally shown to be pure anecdotal prank, for not only does Marcel fail ever to locate this alluring creature, but he and we also learn that he did once know her, long ago, as a child in Combray (III, 307). In the scene above, the Duke's costume-ball motif displays the unwavering selfishness of Marcel's protectors in high society and provides a sardonic commentary on all the magnificence.

It is natural enough that such society scenes should be decked out in comic accouterments. But there's something more disturbing and complex in the third of the four scenes I am examining. In it we learn, beyond a doubt, that Charlus is an active and obviously experienced homosexual. Proust warned his prospective editors that the scene was shocking—as indeed it was over fifty years ago. Out of sight in the stairway, Marcel watches Charlus and Jupien identify and approach one another in the courtyard and finally retire for half an hour to an inside room. Comic details and lines keep cropping up, though they remain a quiet obbligato. (At one point Jupien, suspecting Charlus may be a bishop, is himself scandalized.) Proust asks us to see the scene in three perspectives: as the demonstration of a set of scientific laws of attraction, here presented in precise botanical terminology; as a scene having a special kind of esthetic tone, comparable to the music of Beethoven; and as a comedy of shifting identities. The weave is very tight, and he maintains a careful balance among the three. The Narrator is more explicit than usual. "This scene, moreover, was not positively comic, it was overlaid with a strangeness or, if you will, with a naturalness, whose beauty kept growing" (II, 605). Now Proust's book has no villain; his psychology is too subtle for so static a classification of character. Charlus increasingly grows into an evil genius. He abandons health, reputation, and fortune for his vices. Nevertheless, even in the depraved scene near the end of the book, where he is being flagellated by a young man in Jupien's male bordello, a curious innocence hangs over the events. We are told that Charlus really has a good heart. None of the hired hands is vicious enough to get any kick out of whipping the old man; they do it reluctantly, only for money. And in the penultimate moment when Marcel meets Charlus on the Champs Elysées after the latter has had a ravaging heart attack, Proust paints the semiparalyzed Baron both as an indomitable Lear and as a senile puppet bowing to old enemies at

Jupien's prodding. The basest vice is not excluded from the comic vision.

We can now move back to the first of the four crucial scenes. Proust brings to bear on the grandmother's death in her family's Paris apartment his broad medical knowledge and a devastating insight into what happens to people in the presence of death. These forty pages contain one of the most unsparing descriptions of a death agony in all literature. Her loss confronts Marcel with the full burden of selfhood. And the week-long sequence displays the heroism of the grandmother as she faces death and tries to sustain her disintegrating humanity, and the courage of Marcel's mother. Her grief surpasses words and gestures, and at the same time she must try to control a household gone mad. Everything is brought to bear on this test of mortality. Yet, against all odds, even this is essentially a comic scene, drawing on deep-seated traditions of danse macabre and gallows humor. Without comedy, the heroism would be strained and unconvincing. As things stand, the courage and dignity of the two afflicted women shine out through multiple layers of burlesque.

Most obviously there is Françoise whose devotion and feeling cannot be distinguished from peasant insensitivity. She keeps acting as if the whole affair were a special holiday, a *jour de gala* for which her most important mission is to have her mourning clothes properly fitted. Over everyone's objections, especially the victim's, Françoise wants to set the grandmother's hair. "By dint of repeatedly asking her whether she wouldn't like her hair done, Françoise managed to persuade herself that the request had come from my grandmother" (II, 333). The faithful servant never stops massacring the French language. Having no adequate way to express deep feelings in words, she comes out with this urgent signal of moral distress. "I've got this heavy feeling on my stomach" (II, 340).

Meanwhile, Proust keeps wheeling in unlikely visitors. When the still articulate grandmother refuses to see the specialist, he insists on examining everyone else in the household instead—and infects them all with head colds. Françoise is then distracted by an electrician whom she cannot bear to send away. She talks to him for a quarter of an hour at the back door just when she is needed in the sick room. The Duc de Guermantes arrives, insists on speaking to Marcel's stricken mother, and is unable to get over his own graciousness in visiting this bourgeois family. A mysterious and distantly related priest comes to read and meditate by the bedside; Marcel catches him peeking between the fingers he holds folded over his face. Finally, when the celebrated consultant, Dr. Dieulefoy, makes his ceremonial entrance *in extremis*, the text blurts it right out: "We thought we were in a Molière play" (II, 342). Indeed they are—in a Molière play written by Proust. Right up to the time one reaches the sudden surge of stage movements and missed cues that surrounds the actual death, laughter is one among the strong conflicting responses.

A MATTER OF TEMPERAMENT: THE OPENING STUMBLE

Proust is conventionally portrayed as a brooding figure, bedridden and sinister, given to devious sentiments and suspicious medications. Because his psychological analyses never move briskly but swing slowly back and forth like the long-stemmed neurasthenic water lilies he describes near Combray, we tend to find him solemn. Brevity is said to be the soul of wit; a work as lengthy as the *Search* must be directed toward high seriousness or gloom. Even sympathetic and intelligent critics have been blinded. "The normal, middle-distance view of human comedy," states Stuart Hampshire, "is altogether lacking in [Proust's] novel."

Proust had many vices, and at times his behavior

seems a little spooky. But no reliable account of his life could picture him as an old sober-sides. Many of his most revealing letters, once past the ingratiating phrases and the self-deprecation, take on a bantering tone. He seemed to nourish his restless intelligence on a diet of gossip about everyone he knew, including those closest to him; yet his curiosity was not so much malicious as finely sensitive to all human foibles. In a letter to Antoine Bibesco he reports this telephone conversation with the Marquis Louis d'Albufera, an unbookish young rake who fascinated Proust:

"Well, Louis, have you read my book?"
"Read your book? Did you do a book?"
"Of course, Louis, I even sent it to you."
"Ah . . . Well, if you sent it to me, my dear Marcel, I've surely read it. Only I'm not sure I received it."

Proust apparently had a special propensity for *le fou rire*—uncontrollable laughter. Lucien Daudet, a close friend from Proust's early twenties, makes much of the fact that even in later years he and Proust sometimes could not contain themselves. It happened not only when they were tweaked by a specific comic incident or expression, but often because, in a mental set created by an unexpected shift in their sensibility, *everything* suddenly became hugely funny. It is a precious state of mind.

Careful attention to biographical accounts reveals a gay, often mischievous Proust, endowed with tremendous verbal spontaneity. He carried his friends along with him in perpetrating elaborate verbal pomposities, like saying "Albion" for England and "our loyal troops" for the French Army.

The waggishness that runs through Proust's conversations and correspondence entered his literary works slowly. His first book, *Pleasures and Days*, attempts only the gentlest of comic effects. In the heaped up materials

of the projected novel *Jean Santeuil*, the comic touches
are much more frequent, yet still tentative. The most
amusing sequence comes at the very start, where the
young narrator describes and implicitly ridicules his
own excitement on discovering that a famous author is
living in the same rustic hotel on the Brittany coast.
The whole section mocks the literary convention, to
which it belongs, of the manuscript found in a bottle.
Fully matured, the same attitude guides the masterful
Pastiches, which Proust wrote for practice and for publication. They are so fully controlled that it is impossible
to do them justice by fragmentary quotation. Proust's
sly mimicry of an author belongs to his text as a whole;
its individual parts seem perfectly normal. The pastiches
demonstrate that style as a self-conscious personal mode
tends fatally toward the ridiculous. The greater the
stylist, the more vulnerable he is to pastiche. Yet far
from inhibiting Proust, that discovery apparently liberated him to write according to his own bent and face
the consequences. He acknowledges the perils of a personal style by incorporating into the *Search* passages
that function in part as self-parody. As I have tried to
show, the "Kissing Albertine" sequence is one such passage. Proust referred to his published pastiches as "a
matter of hygiene" (*CSB*, 690) which purges him of
other writers' influence. Self-mockery helped him navi-
gate among his own excesses.

The brooding and even grim image of Proust's work
is inappropriate. Released from it, one soon discovers
a novel overlaid with amusing scenes and details.[3] The

[3] The eighty pages (III, 478–558) in which Marcel, as if by
sheer exercise of his mental powers, gradually recovers from
the shock caused by Albertine's death, come closer than any
other in the book to being devoid of humor. In fact the
grimness of this section (in a letter to his editor Proust once
described it as "the best thing I've written") provides a
problematic reading on the extent of Marcel's trauma. In
the case of the grandmother's death, the shock is long de-

benevolent Princesse de Luxembourg has difficulties adjusting to the social distance that separates her from Marcel. When he is presented to her, she almost pets him, like an animal at the zoo, out of sheer kindness. The celebrated wit of the Duchesse de Guermantes jeers at the world, and is itself jeered at in turn as self-centered and artificial. Verbal comedy, in fact, permeates every scene and every character, major and minor. Dr. Cottard is an unstoppable machine for producing the most cobwebbed cliché for any situation. Françoise's endless howlers prevent Marcel from ever taking his own language for granted. And she is helped by a small cast of characters whose principal role seems to be exclusively that of fracturing French. To the elevator boy in Balbec, Mme de Cambremer will never be anything but Mme de Camember—Mrs. Cheese. To process everything novel back into familiar terms is a form of intellectual deafness most prominently displayed in language. The elevator boy's director, a Rumanian émigré out of his depth in his adopted tongue, produces solid paragraphs of untranslatable barbarisms: *"fixure"* for "fixture," *"granulations"* for "gradations." Proust sometimes allows the director to carry on his word-scrambling for too long. Yet one cannot help laughing aloud.

There is a scene in which Mme Cottard falls asleep in her chair after a big dinner at the Verdurins' summer place. Proust rides the crest for three pages, obviously enjoying himself. Spoofing all his own earlier scenes about sleep, he runs through a learned medical discussion on the subject and has Dr. Cottard cruelly keep waking his wife to tell her it's time to leave, only to let her relapse again. When she finally comes up blinking out of the depths, she is still talking in her dream. The guests enjoy the performance.

layed, probably deeper, and surrounded by comic circumstances. Even in the "Albertine Is Dead" section, Aimé's work as a private detective for Marcel introduces some discreetly scabrous comedy (III, 515–16, 525).

"My bath is just right," she murmured. "But the feathers on the dictionary . . ." she cried, straightening up. "Oh, Good Lord, how foolish I am. I was thinking about my hat, and I must have said something ridiculous. Another minute and I would have dozed off. It's the heat from that fire that does it." Everybody began to laugh, for there was no fire (II, 962).

Mme Cottard looks ridiculous because she has confused waking and dreaming and produces the anomaly of "dictionary feathers" as a souvenir of her trip. But this little scene tucked away in the middle of the novel reveals unexpected links with the opening of the book. Both moments are located in the precarious zone between sleep and waking, and Mme Cottard's very human behavior sets the novel's first three sentences in a new light. Listen to them again. These are the first words Proust offers us, a subtle gambit, the flash of mental and physical movement which will influence every moment to follow.

> For a long time I used to go to bed early. Sometimes, when I had barely put out my candle, my eyes would close so quickly that I did not even have time to say to myself, "I'm going to sleep." And half an hour later the thought that it was time to go to sleep would awaken me.

When we first see him, Marcel is as confused as Mme Cottard. His attention, his grasp of what he is and what he is doing, collapses under him. I interpret this incident as an epistemological stutter or stumble, deliberately placed ahead of all other incidents. It functions like a standard vaudeville routine: the curtain opens; an actor walks out on stage; before he can open his mouth, he trips hugely and barely saves himself from falling. Laughter. Proust's *I* does something very similar. He stumbles over his self-awareness before the book is under way. According to one scale of events, he regains his balance forty pages later as Marcel in the "Combray" section. According to another, more basic scale, the equilibrium of self-recognition does not occur until 3000 pages later. And even then Marcel, metamorphosed into the Narrator of his own life, is perched on grotesque stilts which reach back into his past and on which he can barely stand. Montaigne uses the same carnival metaphor in the closing lines of his last essay, "On Experience," and tells us to keep our feet on the ground. Proust does not shrink from portraying the elevations and pratfalls out of which our deepest insights may emerge.

THE USES OF THE COMIC

Beyond its own life as sheer exuberance and celebration, the comic has earned a place in "serious" literature through three potential roles: as social corrective, as relief from the tensions of plot or implacable fate, and as a vehicle for forbidden content. These categories will shed some light on Proust's practice.

What is excessively individual or conformist in us usually comes out as rigid, mechanical behavior. A natural Bergsonian, Proust brought on his characters both masked and revealed by their tics. Mme Verdurin has a sobbing ritualized laugh that betrays the artificiality of her feelings. Saint-Loup, though favored with elegance and *savoir-faire*, slips sideways through all doorways, as if he has something to hide. (He does.) Proust excels in depicting exaggerated, socially compromising conduct, but the corrective edge of the comic in the *Search* is constantly blunted by uncertainty about what represents appropriate behavior in a society coming apart before our eyes. The grandmother's death is a Molière play in that large portions of the action veer toward satire and even burlesque. But in Proust there is no assumed universe of harmonious manners to appeal to, no *juste milieu*.[4] Awkwardness is simply part of our lot. Corrective action will not avail.

Many of the comic elements I have cited earlier are undeniably diverting and may provide "relief" from a highly extended story. A superb two-page caricature of monocle styles in the middle of a social scene (I, 326– 327) seems to serve such a purpose. Yet a monocle described by Proust reveals social manners as well as individual character. And from what could we be relieved by comic elements merely inserted or pasted on? For Proust has jettisoned most conventions of linear plot and character development. We are rarely sure of motivation and intention, or of where events are headed. When the Narrator proposes three or four possible explanations for what happens, and an equal number of possible results, a sense of dislocation and anomaly becomes the very ground out of which the action springs. This sense does not just raise its head at long intervals as "comic relief." As I have tried to show, it weaves tightly through scenes one would usually consider serious or emotional.

The third role conventionally assigned to comedy figures more importantly in the *Search* than the first two, and Proust explicitly recognized this function. By depicting a "depraved" character like Charlus as comic, ultimately as a mock-heroic figure, Proust seems both to pass sentence on him as a deviation from the norm,

---

[4] In a text not incorporated into the novel, Proust gave a notion of how far the comic sense of life, free of moral overtones, invaded his sensibility. He described Bergotte as leading an unrepentantly dissolute life, yet writing books which set very demanding moral standards. The morality of such people, the Narrator states, "makes the good consist in a sort of painful consciousness of evil . . . rather than in abstention from it" (Maurois, pp. 146–47). The revealing yet disturbing thing about this fragment is that Bergotte's friends find his inconsistent behavior, not in bad faith or hypocritical, but "comic."

and simultaneously to grant him pardon for that deviation. Charlus's vices look like a grotesque caricature,
and thus Proust sought dispensation for the forbidden
content he felt compelled to deal with. He wrote to the
publisher Fasquelle to say that nothing was really shocking in his novel, and then corrected himself in a parenthesis: "(or rather it is saved by the comic, as when the
concierge calls the white-haired Duke [sic, for "Baron"]
a 'big kid'. . . .)" As Freud insisted, in writing about wit,
the comic furnishes protective coloring for themes that
cannot be introduced without it. Social corrective and
comic relief do not help much in understanding the
Search, but the novel does rely sometimes on the camou-
flage effect of the comic.

From the start of the *Search* we are given the record
of a sensitive consciousness eager to discover and enter
the outside world of appearances, and apparently unable
to do so in any satisfactory way. Marcel remains confined inside a pliable but impenetrable membrane of
self-consciousness. Yet he cannot turn away from the
universe of attractive enigmatic beings that present
themselves outside his consciousness and his identity.
The comic element in the novel follows this division into
outward and inward.

In the external world the comedy arises from many
sources. The French critic Gilles Deleuze has recently
emphasized the way in which Proust presents people
inhabiting a world of signs and clues needing astute
interpretation. One result of this constant decoding, a
result Deleuze fails to bring out, is a parade of *gaffes*, a
comedy of errors. Marcel is forever getting his signals
switched and confusing identities. He even mistakes the
color of Gilberte's eyes and falls in love particularly with
her "azure" eyes, when in fact they are black (I, 140–
141). Yet there is no surer path to the truth than through
such foolish blunders. "An error dispelled gives us a new
sense" (II, 613).

Most tellingly, however, the comic tone in outward

events results from botched timing. Few things happen when expected, or as desired, or as might be appropriate. Usually things come too late; by the time their charms become available to him, Marcel has half lost interest in the haughty Guermantes family and in the person of Albertine. At other moments the timing is too perfect; the unlikely coincidences and windfalls which favor Marcel usually paralyze him. Both kinds of timing make him look ridiculous. Combined and reinforced, they persist into the novel's closing sequence, which relates Marcel's encounter with death.

After long absence from Paris, now aging more than he realized, Marcel attends the last great Guermantes reception. With difficulty he recognizes his old friends and, through them, the tortuous track of his own life. He resolves once and for all to sit down and write the book he has been carrying inside him all these years. Françoise, the only surviving witness, recognizes the change in him and at last "respected my work" (III, 1034). Immediately, however, Marcel finds himself blocked. The discovery of the essential truths about time that give him the confidence to begin his novel also makes him aware of his vulnerability to contingent time. For time can inflict death on him at any moment, wipe out "the precious deposits within him," and prevent him from completing his work. At the start of the book, Marcel fumbles his timing in falling asleep. At the close, he picks the wrong time to settle down to producing a work of art. Yet this worst of all threats is given detached, almost amused treatment.

> Now, by a bizarre coincidence, this carefully considered fear [of death] came alive in me at the moment when the idea of death had just recently become indifferent (III, 1037).

Marcel appears always out of step, always the victim as he confronts the external world.

Yet inwardly he remains undiscouraged in spite of all. Resignation and lucidity give him strength. Self-deprecation is his form of courage. In later years he finds it incredible that he should ever have bestowed special status on the Guermantes clan. And it is even more ludicrous that anyone, particularly a Guermantes, should see merit *in him*.

> Later, I learned that the Guermantes believed that I belonged to a race apart, but a race that aroused their envy because I had merits unknown to me and that they prized above all others (II, 439).

Marcel cannot believe in his own accomplishments. When he happens upon an article he wrote, finally published in the *Figaro*, he fails for a time to register the fact. "I opened the *Figaro*. How annoying! The lead article had exactly the same title as the article I had sent them and that they hadn't printed yet" (III, 567). Self-deprecation turns into slapstick when the Narrator describes Marcel's first entrance into a very chic café.

> . . . I had to go in alone. Now, to begin with, once I had ventured into the revolving door, a device I wasn't accustomed to at all, I thought I'd never get out again (II, 401).

Such incidents have a theatrical flavor. Proust carries the effect even further in the carefully planned double incident of Mme Swann walking at noon in the Bois de Boulogne surrounded by her reputation and her admirers. In the first version (I, 419–21), Marcel is "an unknown young man whom no one noticed." Palpitating yet resolute as he sees her approaching, acting on the dubious basis of his acquaintance with Mme Swann's daughter and his parents' acquaintance with her husband, "I raised my hat to her in so exaggerated a gesture that she could not help smiling. People laughed." Though merely an "extra" on the fringes of her performance, Marcel feels more pleasure than humiliation in accomplishing this exploit. A few years later, when Marcel has come to know Mme Swann quite well, the scene is restaged with Marcel placed inside the magic circle, under Mme Swann's parasol, talking confidentially with her, holding her jacket. Looking out at the public, he sees one or two unknown young men summoning up the courage to greet her. Then, in fascination, he watches the ceremonial entrance of the most elegant aristocrat of the era, historically the genuine article, the Prince de Sagan. "The Prince, turning his horse's head toward us as if for an apotheosis on stage, or in the circus, or in an old painting, addressed to Odette a grand, theatrical, almost allegorical salutation" (I, 640). It is all *performed* —both vivid and unreal, thus held far enough away for a subtle destructive element to seep in around the edges. When Marcel first greeted Mme Swann, people laughed. Now that he stands among the mighty, there is no open laughter. But having reached the apparent center of the universe in this scene of apotheosis, Marcel still seems vaguely out of place—and this time the others along with him.

At least this is how the Narrator paints things. And it may be evident how the double *I* of Proust's narrative helps create the novel's gently mocking tone. Marcel and the Narrator form a contrasting pair like comic and straight man—*clown et auguste*. Either one without the other would not hold our attention for long. Together they combine innocence and wisdom. The jokes are on Marcel, told by his alter ego, the Narrator, looking back on his former self. The syntax of the story carries inside it this enlarged and ultimately comic perspective of reflection and memory. That perspective cannot be peeled off the body of the narrative as incidental entertainment or social commentary. It constitutes one of the most human aspects of Proust's vision. This is a far cry from the gloomiest book ever written.[5]

[5] Among standard works on Proust, those by André Maurois and Léon Pierre-Quint take time to consider his comic side. Neither does much more than introduce a chapter on how Proust achieves amusing effects through character, language and situation. Two scholarly-critical works have developed the subject along similar lines: Roland André Donzé, *Le Comique dans l'œuvre de Marcel Proust* (Neuchâtel, 1955), and Lester Mansfield, *Le Comique dans Marcel Proust* (Paris, 1953). Only Germaine Brée, in a chapter of *Marcel Proust and Deliverance from Time*, does justice to the pervasiveness and the organic role of comedy in the *Search*.

Proust's Complaint

iv

FALSE SCENTS

Like the youngest son in a fairy tale, Marcel is given three chances to succeed. He tries three solutions to the puzzle of life, and one after the other they fail. Of course it turns out in the end that he has won without knowing it, as if he had walked backward into paradise. The three magic stones, the three wishes he was allowed, come to naught. But since error recognized is a source of personal knowledge, the years of quest have not been wasted.

The first false scent leads to the Faubourg Saint-Germain, the quarter of Paris inhabited by the oldest families of the nobility. Marcel smells from far off the legendary amalgam of birth, title, and landed property that forms aristocratic society. It showed its last spark of life in France during the prewar years in which the *Search* is set. Marcel supposes that there is a fourth ingredient as well: nobility of character. Instead, he finds totally human lineaments exaggerated and distorted by the setting. The *prestige* (a key word in Proust) of the rich and titled turns to tinsel when approached close up.

After preliminary trials and rehearsals, Marcel enters the select domain on the evening he is invited to dine with the Duc and Duchesse de Guermantes. The Duke himself displaying his most considerate politeness meets him at the door. After visiting the collection of Elstir paintings, Marcel is presented to the Princesse de Parme. She seems to radiate a Stendhalian aura and a gentility all her own. Then, before Marcel can begin to identify the other guests, dinner is announced, the machinery starts, the Duchess circles the salon like a protective huntress to take his arm, and they enter the dining room "in a rhythm of exact and noble movements" (II, 434). At this point the action freezes, and the Narrator opens an unsparing fifty-page digression on the wit and politics of the Guermantes. Marcel tries to find some ground on which to resist his initial negative reaction to his hosts.

> But just as in the case of Balbec or Florence, the Guermantes, after having first disappointed the imagination because they resembled their fellow men more than their name, could afterward, though to a lesser degree, hold out to one's intelligence certain distinguishing particularities (II, 438).

By the end of the dinner a hundred pages later, it is the remarkable genealogy of their names and the history of their titles that re-endows these vulgar citizens with fascination, with "their lost poetry" (II, 532).

Thus the prestige of the Guermantes and their kind survives essentially as an established form of *snobbery*. For Proust, snobbery is the great cohesive force that holds society together. He studies it tirelessly at every social level. The word itself covers two major attitudes or classes of snobbery. Proust contrasts them in a semimathematical formula while describing the Duchesse de

Guermantes when she still had the title of Princesse des Laumes.

> She belongs to that half of humanity in whom the curiosity the other half feels toward the people they don't know is replaced by an interest in the people they do know (I, 335).

The sentence bears expansion. Persons securely favored with high rank and wealth are prone to a snobbery of self-satisfaction, expressed in their exclusive attention to their own class and milieu. Those not so favored, but who aspire to social position, are prone to the snobbery of social envy, a desire to spurn their own class and milieu. Of course the snob rarely occurs in the pure state, without a tincture of the other category. Charlus "combined in himself the snobbery of queens and that of servants" (III, 598). Proust is using the word in the second sense when he refers to a woman as "snobbish even though a duchess" (III, 266). The varieties of *mondanité* gradually give Marcel an understanding of the springs and wheels that turn the social machine.

One of Proust's early titles for the first volume of his novel was "The Age of Names." He means *proper* names, of places and of people. Only such names seem to stand for "something individual and unique" (I, 387). The false scent of social success corresponds closely in the novel to the age of names. For years, what ignites Marcel's imagination is always in a name. A train timetable reads like poetry, just as a noble title has the magic power of "a fairy" (II, 11, 533). As times goes on, these names, the most eminent and effective vehicles for prestige, wither and almost die. The "semantic illusion" of social prestige, despite its poetic origins, hardens into the dry husk of snobbery.[1]

The second false scent is love, both as sentimental at-

---

[1] The best description and analysis of this "semantic illusion" can be found in "Proust et le langage indirecte," by Gérard Genette, collected in *Figures II* (1969).

tachment and as physical desire. The two can be distinguished, but neither leads to true gratification. Swann's
famous last words on the death of his love for Odette
catch the mood of disappointment.

> To think that I wasted years of my life, that I hoped
> to die, that I had my greatest love affair with a woman
> who didn't appeal to me, who wasn't even my type
> (I, 382).

Proust extends to the verge of solipsism what Stendhal
and Nerval knew about the imaginary subjective nature
of love. In his liaison with Albertine, Marcel makes his
own special variation of Swann's pattern. In both cases a
transformation takes place not unlike that which we
have seen modifying the dynamics of the social sphere
and turning respect for rank and honor into snobbery.
By a kind of psychological fate, love decays into the very
different yet equally powerful force of *jealousy*. It happens to Swann and Marcel (and to Saint-Loup and Charlus) before love has achieved fulfillment or equilibrium.
Why must it be so? It is as if the capacity of physical
actions and ordinary words to reach behind appearances
and touch another person fails us when we most need it.
Communication falls short—whereupon love and desire
yield to a kind of emotional envy which feeds on the pos-
sibility that the loved one is communicating better with
someone else. Given its head, the imagination then runs
away with everything. ". . . the mind goes to work; instead of a need one finds a novel" (III, 1022).

What disturbs many Proust readers more than his
uncompromising criticism of love is the fact that he does
not spare friendship. Gradually we are forced to perceive
that egotism, distraction from boredom, and insecurity
reign over the only friendship Marcel allows himself,
that with Saint-Loup. And the Narrator leaves no room
for doubt. Friendship tends to make us

> sacrifice the only real and incommunicable part of
> ourselves . . . to a superficial self which does not,

like the other one, find any joy in its own being, but is touched to find itself held up by external props, taken in and sheltered by an individual foreign to itself (II, 394).

Proust's correspondence and biography demonstrate the importance that friendship held for him and the steadiness with which he observed its rituals, if not its realities. Thus it is perplexing to read a letter he wrote in 1901 to Antoine Bibesco (who became one of his closest friends) upbraiding him for abusing the code of friendship and in the same breath affirming that friendship is "something without reality." We will simply have to live with the fact that profound skepticism about generally recognized sets of human feelings can coexist with a yearning for those feelings. In the *Search*, the Narrator's description of Marcel's long detour through the false promises of love and friendship is virtually congruent with the story itself.

The third false scent in the novel will be much harder to deal with than the other two, because it carries us into the domain of the intellectual and the esthetic. Not only did Proust's thinking in this area shift and evolve as he wrote, but he often presented and dramatized views opposed to those in which the Narrator ultimately puts his faith.

The third path of error is art—not all art, but art misconstrued and given false value. A dilettante and esthete in his youth, Proust developed his own convictions in the crucial period when he won his independence from Ruskin. In the postscript he added to his introduction to *The Bible of Amiens*, and in the later introduction to *Sesame and Lilies*, a series of references single out as "intellectual sin" what begins as a form of artistic "snobbery" (*CSB*, 183). This "essential infirmity of the human mind" (*ibid.*, 134) is attributed to Ruskin as well as to Montesquiou, Proust's two intellectual heroes at that time. They are guilty of esthetic "fetishism" (*ibid.*, 117), a veneration of the symbol instead of the reality it represents, a worship of esthetic beauty without approaching the "discovery of truth" (*ibid.*, 132) that gave it birth and significance. *Idolatry* is the word Proust finally settles on to carry his full condemnation of this esthetic attitude (*ibid.*, 129–41).

In the *Search* we are given so much varied discussion of art that it is difficult to sort out false or provisional attitudes from the deepest insights. The book closes with a great philosophical affirmation of art as a means of discovering and communicating truth. But art objects set up as fetishes, removed from life and from moral meaning, come under steady attack. A sensitive and intelligent amateur of the arts, Swann is nevertheless a victim of "idolatry of forms" (I, 852) because he tries to arrange his life—even his love life—according to the narrow beauty he sees in art. Bergotte, a genuine though limited artist in his writings, has, when he dies, a glimmering sense that he has taken the wrong course, that he has been "imprudent." Looking at a little yellow patch in the Vermeer painting he has gone to see ("That's how I should have written"), he has a heart attack.

> A celestial scales appeared to him which carried on one side his own life and on the other the little patch of wall that was so beautifully painted. He felt that he had imprudently given up the former for the latter (III, 187).

He had been a fetishist, and he dies as one. In the curious image that follows, his books are arranged by threes in bookstore windows, "like angels with unfurled wings . . . the symbol of his resurrection" (III, 188). But by now we know better. Such a resurrection can take place only among the cultists of esthetic idolatry. Proust's tone is deeply ironic. Bergotte had wasted his life and therefore compromised his art.

What I am arguing here differs from much prevailing criticism. Therefore, I shall document it further. Though there are long passages of conversation in the novel,

Marcel's words are rarely given in direct discourse. What he says is barely summarized, and often passed over in silence. (Possibly this is further evidence that we cannot be ourselves with others.) Exceptionally, Marcel is quoted at some length in a conversation with Charlus, who is bemoaning the wartime destruction of the Combray church. "The combination of surviving history and art that represents France at her best is being destroyed" (III, 795). (It also represents Marcel's childhood.) Charlus goes on to wonder whether the statue of Saint Firmin in Amiens has also been destroyed. "In that case," he adds, "the highest affirmation of faith and energy in the world has disappeared." Marcel raps his knuckles.

"Its symbol, Monsieur," I answered. "And I adore certain symbols as much as you do. But it would be absurd to sacrifice to the symbol the reality it stands for. Cathedrals should be venerated until the day when, in order to save them, one would have to renounce the truths they teach. The arm of Saint Firmin raised in a gesture almost of military command, declared: Let us be broken if honor requires it. Do not sacrifice men to stones whose beauty has caught for a moment a few human verities" (III, 795).

There is no other passage quite like it in the book. The Author has thrust his head through the text in order to speak to us directly. In his desire to refute idolatry, he violates the conventions of his own work. As a character, Marcel is never so resolute and categorical as this speech suggests. Even the Narrator speaks more softly. In fact, Marcel inherits from Swann and Bergotte a sense of the privileged status and calling of art. Its elevated position has made it impossible for him to believe he could ever become an artist. How could he lift his lowly insights and impressions to the exalted regions of literature? Esthetic snobbery, or *idolatry*, has kept him from pursuing his own vocation.

Another illustration of this mental cramp of Marcel's occurs in the section early in the final volume where he reads himself to sleep over a passage out of the Goncourt brothers' journal. This scene, which includes Proust's masterful nine-page parody of the Goncourts' arty journalism, suddenly turns the action of the story back on itself, as when a passenger is startled to see the other end of his train while going around a curve. The false scents and lost quests seem to lead here, and produce a deep feeling of discouragement.

In the Goncourt "extract," Marcel finds himself reading about a dinner at the Verdurins. The apartment, the people, the stories are all familiar. Yet, as now described, they appear bathed in miraculous glow of literary and historic importance. The Goncourts have observed everything, right down to the elegant plates the meal is served on. Every detail of that life seems exciting and significant. In consequence, as he reads, Marcel feels everything tumbling down around his ears. He knew all these people. How could he have gone so far astray as to consider the Verdurins a couple of mediocre bourgeois social climbers and bores if they can inspire these lyric pages? The people he had classified as mere bit players (*figurants*) turn out, in the Goncourts' authenticating account, to be the leads (*figures*). The closing sentences of the passage describe Marcel's quandary as belonging both to life and to literature.

> . . . it amounted to wondering if all those people whom one regrets not having known (because Balzac described them in his books or dedicated his works to them in admiring homage, about whom Sainte-Beuve or Baudelaire wrote their loveliest verses) or even more if all the Récamiers and the Pompadours would not have struck me as insignificant people, either because of some infirmity in my nature . . . or because they owed their prestige to an illusory magic belonging to literature (III, 723; cf. II, 30).

Everything is now in jeopardy. Either Marcel has misjudged all the apparently tiresome and fraudulent people of fashion he knew and has been blind to their real importance; or else they are indeed as ordinary as they appeared and it is the magnifying, transforming power of literature that has raised them to an imaginary and fraudulent prestige.[2] He is unable to reject either alternative. Both ways, he loses. Marcel perceives that the Goncourts write as snobs and idolators, and that at the same time their mannered style affects his sensibility more forcefully than he would like. This lucid grasp of a contradictory dilemma affords him no comfort. It is precisely at this point in the story that Marcel takes refuge "for long years" in a *maison de santé* outside Paris.

Everything seems to go wrong for Marcel. Social success is empty. Love and friendship carries him not to the discovery of another person but into closer quarters with himself. Art may be a lie, getting in the way of reality. The passage about Marcel reading the Goncourts' journal is particularly revealing. When he closes the book, Marcel's first exclamation to himself is, "The Prestige of Literature!" (III, 717). There is something about a written text—its vision, its transparence, its metaphoric quality—that makes it very strong magic. Even against our will it can enter our mental system and exert a lasting influence. Prestige in this sense begins to look little different from snobbery in the social domain. If the patina of heightened existence that hangs over certain lives can be attributed to the secret power of literature, then we can accept the need for a certain portion of artifice to save reality from triviality and platitude. But the converse case that Proust puts forward and that troubles Marcel seems far more devastating. Is there a

[2] Confronted by a similar problem in social relativity theory, Marcel's grandmother has no trouble finding a solution. She discovers that their nice but slightly disreputable neighbor in Combray, Swann, is a close friend of the nephews of the Marquise de Villeparisis, her most aristocratic schoolmate. "Now, this information about Swann had the effect, not of raising him in my grandmother's estimation, but of lowering Mme de Villeparisis" (I, 20).

quality in some people that makes them highly suscepti-
ble to the prestige of literature and yet incapable of
finding its counterpart in their own existence? The
crucial phrase in the last passage quoted, a phrase which
opens in Marcel's line of thought a crevasse falling away
to unknown depths beneath, is *some infirmity in my
nature.*" What precisely is this infirmity that makes
Marcel incapable of taking full account of the very
scenes he has lived through? The answer will tell us
what has made Marcel so prone to the false scents of
society, love, and art.

FROM PLACES TO PEOPLE:
THE "INFIRMITY IN MY NATURE"

During the extended nocturnal musings at the start of
the *Search*, the voice of Proust's Narrator first gathers
strength and identity in a kaleidoscopic description of
bedrooms. He is trying to orient himself, to establish
where he is. Wallace Stevens in his "Adagia" could have
been speaking for Proust: "Life is an affair of people not
of places. But for me life is an affair of places and that
is the trouble." Proust's universe hangs together at the
start more substantially by places than by people, who
are forever disappearing behind new incarnations of
themselves. Each important place takes shape as a
vividly experienced and basically stable association of
light effects, smells, tastes, sounds, history, habitual
behavior patterns, and predictable deviations. Combray
forms a "closed society" (I, 110) with its own laws and
legends. Marcel comes to rely on a similar ritual of
familiar place when he plays in the Champs-Elysées
gardens in Paris. Balbec also stands for a reassuring stability of life. When Marcel returns for his second visit to
this alluring seaside resort, only his outlook on things
has changed. Balbec with its familiar landmarks and
leisurely life seems motionless in time. The early vol-

umes of *Search* depict in convincing detail what Proust states bluntly in *Jean Santeuil*.

> Places are people, but people who do not change and whom we often see again after a long time in wonderment that we have not remained the same (*JS*, 534).

One can rely on places, above all on landscapes like Combray and Balbec where man's handiwork blends with nature.

But as time goes on Marcel loses this security. Paris apartments and fashionable salons replace countryside and landscape. These city interiors frame not the durable objects of nature but the inscrutable metamorphoses of men. Even the attractions of Balbec fall victim to this movement. After a summer full of visits to sites in the area, Marcel realizes that the exotic local place names have slowly been "humanized" (II, 1098). He decides to leave this "much too social valley" (II, 1112). When his special sensibility to landscape has withered away, only Venice, still unvisited and unknown, seems to hold out the power to move him.

The last exterior in the *Search* comes only a few pages before the last Guermantes reception. Marcel's train stops in the countryside next to a line of obliquely lit trees. A sensitized reader will at this point see several hovering images—the half-lit tower of the Combray church, the trees the Narrator reflects on in the Bois, the three trees from which Marcel receives mysterious signals in Hudimesnil near Balbec (I, 64, 423, 717). But not Marcel. His light has gone out.

> "Trees," I thought, "there's nothing more you can say to me, my chilly heart can no longer hear you. Yet here I am in the very lap of nature. Well, I feel only indifference and boredom when my eyes follow the line that separates your illuminated forehead from your shadowy trunk. If I could never before fully

believe myself a poet, I now *know* that I am *not* one"
(III, 855).

Landscape serves no longer, even in retrospect. During
the novel's long meandering, the collection of vivid
scenes which Marcel formerly possessed and which he
could more or less at will slide into his interior stereo-
scope has been subordinated to the characters and absorbed by them. Albertine, an unknowable mixture of
innocence and vice, takes shape out of the exotic topography of Balbec and then displaces it. The richly colored
landscapes of Combray and Balbec fade into the background as the cast of characters moves forward. People
have taken over from places.

This large-scale shift from place to person as the
focus of the narrative provides the background for Marcel's long dedication to society, love, and art. Though
these pursuits may not bring him the rewards he hopes
for, they do seem to lead him out of childhood and toward maturity. Haltingly, he begins to make his way in
the world outside the family unit. Yet Marcel has the
desperate feeling that life is escaping him precisely
when he can for the first time find friends and protectors
and lovers. What has gone wrong? We are dealing again,
I believe, with a quirk of mind that begins very early in
the story as a kind of contrariness, of perverseness in a
spoiled boy.

As a child in Combray, Marcel goes to Machiavellian
lengths to lure his mother up to his bedroom to say
goodnight when she should be downstairs attending to
her guests. The scene is justly celebrated, for it sets the
novel in motion and anticipates many themes to be
developed later. The close of the incident brings its most
revealing moment. When finally his mother does come,
Marcel's father indulgently persuades her to spend the
night in Marcel's room and read him to sleep—thus compromising her principles and her authority. Marcel cannot cope with so great success and inwardly reverses

himself. "If I had dared to now, I would have said to maman: 'No, I don't really want you to, don't sleep here with me'" (I, 38). Her capitulation unmans him.

From this seed will grow a vine of constrictive experience, a vertible tree of forbidden knowledge. In a letter to the Princesse Bibesco, Proust generalized the same reaction. "A sensation, no matter how disinterested it may be, a perfume, or an insight, if they are present, are still too much in my power to make me happy." Steadily and disturbingly, the novel develops this mental set: it is the same "infirmity in my nature" that troubles Marcel when he reads the Goncourts' journal. Toward the end of the evening when he dines for the first time with the Duc and Duchesse de Guermantes, Marcel tries to take stock of his disappointment. I have described how his entry into this most elegant and inaccessible layer of society fails to meet expectations. He finds the explanation not in the other people but *in himself.*

> Several times already I had wanted to leave, and, more than for any other reason, because of the insignificance which my presence imposed on the party. . . . At least my departure would allow the guests, once rid of the interloper, to form a closed group. They would be able to begin the celebration of the mysteries (II, 543–42 . . .).

Because this is still a young dilettante among the dowagers, we might easily laugh off such a moment as something like a failure in social depth perception. It should all straighten out as Marcel gains experience and confidence. Yet he and we remain apprehensive. Even Swann fell victim to this vision of his own presence blighting reality. The part of Odette which he longs above all to know is her "real life as it was when he wasn't there" (I, 299). Marcel feels the same way toward Albertine, and could barely bring himself to kiss her when available.

It is this clouding of the mind at the moment of achieving what it most desires, this "infirmity in my nature," that I call Proust's complaint. He was not the first to discover it, of course. He did not even give it a consistent name. But more than any other writer, Proust explored this distressing perverseness that dogs the most enterprising activities of the human mind and seems to deprive it of satisfaction. One finds, knit tightly into the comedy of the *Search*, a long lament of self-deprecation.

SOUL ERROR

Throughout the seventeenth and eighteenth centuries, in England and on the Continent, the psychological investigations of men's motives concentrated on the theme of pride and the search for fame. The French rolled the two together into the term, *la gloire*. It haunts the work of La Rochefoucauld and La Bruyère, of Corneille and Racine. Milton knew that "Fame is the spur. . ." (*Lycidas*) yet proceeded to condemn it in all its forms except the divine. When Voltaire, Hume, and Kant picked up the theme in an age less concerned with a Christian God, they treated the desire for esteem in the eyes of others as a socially beneficial infirmity. This powerful doctrine accepts human vanity or pride as the necessary engine of culture and as the source of the fair edifices of civilization. The current still runs strong in the nineteenth-century novels of Stendhal and Balzac, who were absorbed by the myth of the young adventurer out to make his mark in the world.

Against this background of *gloire*, Marcel's "infirmity in my nature" looks ludicrous. He hopes for success and fame; what holds him back? Why is he such a miserable hero? Considering his accomplishments, why does he feel this way? The answer is confounding. Marcel cannot win; not because he lacks talent or looks, but *simply because he is Marcel*. His very presence discredits, in his own eyes, whatever he does. After the most elaborate efforts, he attains goals that turn out to be valueless—precisely because he has reached them. When he kisses Albertine, he confronts ten Albertines, no one of whom he desires. The Guermantes don't live up to expectation. By a fatality that lodges in his bones or his name or his being, Marcel carries a pall wherever he goes.

The pattern is endlessly repeated. Having heard from Swann about the beauties of the Balbec church, Marcel visits it before going on to the hotel and the beach. When he finds the church surrounded by ugly buildings and "reduced to its own stone countenance," he is bitterly disappointed. The precious work of art is overwhelmed by the proximity of a pastry shop and the branch office of a bank. The promise of its name crumbles under "the tyranny of the Particular" (I, 660). Later, near Balbec, Marcel accosts a pretty fishergirl in such a boasting manner that he knows she will remember him. For a moment he desires her and forces himself on her attention.

And that capturing of her mind, that immaterial possession, was enough to strip her of mystery as fully as physical possession (I, 717).

In his success is his failure.

Does the flaw that causes this condition lodge entirely in Marcel's sensibility, as is implied by the phase "infirmity in my nature"? Before accepting this verdict, we would do well to look again at the pattern of events that surrounds Marcel. One persuasive answer to the question would be that the real flaw is not simply a character trait but arises out of the relation between subjective and objective. We already have the terms available. When the intermittence of our natures meets the perverse timing of events, the result is a puzzling disarray.

Our desires interfere constantly with one another, and, in the confusion of our existence, it is rare that happiness coincides with the desire that clamored for it (I, 489).

The two series will not mesh. Odette falls passionately in love with Swann when she first meets him, yet those feelings fade before his infatuation begins. This explanation of Proust's complaint by intermittence and timing appeals to an unexamined fatalism. It posits that we must simply accept the fact that his (our) condition springs from an inevitable semicomic discrepancy between subjective desire and objective reality.

I believe we can go further in seeking the origins of Marcel's habit of self-doubt. It seems fully appropriate that one of the keenest descriptions of this temper was written four centuries ago by Montaigne. In the first version of the essay "On Presumption," he is speaking of the outward signs of vainglory. That vice arises, he says, either out of too high an opinion of oneself or out of too low an opinion of others. Then suddenly—at least it feels sudden when you come upon the passage Montaigne inserted many years later into the original text—he shifts his ground. Now it is a sixty-year-old man speaking a deeper truth than he knew at forty.

> I feel oppressed by *an error of mind* which offends me both as unjust and even more as annoying. I try to correct it, but I cannot root it out. *It is that I attach too little value to things I possess, just because I possess them; and overvalue anything strange, absent, and not mine.* This frame of mind extends very far. As the prerogative of authority leads men to regard their wives with monstrous disdain, and sometimes their children, so too am I afflicted. Whatever I am responsible for can never, as I see things, meet the competition. To an even greater degree, any desire for advancment and improvement clouds my judgment and closes off the path to satisfaction, just as mastery in itself breeds scorn of whatever one holds in one's power. Exotic societies, customs, and languages attract me, and I realize that the dignity of Latin impresses me more than it should, just as it does children and common folk. My neighbor's house, the way he runs his affairs, his horse, though no

better than my own, are all worth more than mine precisely because they are not mine [italics added].

In this passage Montaigne is right on pitch, perfectly in tune with himself and with that human condition we share with him. Here is the subtlest and most far-reaching fault of all. It strikes at our very sense of reality. *Soul error*[3] is the incapacity to give full value or status to one's own life and experience. This quiet southern gentleman, former mayor of Bordeaux and companion of kings, retired to a tower and devoted his life to writing about himself. One would expect to find the most self-satisfied, the least self-deprecating of men. Yet it is he who tells us in the same essay: ". . . it would be difficult for any man to have a poorer opinion of himself."

Here then is the "tyranny of the Particular"—but directed by Montaigne back at ourselves. For we are our own principal particular. We find ourselves and all that belongs to us very hard to live with. Soul error: Proust, the Narrator, and Marcel wrestle with it. The only escape Proust suggests is to seek an impossible perfection (II, 46) or the inaccessible (III, 384). That way one keeps one's face averted from the real. But in his writing, soul error is never far away. In one of the early texts published in *Pleasures and Days*, Proust writes of a ten-year-old boy who tries to kill himself out of love for an older girl. Has she scorned him? No. "He felt disappointment every time he saw the sovereign of his dreams; but as soon as she had gone, his fertile imagination gave back

---

[3] Montaigne's phrase is *une erreur d'âme*. Florio and J. M. Cohen translate it as "an error of the mind." Donald Frame tries "an error of my soul." Montaigne does not use the genitive, which would be *erreur de l'âme*. The French syntax implies substance, essential composition, as in the forms *crise de nerfs*, *état d'esprit*, or even *chemin de fer*. My own translation proposes "an error of mind." However, English and American usage of both sixteenth and twentieth centuries offers a tighter version than any of the above: *soul error*.

to the absent girl all her charms and he wanted to see her again" (*JS*, 111). At the restaurant in Rivebelle, the elegant customers act as compulsively as Marcel. ". . . at each table the diners had eyes only for the tables at which they were not seated. . ." (I, 811). When Mme de Stermaria accepts Marcel's invitation to an intimate dinner in the Bois, he finds he would prefer to have the evening free to try to see other women (II, 391). *Whatever bends to our desire disqualifies itself by becoming a part of ourselves.* Whence the flat statement from the Narrator during Marcel's agonizing separation from Albertine: "Man is the being who cannot get out of himself, who knows others only in himself, and, if he denies it, lies" (III, 450).

Once it has attacked, there is no escape from the worm of self-contempt. For Marcel, only one set of experiences remains immune: the closed world of Combray, where place, family, and nature congeal into a vision barely shadowed by advance warnings of dangers to come. For a precious moment Marcel was content to be himself. Childhood provides the standard of things as they were before the worm attacked them.

Still it is too imprecise simply to say that soul error arises from a loss of the unified world of childhood. For just how does it come about that reality and appearance part company? Combray exists retroactively for Marcel as a benevolent but inflexible routine, a *train-train*, within which he discovers for himself the catastrophic factor of time. His goodnight kiss is withheld when he needs it and granted when he wants it no longer. That incident breaks the spell of Combray and infects his experience with the decay of time. Marcel has to face what Proust had already expressed in *Pleasures and Days*. "No sooner has an anticipated future become the present than it loses its charms." Temporality introduces "an incurable imperfection into the very essence of the present" (*JS*, 139). When Marcel gets high on wine while dining with Saint-Loup at Rivebelle, the euphoria or "pure phenomenism" (I, 816) he feels, approximates a return to total immersion in the present. Exalted tipsiness annuls the discovery of time. While tingling with wine he could forget everything but the intensity of the moment. However, this state represents not a conquest of temporality but a surrender to it.

The "imperfection" in reality imposed by time is accompanied, Proust shows us, by an increased (but far from compensating) power of the imagination. It is the principal internal organ of desire. When Proust describes the young boy in love with a girl who disappoints him every time he sees her, he attributes the boy's malady to his precocious imagination (*JS*, 111). Albertine's "mystery, which she had for me on the beach before I knew her" (II, 363) is a pure product of the imagination. And its functioning observes a precise relation to presence and absence. "Man of imagination, you can find enjoyment only through regret or expectation, that is, in the past or in the future" (*JS*, 54). Twenty years later, Proust was even more categorical. He sees "an inevitable law which arranges things so that one can imagine only what is absent" (III, 872). We may have learned why. Thwarted by intermittence and the warped timing of experience, the imagination falls victim to soul error and seeks its object forever elsewhere.

THE PARADOX OF CONSCIOUSNESS

All literature may aspire to the condition of the proverb. Proverbs appear to record a state of things so compact and definitive that we can tuck them away and forget them until their turn comes around again—as it always does. The one dimension they lack is the dramatic. On the other hand, the manner in which Proust (like Montaigne) devoted the last fifteen years of his life to a single monumental work, and with such intensity as to signify that the work *took* his life, has a clear dramatic ring that echoes through the *Search*. Nevertheless, *roman-fleuve* and proverb are by no means irreconcilable modes. Raymond Radiguet, a sage at seventeen when he wrote *The Devil in the Flesh*, spoke cannily of literature as a means to "*déniaiser les lieux communs*."[4] There is much to be learned from the wisdom worn into the folds of language itself. It is not surprising to find a pair of matched proverbs in English to elucidate Proust's complaint. A comparable pair exists in many languages.

The romantic version has a strong ironic counter-thrust, and its pastoral metaphor makes it suitable for hymns and popular songs: *the grass is greener on the other side of the fence—or hill.* The realist version is terser and has an edge of cynicism: *familiarity breeds contempt.* Once heard, they remain. Of all the major characters in the *Search*, Françoise has the most humble origins, yet she outlasts all the others, including the Narrator himself. Similarly, Proust finally leads us to proverbs, sturdy little shrines in the landscape of human experience. They cannot replace his novel, but they may well outlast it. And they also caution us not to dismiss or underrate the state of mind I have been describing. Through Marcel, Proust places soul error at the crossroads of his novel and develops it as a powerful metamorphosis of the flaw we knew first as Greek hubris and Christian pride. The *Search* makes a man of its maxims by gradually laying bare several closely joined aspects of Proust's complaint. I shall distinguish here between three: the pathos of thought, the pathos of self, and the paradox of individual consciousness.

If, as I wrote earlier, Proust shows temporality and the imagination working together to infect the present with unreality, then we confront an essential character of thought: our incapacity to conceive and assimilate

---

[4] Here lies a translator's nemesis—or fortune. "To give meaning to the commonplace." "To teach clichés the facts of life." "To make a man of a maxim."

what immediately confronts us. The pathos of thought begins with the realization that thinking always operates at a distance, at one remove. The subjective mind cannot fuse with objective reality. All the examples I have been giving outline an attitude very close to the one Rousseau has Julie express in *La Nouvelle Héloïse*: "In this world the realm of fantasy or of fiction [*chimères*] is the only one worth living in, and the emptiness of human things is so great that, except for Being itself, nothing is beautiful but what does not exist." This is an extreme form of our yearning for elsewhere, of our squirming against being where we are. The mood creates around it an aura of anxiety, emanating from the knowledge that our very presence anywhere is a form of intrusion. An added consciousness interferes with the goings-on. Whence Marcel's eternal desire to spy on people, to be simultaneously present and absent.

As is often the case when he wants to give particular emphasis to his point, Proust finds a scientific comparison for the pathos of thought. Marcel is reading, hidden in a little shelter or recess in the depths of the garden.

> And didn't my thinking resemble yet another recess in the depths of which I felt caught, even if I wanted to look out at things around me? When I saw an external object, my consciousness that I was seeing it remained between me and it, outlining it with a narrow mental border that prevented me from ever touching its substance directly; in some way the object volatilized before I could make contact, just as an incandescent body approaching something moist never reaches moisture because of the zone of evaporation that always precedes such a body (I, 84).

Mere awareness volatilizes what it seeks and hampers its own functioning. The most reflective of us are endowed with the antithesis of Midas's touch; it turns the things we want, or want to know, into dross. In the sphere of love, Stendhal gave a name to the common and distressing weakness that renders a man physically incapable of doing precisely what he most desires to do. *Fiasco*, in any language, can no longer mean just a jug of wine. But Proust felt fiasco writ very large. He comprehended a greater disaster: not only that familiarity breeds contempt, but also that merely to think something diminishes the dimensions of its reality. Imagining impedes realization. It is impossible to be present at the coronation of one's own happiness: recall Marcel kissing Albertine. No wonder Proust spent his years writing his way out from under the burden of being alive, and of being aware of being alive.

For our culture, Faust represents this pathos of thought. There is no happiness or repose for his overactive mind, only for the new community of citizens he creates by draining swamplands. In this perspective of restlessness, Faust's lot looks very similar to that of Don Juan, who embodies the pathos of self. Both their stories arise from a perception of life as flawed. We are born into dissatisfaction with our estate. Society constrains us to limit our behavior to patterns assigned not only by our public role but also by expectations of consistent character. We are usually barred from acting out all our conflicting feelings and responses. But even without social conventions, our behavior displays the features of what I have referred to as intermittence. It is beyond our power as humans to be all of ourselves at once. Our finite capacity for existence makes our character successive, dependent on time to reveal itself in any depth. Impatient with this inability to assume ourselves entire at any point in time, we react by yearning to enter into or become someone else, to escape the limits of our own body and being. What Marcel shares with Don Juan is a gnawing dissatisfaction with himself, compounded by the feeling that he cannot fully possess the persons he desires. The urge for self-transcendence burns a hole in our being without ever attaining its goal: true otherness.

Proust's Narrator comes back many times to the dynamics of this process. He describes it in fact as a consequence of the pathos of thought. The "narrow mental border" that isolates us from the world around us has an effect on our sense of self.

> For even if we have the sensation of being always enveloped in, and surrounded by our own soul, still it does not seem a fixed and immovable prison; rather we seem to be borne away with it, and perpetually struggling to break out of it into the world, with constant discouragement when we hear endlessly, all around us, that unvarying sound which is not an echo from without, but the resonance of a vibration from within (I, 86).

We are stuck inside ourselves. Two thousand pages later the narrator has still not found his way out. He says that even a pair of wings and a new respiratory system that would allow us to survive on Mars would not take us out of ourselves so long as we had to use the same senses and our own consciousness. The conclusion has a desperate ring.

> The only true voyage, the only Fountain of Youth, would be found not in traveling to strange lands but in having different eyes, in seeing the universe with the eyes of another person, of a hundred others, and seeing the hundred universes each of them sees, which each of them is (III, 258).

The desire of the imagination to outstrip the self is as urgent as it is hopeless. Marcel moves through the world in a kind of tightly enclosed, yet partially transparent gondola. This confinement, and the intense spiritual and even physical activity it provokes, is what I mean by pathos of self.

My third gloss on the proverb version of Proust's complaint departs only slightly from the other two. Yet it introduces a now familiar concept that may illuminate a key segment of Proust's thinking. It also displays the way our universe seems to fold back on itself when one reaches one of its remotest corners.

When modern physicists began to explore elementary particles of matter, they realized that certain things were happening which ran counter to accepted laws or regularities of determinism. In order to explain these events, Werner Heisenberg formulated the indeterminacy principle. Fully developed, that principle combines two very different sets of phenomena, on an atomic order of magnitude. First, submicroscopic events like the radiation of a specific particle of radium cannot be predicted. Even statistical probabilities can be calculated only for significant quantities of particles. Single particles appear independent of traditional determinism. Second, the impress of energy required for accurate observation (i.e., some equivalent of light on the subject) is in itself sufficient to modify the event under observation. Thus, at the level of atomic magnitudes, we can neither predict nor observe with accuracy.

I would suggest that probers of the human consciousness like Proust reveal a comparable indeterminacy principle that describes processes on the level of individual thought. The disruptions and irregularities of one man's thinking cannot be predicted. General statements about a statistically significant sample of individuals are another matter. Furthermore, observation (including self-observation) close enough to penetrate inside a person's consciousness provokes a disturbance sufficient to vitiate the observation. (See Proust's second answer to the question "Your ideal of earthly happiness?" cited above, p. 12.) Mere witnessing modifies the course of human actions. Many authors, from Rousseau to Dostoevski, lead us toward an awareness of this double bind. Proust's exploration of the psyche makes it almost impossible to deny the validity of something like an indeterminacy principle at the level of individual thought. This paradox of consciousness fetters us to a modicum of ignorance about what we might otherwise expect to know best: our kind and ourselves. Proust is describing the condition in the passage quoted on page 101, particularly with the word *liséré*—border, or outline, or margin. He uses it one other time, near the end of the novel, unforgetful of the earlier passage, and now making perfectly clear the double thrust he means to give the word. Uncertainty inheres both in things (contingencies) and in consciousness (perception).

> For there exists between us and all beings a border [*liséré*] of contingencies, just as I had understood while reading in Combray that there is a border of perception which prevents perfect contact between reality and the mind (III, 975).

The origins of Proust's complaint reach back to this dark region of mind where, alone, we face the problems of reality and communication.

Marcel's efforts to break out of these confinements of self have already been described in terms of social climbing, love, and art. Those three false leads throw him back even more desperately on himself. He is left with few resources, one of which we hear about very early in the *Search*. "Habit! that skillful arranger" (I, 8). As the novel opens, and repeatedly thereafter, Marcel imagines his life as a series of bedrooms to which he becomes accustomed. Their familiarity as places sustains his identity as a person. The accomplishment of life's major tasks, the Narrator tells us, relies more on habit than on "momentary transports" (I, 93). It also provides our security, for habit "drapes over things the guise of familiarity rather than showing their true being, which would frighten us" (II, 764). Marcel's psychic survival under the curse of soul error depends on the defense of habit which "regulates the economy of our nervous system" (III, 918); but it is survival on a low level of being and happiness. Marcel clings to routine and blesses the comforts of the familiar even while another part of his mind knows that he is missing the truths and satisfactions he seeks from life.

The Narrator's steady presence in the text embodies a different response to the paradoxes of consciousness and self. (Marcel gradually approaches this attitude, which is more flexible and rewarding than his reliance on habit.) It is the opposite of intolerance and defiance of those inward failings in an effort to overcome them. In seeking to transcend their humanity, Faust and Don Juan aimed at glory and immortality as ambitiously as any Pharaoh or world conqueror. Yet their aspirations to divinity by means of surpassing the human condition contain the seeds of a tragic fall.

What Proust portrays in the Narrator is a more direct and modest attitude toward mortality. The descriptions of consciousness as rarely whole and beset by impossible desires for otherness show how deeply flawed life is. The *Search* as a whole seeks not to transcend that condition but to encompass it. *Intermittence* is the guiding principle. The action transpires by lingering seasons and stages. The book becomes oceanic in scale in order to contain the changing weathers and tides and crosscurrents of a long voyage. There is no synthesis, no higher calculus to which these manifold cycles can be reduced. Intermittence describes a sequence of variations without prescribing their course or regularity. Correspondingly, since we cannot assume all parts of our character at a particular moment or grasp the full significance of our experience as it occurs, it is wise to recognize and tolerate this temporal aspect of our humanity. To oppose it is folly. As a basic insight into the pulse of life, intermittence means that Marcel gradually learns to bear and reflect upon fluctuations of self and experience through periods of long duration. He speaks occasionally and misleadingly of general laws, but he lives with, and through, vividly alternating particulars. The same applies to the reader following the text. In letters to two prospective editors in 1912, Proust proposed a general title for his unpublished novel: "Intermittences of Heart." He would have done well to keep it.

Without shuffling off the tribulations of soul error, we have reached a universe of sympathy and understanding far removed from the fanaticism that propels tragedy. In this universe where everything connects, the next observation should seem natural. "The infirmity in my nature" that convinces Marcel he is always a wet blanket, and "the narrow mental border" that intervenes between his subjective perceptions and the objective world he longs to reach, are extensions of the comic vision. Consciousness itself partakes of the comic. Marcel, watched patiently by the Narrator, stumbles over his mortality both when he ventures out into society or tries to kiss a girl and also in the innermost workings of his thought. Intermittence links the conflicting segments of his life through age and cumulative experience without invoking a transcendent vision out of time. Fully understood as part of our lot, Proust's complaint leads not to despair but to a gentle smile at the vagaries of men and at the time it takes them to recognize themselves for what they are.

Spinning a Yarn

Many years ago a New York publishing firm
issued a collection of orchestral scores with ar-
rows prominently overprinted to designate the
instrument carrying the melody. Presumably this
was the line one should follow. Intelligent musicians immediately criticized these "Arrow Guides"
as a travesty of music. One must listen to the
entire texture of relationships, they insisted, and
not just pick out a melody.

What forms and directs Proust's work is not
any one strand that can be singled out and followed through the entire fabric. It is rather a sustained mental movement producing tension,
comparable to the spinning of many fibers into
thread or yarn, into the clothes on our backs, into
the very struts and cordage of civilized life. The
thickest rope is worthless unless its filaments
have been twisted tight. Friction sustains us. The
strength of Proust's work resides in the turning

and tossing of a mind engaged with many recurring themes. That inexhaustible activity did finally weave a fabric sturdy enough to intertwine the comic and soul error. In fact, I have emphasized those two strands of the *Search* because they reveal the perpetual motion of Proust's sensibility. He never stopped spinning, and pulling the strands snugly together. I have passed over several elements whose significance in his work is widely and properly recognized. The time has come to deal with them.

A CASE HISTORY

Because of its constant preoccupation with states of mind and hidden motivation, the *Search* seems to qualify as an exhaustive psychoanalytic case history. Of course, Proust did not discover the unconscious and the influence of long-forgotten or suppressed events by reading Freud. Furthermore the novel does not simply record Proust's own case (see above, pages 20–21).

Beginning with recognizable symptoms of anxiety, the Narrator of the *Search* carries his explorations back into the past until he locates the magnetized and luminous event that lies at the source of everything. Then the case history moves forward through successive revelations that grow in scale and detail until they seem to lay bare the patient's life. "Analysis" is constantly going on, probing toward the functioning of the psyche. Can we distinguish patient from analyst in this narrative? The two persons of the drama are not separated here by professional competence, signified by the paying of a fee; they are separated by age and experience, as signified by various overt and covert signals in the narrative voice. The *Search* records the achingly sustained self-analysis of a fictional character projected into the double role of Marcel and the Narrator. Both of them contribute passages of deep analysis that sometimes seem to bring the action to a full stop. Yet it always moves on. The *Search* remains fundamentally a story—a temporal, linear narrative in which the reader feels a pressure of events propelling him from a beginning toward an end. The general movement is a growing up and a growing old.

Marcel's specific case circles around the question of resolution, of will power. When the lens of the narrative comes into focus in the opening pages, it fixes on Marcel's first self-affirmation as a child. "I had just made the resolution not to try to go to sleep without seeing maman again, and to kiss her whatever happened" (I, 32). This resolution leads to a double abdication: his mother's, when she indulges his whim; and his own, when he cannot confess that he doesn't really want her to spend the night in his room after all. The story begins with a compound failure. Near the end of the novel, Marcel goes through an analogous sequence, but in reverse order and at another level. Arriving at the Prince de Guermantes's reception, he begins his long meditation on literature as a vocation. Here Marcel explicitly abstains from any rash resolution. "In the middle of all this I realized that, in the work of art I felt ready to undertake without having consciously resolved to do so, there would be great difficulties" (III, 870). His skepticism lasts through one hundred fifty pages of soliloquizing and anguished socializing until he suddenly confronts the incarnation of his past and of lived time in the form of Mlle de Saint-Loup. This "goad" to his will tells him that it is time at last to begin writing the book that will show his life as worth living (III, 1032). And he does begin. Skepticism gives way to dedication. The moral strength that abandoned him and his mother in the opening pages comes back here at the end and allows him to record its case history.

Between these two events lies a lifetime full of personal experience and suffering. Marcel has to learn all his lessons for himself. But how does he survive the voyage? And why does the action seem to face the past so steadily as it moves forward in time? The earliest events of the story in Combray are bathed in a feeling of reverence that the accompanying comedy does not diminish. Aunt Léonie's house has as magical and symbolic an existence as the village church. Is there an authority that ties us to our childhood more than to any other period? On this point the novel is clear: *faith* makes the difference. As children, *we believe in the world around us* as we never shall again. The Narrator states the case in the closing pages of "Combray."

> But I regard the Méséglise and the Guermantes's ways primarily as the deepest layer of my mental soil, as firm ground on which I can still stand. It is because I used to believe[1] in things and in beings while I walked along these two paths that the things and the beings they made known to me are the only ones that I still take seriously, the only ones that bring me joy. Whether it is because the faith which creates has ceased to exist in me, or because reality will take shape in the memory alone, the flowers that people show me nowadays for the first time never seem to be true flowers (I, 184).

In spite of strong family tensions and dark forebodings, Combray possesses the one essential quality that transforms it into Eden for Marcel. The congruence of his faith in desired things with the real presence of those things close to him produces a wholeness of experience that stays in his memory. It provides the eternal standard of a world not yet sundered by soul error. Once upon a time we were all believers in the completeness of our own existence. Faith in one's own experience: do we need any further description of Eden? As an old man at the end of the novel, Marcel imagines how a young student, like himself many years before, might still be

---

[1] Unfortunately, Moncrieff here mistranslates *croyais* as "think of" instead of "believe in" and obscures a crucial point.

enchanted by the Guermantes mansion on the Avenue du Bois. "It is because he is still in the age of belief, which I had left far behind" (III, 858).[2]

Combray means a time of life, an age of belief. It represents not only wholeness of experience but also the domain where the child remains in close proximity to unmediated sensation in the form of impressions. The narrative uses the two ways as a topographical scheme (almost like the mnemonic devices actors once relied on to learn their lines) of sorting out impressions into two contrasting sets. We later learn how inadequate the two ways really are as an organizing principle. They stand firm because Marcel once believed in them. On the other hand, his first impressions, in which he loses faith all too soon as he grows up, turn out to be accurate. Twice toward the end of the novel the Narrator points out that Marcel's first impressions of Gilberte and Albertine as precocious and lascivious young hussies were right after all (III, 609, 694). Proust was not so misguided as to believe we can revert to childhood or naïve sensation. Yet his literary imagination and stylistic power were bent on capturing the reverence of childhood experience. The important thing about the *Search* as a case history is not its presentation of Proust's neuroses or coenesthesia or homosexuality. It is the way Marcel keeps the faith in spite of terrible reverses and finally finds the resolve to create a present for himself that encompasses the past. Living is nine-tenths endurance.

TWO DISPUTES

For many years the length and title of the *Search*, its depiction of age, and its emphasis on memory convinced

[2] The German writer Hugo Ball also discovered the meaning of this kind of belief. In his deeply meditative journal, *Die Flucht aus der Zeit*, he describes Adam as the man "who believed in his surroundings."

most readers that the book's essential subject is time and temporality. It conveys above all a sense of time deeply penetrated and linked back to itself in wide loops of recall and recognition. This approach lends weight to the order and pacing of events and endorses the conception of a story as basically linear, or perhaps circular, like time itself. In recent years, however, a number of critics have taken up their cudgels to make the opposite case. When one has finished the novel, they contend, when one can hold its parts together in the mind, its true character reveals itself as that of a single whole which stands free of temporal order and lies spread out before us in space, like a painting.

In this case, as usual, Proust speaks eloquently on both sides of the questions. In the "interview" he supplied in 1913 for the journalist Elie-Joseph Bois (the text appears in the Appendix, pages 167–172), Proust justifies the still undivulged length of his novel by saying it will portray "psychology in time. It is this invisible substance of time that I have tried to isolate." And when the last volume appeared fifteen years later, he insisted all over again that the book was cast in "the form of Time" (III, 145; *cf.* III, 1149). The opening sentence of the entire work as well as its title indicate a constant cohabitation with time. The case would seem clear from the start. Yet, particularly in the decisive closing pages, Proust uses figures that describe a reaction against temporality. In the sentences that immediately precede the moment when the tide of the action turns and Marcel steps on the uneven paving stones, he complains that living to be a hundred would bring no reward. For it would mean nothing more than "successive extensions of a life laid out along one line" (III, 866). Images of height and architectural construction in the final pages seem to imply a new perspective. Proust had formulated the shift most tersely when speaking of architecture in an early draft of the novel: "Time has assumed the form of space" (*CSB*, 285). A building in different styles displays time as simultaneous. To what degree does the *Search* aspire to the condition of architecture?

Now time poses the crucial problem of how we know things, particularly how we know people, over a period of days or years. Proust never wandered far from this problem. Exasperated by his uncertainty over Albertine's and Andrée's unstable feelings toward him, Marcel tells himself in desperation that the only way to find out about their sentiments would be for him to "immobilize" them in order to examine the pattern of their behavior. But he could do so only by ceasing to desire them, for desire provokes change. Without desire he would no longer care about their feelings. The passage concludes glumly: "the stability we attribute to natural things is purely fictive and serves the convenience of language" (III, 64–65). Immobility may permit knowledge, but it arrests life and love. Hence we can never know anyone we love. Such paradoxes of temporality permeate the incidents of the story.

Chronology itself raises parallel problems. Just how far does experience arise from or conform to the temporal order of events? While falling out of love with Gilberte, Marcel finds calendar time utterly meaningless.

> Often (since our life is chronological to so small a degree and inserts so many anachronisms into the sequence of our days) I found myself living a day or two behind myself, going back through stages when I still loved Gilberte (I, 642).

Yet in a later passage about what happens to Saint-Loup and Charlus as they grow older, the Narrator proclaims the opposite dogma: "Everything is a question of chronology" (III, 737*n*).

In the face of these contradictions, and with strong leads from Ortega y Gasset and Raymond Fernandez, two recent critics have taken a categorical position. In an essay called "Spatial Form in Modern Literature"

(1945), Joseph Frank lumps Proust with Pound, Eliot, and Joyce as overdeveloped Imagists. They all incorporate in lengthy works Pound's original definition of an Image: to present "an intellectual and emotional complex in an instant of time." The length and temporal narrative of the *Search* should not deceive us, Frank argues. "Proust's purpose is only achieved, therefore, when these units of meaning [impressions and views of his characters] are referred to each other reflexively in a moment of time." A moment of time Frank interprets as not time at all but as space. Almost twenty years later the Belgian critic Georges Poulet defended the same thesis at greater length. Proust's narrative "juxtaposes" discontinuous images "exhibited side by side" as in a museum. "Thus time yields to space."[3]

Both these critics have much to say on Proust that is revealing. However, on this major point about time they are as misguided as pre-Darwin (and pre-Lyell) biologists trying to develop a theory of the origin of the species without a huge tract of prehistoric time during which variations and selection could occur. How does a mind achieve this spatialization of time? The events and thoughts of Proust's novel, if they are genuinely spatial in Frank's sense, would have to conform to the principle that binds the units of meaning in Pound's *Cantos*: ". . . while they follow one another in time, their meaning does not depend on this temporal relationship." Poulet argues the same case in more homely terms.

> Intact . . . caught in their frames, the episodes of Proust's novel present themselves in an order which is not temporal since it is anachronous, but which cannot be anything other than spatial, since, like a row of jam pots in the magic cupboards of our childhood, it sets out a series of closed vessels in the caverns of the mind.[4]

[3] *L'Espace proustien*, p. 130.
[4] *Ibid.*, p. 134.

In order to persuade us that the order of events in Marcel's life has no significance, Poulet shows him storing those events in a kind of mental larder, with no temporal sequence. The figure applies fairly well to *Jean Santeuil* or to *Against Sainte-Beuve*. But we are dealing with a linear story which Proust carefully and properly called a *search*. Far more aptly it could be represented as a climb to the top of a mountain. The view from the summit does indeed set out before one an arrangement of the landscape that allows one's gaze to move at will from feature to feature and to take it all in at once. That view is essentially spatial. But it does not and cannot abolish the climb that took one to the summit, and the temporal order of events in that climb. One cannot climb the last hundred feet before the first. Marcel could not have loved Albertine before Gilberte, nor could he have become a writer without the years of discouragement and disillusion that seemed to be leading him in quite another direction. Marcel remains the creature of a temporal order of events that obtains even in retrospect. "Just like the future, it is not all at once but grain by grain that one tastes the past" (III, 531).

But we must go beyond isolated quotations picked shrewdly out of 3000 pages of waiting prose. If a spatial simultaneous vision of the past were Proust's fundamental purpose, then all the early pages would become strictly preparatory and subsidiary. They would in effect drop off, and we would be left with an intense hundred-page essay on the rewards of memory and the nature of literature.[5] Everything I shall have to say about the esthetic attitude and the composition of the *Search* will weigh against this one-sided interpretation.

[5] I believe that Proust had such an expository, nonnarrative plan in mind when he began to work on *Against Sainte-Beuve*. As I have already suggested, the Preface sets down his basic philosophic attitude with only a highly abbreviated version of how he reached it. He abandoned the plan almost as soon as he began writing.

The *Search* affirms *both* perspectives. On one hand, it insists on the lived temporal order of things, which combines individual development with a sense of the gradual modulation of reality itself. On the other hand, it focuses on occasional resurrections revealing a glimpse of the past outside of contingent time and creating patterns so convincing as to be called essences. A mass of evidence, passed over by Frank and Poulet, suggests that the temporal sequence dominates most of the narrative and withdraws conditionally in favor of the spatial arrangement only at the start and again as its end approaches. This close relation between time and space in the novel as a whole parallels the art of description insisted upon by the Narrator (III, 319, 591). True description follows the temporal order of impressions—a kind of innocence reintroduced into experience otherwise encrusted by habit—before accepting a ready-made concept or a word. The interchange never stops. The *Search* creates a predominantly temporal perspective, scored through deeply at crucial moments by arresting spatial insights. The only synthesis resides in the full dimensions of the work itself.

These concerns led Proust to give serious attention to music, an art whose performance is entirely temporal, yet whose form may be spatialized by repetition and memory. In two closely related passages, one toward the beginning and the other toward the end of the novel, Proust describes that double experience. In the first, Marcel is listening to Odette play the piano.

> It was on one of those days that she happened to play for me the part of Vinteuil's sonata that contained the little phrase of which Swann had been so fond. But often, if it is a complicated piece of music to which one is listening for the first time, one listens and hears nothing. . . . That gives rise to the melancholy that clings to the knowledge of such works, as of everything that takes place in time. . . . Since I was able to enjoy the pleasure that this sonata gave me only

in a succession of hearings, I never possessed it in its
entirety: it was like life itself. But great works of art
are less disappointing than life, for they do not begin
by giving us the best of themselves (I, 529–31).

The passage contains a tentative esthetic. The experience of complex music is cumulative, subject to time,
never exhaustive. It differs from life in that its greatest
rewards come late and not early. The *Search* itself, we
realize, observes this rhythm of delayed revelation. The
time needed for gradual initiation to a work of art belongs to and forms part of its experience. An instant
does not contain it, though art may contain exalted
instants.

In the counterpart scene many years later, Marcel discovers in music an even deeper synthesis of temporal
and spatial experiences. Albertine is selecting to play
for Marcel on the pianola, not familiar works, but new
pieces whose shape is still obscure for him. The Narrator
distinguishes carefully between two experiences of these
unfamiliar pieces. First comes a slowly built-up deposit
of successive playings, which he describes as "a volume, produced by the unequal visibility of the different
phrases." Later, Marcel can project and immobilize the
different parts "on a uniform plane," open to inspection
by his intelligence (III, 373). The next sentence tells us
not that one aspect is higher or more final than the
other but that what brings a reward is the movement
between the pathos of temporal experience and the immobility of analytic intelligence.

[Albertine] did not yet go on to another piece, for,
without being really aware of the process taking place
inside me, she knew that at the moment when my
intelligence had succeeded in dispelling the mystery
of a piece, it had almost always, in the course of its
ill-fated work, discovered in compensation some
profitable reflection (III, 373).

The shift from shadowy time to brightly lit space would
be "ill-fated" (*néfaste*), injurious to the sensibility, were

it not for the fact that this shift in psychic levels brings
a reward in some other realm of the mind.[6] Furthermore, the knowledge wrested by intelligence out of the
flux sends Marcel continually back toward temporality
and mortality. There is always another piece of music
to listen to and understand. After the pinnacles of atem-
poral vision at the end, Marcel's reward comes in the
form of the very down-to-earth discovery that "life was
worth living" (III, 1032). Time and space do not try to
elbow one another aside in the *Search* in order to domi-
nate the scene. They perform an elaborate and moving
saraband that leaves both on stage and in full possession
of their powers.

The second dispute that hangs over Proust's work is
partially implicit in the first, and it centers on the nature
of our mental faculties.

I sometimes feel that the long essay on memory, time,
and art in the closing pages of the *Search* does a dis-
service to the understanding of the novel. Proust's discursive, almost magisterial tone in those pages leads one
to expect a final declaration that will weave back together all the raveled ends and resolve all contradictions.
Critics with a hypothesis to support will often pick most
of their quotations from this section, as if it were more
probative than any other. Proust gives them every reason
to act this way. Yet the lesson of unreason many critics
have read into these pages conflicts with the lucidity
and logical sequence of its style.

[6] If I understand Proust properly here, he is taking a step
beyond the approach to art proposed by Ernst Kris in *Psychoanalytic Explorations in Art* (New York, 1962). Kris proposes
that esthetic experience entails a process by which we find
pleasurable in itself a shift in mental energy, a change in
psychic level, if kept under control of the ego. Proust seems
to believe that the mental shift from temporal hearing to
simultaneous understanding of music carries value not as
an ascent to a higher level, and not as a pleasure in itself,
but because it usually released other mental insights. This
undeveloped idea hints at a further argument against the
idolatry of art, against art for art's sake.

Beginning with the earliest reviewers, there has been wide agreement that Proust's portrait of the writer in the *Search* (and, by implication, of himself) presents a man passively responding to experience. Georges Bataille refers to "the rigor with which he reduces the object of his search to *involuntary* discovery." Gilles Deleuze devotes his entire last chapter to Proust's thought as a form of abdication of will. "The great theme of *Time Regained* is that the search for truth is the characteristic adventure of the involuntary. Thought is nothing without something which forces and does violence to it." Most of these critics hunt out the Narrator's commentary on sudden memories near the start of the final commentary.

> I had not gone out looking for the two uneven paving stones in the courtyard which I had stepped on. But precisely the fortuitous and inevitable way in which the sensation had come about determined the truth of the past it resurrected and of the images it set in motion (III, 879).

Fortuitous and *inevitable*. Choice, will, and deliberation thus appear to have no role to play in provoking a reminiscence. Beginning with the Madeleine sequence at the start of the novel, the Narrator insists on the involuntary nature of such experiences.

Do the original impressions, which provide the content of the reminiscences, conform to this pattern? Are they also untainted by any exercise of will? In its full freshness an impression appears simply to impinge on Marcel's senses as an immediate and vivid whole. He never wills an impression, though his mental tonus clearly affects his receptivity. However, it is significant that Marcel does not record as major events—and often omits them altogether—the initial impressions that surge back later in the major reminiscences. He was mildly aware of the starched napkin at Balbec, of the whistles of pleasure boats, and of George Sand's novel *François le Champi*; but none of them struck him as anything more

than an incidental part of the moment. He barely registered any taste or odor of the tea-soaked Madeleine when
his Aunt Léonie offered him a piece (I, 52). It merely
formed a fragment of her world. He apparently took so
little notice of the uneven paving stones in the baptistery
of Saint Mark in Venice that he didn't even mention
them at the time. When he saw the line of trees from the
train (III, 855), he did not consciously hear the train-
man's hammer tapping on the wheels. Yet later on it is
precisely that sound that provides the open-sesame for
total recall of the scene (III, 868). Why this apparent
absence of mind at presumably crucial moments?

In *Beyond the Pleasure Principle*, Freud speculates
that the elements of experience which enter consciousness do not leave memory traces. Consciousness provides
a "a protective shield" against stimuli—or at least a kind
of bypass for them. Only things we do not become conscious of make an imprint that may later be remembered. I find it a dismaying yet arresting theory. Is
Proust saying something similar? Does the obscure
mechanism, or muse, that activates our receptivity to
impressions and reminiscences operate only when left
free and unobserved? Does any effort on our part to
influence its working shut it off and float everything up
into the desiccating air of consciousness? In this view,
the only acceptable activity of mind for the artist is a
passive yielding to contingent forces around him. Many
critics have read the *Search* as the case history of a man
whose intense esthetic experiences issued from complete surrender to the present moment and from a systematic abasement of focused attention. But Proust goes
far beyond the absent-mindedness that Freud glimpsed
at the root of memory. He shows consciousness not as a
protective shield but as a mysterious vital process.[7]

[7] Another great restless mind had ventured this far into the
wilderness almost a century earlier. In the section of *Either/
Or* called "The Rotation Method," Kierkegaard anticipated
both Freud's doubts about the compatibility of memory and

To limit the scope of Proust's literary accomplishment to mental passivity would be like accepting "negative capability" as the full measure of Keats's genius. Neither writer can be so confined. The force and reach of their sensibilities do not shun polarities. I have already insisted on the factor of will power in Marcel's story. It

---

consciousness, and Proust's resolve to surmount any such frailty through a form of psychic delaying action, a stopping-to-look. Here is Kierkegaard:

Enjoying an experience to its full intensity to the last minute will make it impossible either to remember or to forget. For there is then nothing to remember except a certain satiety, which one desires to forget, but which now comes back to plague the mind with an involuntary remembrance. Hence, when you begin to notice that a certain pleasure or experience is acquiring too strong a hold upon the mind, you stop for a moment for the purpose of remembering. No other method can better create a distaste for continuing the experience too long. From the beginning one should keep the enjoyment under control, never spreading every sail to the wind in any resolve; one ought to devote oneself to pleasure with a certain suspicion, a certain wariness, if one desires to give the lie to the proverb which says that no one can have his cake and eat it too. The carrying of concealed weapons is usually forbidden, but no weapon is so dangerous as the art of remembering. It gives one a very peculiar feeling in the midst of one's enjoyment to look back upon it for the purpose of remembering it. (*Either/Or*, trans. David F. Swenson and Lillian Marvin Swenson, Anchor Books, I, 289).

Watching from behind several ironic masks, Kierkegaard has seen everything. Yet he never claims final truth for any of his insights in this deeply cleft and antithetical work that refuses synthesis in any form. What he cannot do so well as Proust is to write a novel. "The Diary of a Seducer," the following section, runs aground on the lame category of "the interesting." Proust works in a different form and tone. Instead of holding them apart in separate volumes, he mixes his Either and his Or into a composite narrative line. Repeatedly along the way we are obliged to "stop a moment" in order, almost, to have our cake and eat it too.

Walter Benjamin touches on this general subject in his essay "On Some Motifs in Baudelaire."

reflects the choice that brought Proust to his full literary calling around 1909. At the beginning of the novel as at the end, the only real sickness afflicting Marcel attacks not his body but his will. The book hinges on the resolve Marcel discovers in himself. One has little difficulty in finding quotations that paint a very different portrait of the artist from the one in the preceding paragraphs. The number of texts Proust devoted to Baudelaire leaves little doubt about the tutelary role the poet played in the development of Proust's sensibility and his theories of memory. There is nothing unintentional about the closing words of Marcel's final meditation before entering the Guermantes's salon.

> In Baudelaire, finally, these reminiscences, more numerous even [than in Chateaubriand and Nerval], are less fortuituous and consequently, in my opinion, decisive. It is the poet himself who, with more choice than laziness,[8] deliberately sought, in a woman's odor, for example, in her hair or her breast, the inspiring analogies that will evoke in him "the azure of a vast encircling sky" and "a harbor thick with flames and masts" (III, 920).

Baudelaire's genius seems to have consisted in his capacity to apply choice and some kind of method to involuntary memory. In Marcel, Proust has created a figure in whose life the fortuitous and fleeting experiences of memory ultimately lead to a deliberately chosen self-dedication to literary art.

The passage quoted earlier on "the fortuitous and inevitable way" in which Marcel stumbled on the uneven paving stones (see above, page 120) is really incomplete. It belongs to a careful discussion of the sequence: impressions, reminiscences, art. The closing sentences cor-

---

[8] The printed text reads *"avec plus de choix et de paresse"*— an incoherent construction resolved by changing it to *"avec plus de choix que de paresse."* Gaëtan Picon certifies the correction, *Lecture de Proust*, p. 176.

rect many of the misconceptions I have been describing
and speak not of passiveness but of *effort*.

> The impression is for the writer what experimentation
> is for the scientist, with this difference: that in the
> case of the scientist the work of the intelligence pre-
> cedes, and in the case of the writer it comes after.
> Something we have not had to interpret, to illuminate
> by our personal effort, something that was clear before
> we arrived on the scene, is not truly ours. Only those
> things belong to us that we draw out of the obscurity
> inside us and that others do not know (III, 880).

In every instance of involuntary memory, from the
Madeleine through the multiple series at the end, Marcel
tries at least briefly to find an explanation of the phenomenon. Otherwise, it would not be *his* experience.
Pulsing beneath the rich textures of the *Search* and
expressive of Proust's whole attitude, I detect a movement toward the mastery of life which is stronger than
his complementary moods of passive resignation to it.

The last quotation and a few earlier ones have already
slipped into this discussion a set of terms which define
a closely related and equally important opposition of
forces. In many contexts Proust names and assigns contrasting functions to two mental faculties: *sensibility*
(or imagination, feeling, instinct) and *intelligence*. It
will not be sufficient to label the former passive and the
latter active, though a loose parallel of this nature can
be discerned. Because Marcel moved through a series of
positions about the separation of powers between these
putative faculties, and because Proust was too canny to
have stayed very long with any schematic description of
the human mind, one can demonstrate almost anything
by quoting from the *Search*.[9]

[9] The same can be said of the implied opposition in the book
between the concrete, highly individual, often monstrous
events of the action, and the general laws which seem sometimes to describe and sometimes to govern them. On occasion

The tradition that divides thought into reason and faith, logic and feeling, goes back a very long way and may well coincide with that partial alienation from ourselves we call civilization. We should beware of these divisions and of the way they are reflected in our language and institutions. In using the terms of this dualism, Proust was not so much approving a conventional division of mind as attempting to reach the seat of thought by any means at hand. His writing—both his style and his story —implies that sensibility and intelligence are not distinct faculties but gradations along a continuous spectrum of mental process.

Now Proust never stops telling us that we can rarely possess or exercise all of our powers at once. According to the last quotation the scientist leads with his intellect, the writer or artist leads with his feeling or instinct. But Proust put forward other proposals. In the early treatment of these ideas that he rapped out as the preface to *Against Sainte-Beuve*, he appeals less to a chronological order of priority than to a subtle and nearly sophistical order of value.

> And as to this inferiority of the intelligence, one must still ask the intelligence to establish it. For if the intelligence does not deserve the supreme crown, it alone can bestow the crown. And if the intelligence holds only the second place in the hierarchy of virtues, it alone is capable of proclaiming that instinct must occupy the first place (*CSB*, 216).

The authority to bestow is also the authority to withhold. I know of few passages in Proust that appear so forthright and remain so ambivalent. This "hierarchy of virtues" is compromised by divided sovereignty. Proust's confidence rings hollow and conveys his frustration over the knottiness of the problem. He never really does solve

---

the Narrator sounds out of character. "Therefore it is useless to observe behavior, since one can deduce it from psychological laws" (I, 513).

it. Rather he dramatized the struggle in the *Search*. Marcel is profoundly torn until, at the end, the revelation of art lifts him bodily out of the impasse.

However, one passage deserves attention. It is frequently overlooked because it occurs in the midst of Marcel's troubled weighing of what course to follow when Albertine leaves him. Is she leaving him in order to stampede him into marriage? He considers this the first hypothesis, the intelligent one. Is she leaving him in order to take up again with her Lesbian playmates? This is the second hypothesis, the instinctive one. He is drawn powerfully to the second.

> But—and what follows will make it even clearer, as many episodes have already suggested it—the fact that the intelligence is not the subtlest, the most powerful and appropriate instrument for grasping the truth, is only one more reason for beginning with the intelligence, and not with an unconscious intuition, not with an unquestioned faith in presentiments. It is life itself which, little by little, case by case, allows us to notice that what is most important for our heart, for our mind [*esprit*], is taught us not by reasoning but by other powers. And then it is the intelligence itself which, acknowledging their superiority, abdicates, by reasoning, before them, and accepts the role of becoming their collaborator and servant. Experimental faith (III, 423).

It is a stunning text, studded with crucial words: *vie, esprit, foi, expérimentale*. The order of events is totally reversed here. Our intelligence must set our existential priorities not after but *before* the fact. On faith. *Reasoned faith*. We come inevitably to paradox, close to the paradoxes of theology. As it is reasonable to have faith in the impressions of childhood, it is reasonable to have faith in presentiments and other feelings that seek the truth. But that faith is experimental. It lies open to the examination and judgment of intelligence. We come back then to an alternation of states or stages, with the implication that reason has both the first and the last say. From his quest for the seat of thought Proust returned with this short version of a long journey: *foi expérimentale.* Scientific belief. Faith-filled experiment. Intelligence and intuition working together, checking and encouraging one another. The *Search* shows a man trying to find his mind —his whole mind. Often it seems to have two opposed parts. Like Plato's charioteer, he learns to control his two steeds and make them pull as one.

COMPOSITION

Against his better judgment Proust accepted serial publication of his novel. Only a little more than half the volumes were published in his lifetime. When the first installment appeared in 1913 with its misleading, false-bottom ending (see below, page 152n), Proust was fully aware that one part would not go very far toward conveying a sense of the whole. At the end of the *Search* he has the Narrator complain bitterly about the reception of *his* early sketches: "No one understood a thing" (III, 1041). In spite of a few discerning critics and his own patient explanations, the complaint applied generally in Proust's case.

His first professional reader (for the Fasquelle publishing house) called the first volume "wandering" and asked irritably in his report: "What's it all about?" He concluded that the book was written by a "pathological case." One of the most perceptive of Proust's recent critics, Deleuze, doesn't sound very different when he insists that the novel's subject is Time: ". . . it brings with it fragments which can no longer be restored, pieces which do not fit into the same puzzle, which do not belong to a preceding totality, which do not emanate from the same lost unity." Proust, on the other hand, never tired of insisting on the unity and totality of his novel. To Louis de Robert he asserted that it displays "very strict composition, though not easy to grasp because of its complexity." As sovereign proof, he frequently cited the fact that the first page and the last page were written together, a demonstration of the convergence or circular form of the story. Is there any way in which these conflicting opinions can be reconciled? One device Proust adopted in the *Search*, to express conflicting principles of fragmentation and unity, is the double *I*. Inside it, Marcel's projects keep going astray and dispersing under the ordering, reflective gaze of the Narrator. The double *I* creates a narrative iridescence that does not resolve itself until the end. But we shall have to explore the questions of unity and composition more carefully.

The opening fifty-page section of the *Search* moves through three distinct stages. The first three pages record the thoughts of an unidentified and unlocated consciousness trying to orient itself while wandering on the frontier between waking and sleep. As it seeks its identity, it describes a movement backward and downward in the evolution of consciousness through sickness, childhood, Edenic innocence, the ignorance of a cave man, and animal existence, to nothingness—*le néant*. When rescued by memory from this collapse, the narrative voice says: "In a second I passed through centuries of civilization" (I, 5). In the most literal and direct sense, the *Search* opens, like *Alice in Wonderland*, with a fall. Consciousness tumbles all the way back to a point before cave men, before creation itself, to the void. The book recoils to zero. Then out of the swirl of images one scene comes clear. It is the second stage. A child in Combray is anxiously awaiting his mother's goodnight kiss. But that vivid spot of awareness cannot expand beyond a strict limit. It remains blocked until the spell is broken in the third stage. Through the unexpected intervention of the *madeleine* incident, a whole segment of the past comes back and gives the protagonist a firm identity, the start of a life, and a story to follow.

Correspondingly at the end of the novel, the narrative comes to a conclusion in three stages. After his long

wanderings Marcel arrives at the last Guermantes reception and experiences a series of reminiscences explicitly
echoing the *madeleine* sequence (III, 866). They too
seem to array the past around him, this time as available
material for his literary undertakings. The second stage
carries him into the salon. Suddenly, all his projects fall
apart because he cannot recognize anyone. For an
agonizing interval he is locked back into the present, into
contingency. It takes a hundred pages for Marcel to
readjust his sights and to focus on past and present
together. Then he moves to the third stage not through
any phenomenon of memory but by recognizing his role
and resolving to write his book. Whereas the imagery
of the opening implied a fall and partial recovery, the
end raises an old man on the stilts of age and time,
awaiting death.[10]

What can we now make of Proust's insistence that the
last page of the novel "comes back exactly to the first"?
A little reflection shows that the three stages of the
opening and those of the close occur in reverse order. In
the first chapter: wandering consciousness seeking identity; the clear outlines of a specific scene; and the release
of involuntary memory. In the last chapter: the release
of involuntary memory; the clear outlines of a specific
scene; and a detached consciousness settling down to
write. In both sequences the second stage works as an
obstacle. Marcel is held captive in a single segment of
contingent time until a new development releases him.
But the narrative movement in these two segments is
flowing in opposite directions. Is there some kind of
pattern here?

In a letter to Mme Scheikévitch in 1915 Proust tran-
scribed nearly verbatim from his novel in progress a

[10] My analysis here owes a good deal to the chapter on Proust
in Jean Rousset's *Form et Signification*. However, where he
sees two stages I see three. And we have markedly different
ideas about the relation between the opening and the close
of the novel.

description of the way Marcel fell in and out of love with Albertine (III, 558). "Before forgetting her completely, like a traveler who comes back to his point of departure by the same route, . . . I had to pass through all the same feelings I had already gone through—but in reverse order." The shape of the action now comes into view. The beginning and the end of the novel are firmly in place, the former leading us into and the latter out of the narrative. In between comes a malleable and infinitely expandable section, which did in fact more than triple its original size. This vast median segment has the resilience of life itself. No incident seems absolutely essential; all are significant when related to the rest. The opening and the close establish beyond challenge an overarching movement that encompasses all digressions and meanderings. After the initial and transient hope of salvation in childhood, the *Search* follows a downward slope toward error, perdition, and death. Only at the end does the action turn out to be a resurrection. And now we may be able to discern why Proust insisted not on the distance but on the closeness between the first page and the last.

A number of modern novels concern a character who is at work writing a novel. A literary convention has grown up implying that we are reading that fictional novel. The convention has something both obvious and contrived about it. A few years after Proust's death, Gide's *The Counterfeiters* and Huxley's derivative *Point Counter Point* developed the scheme into a sustained spoof of the novel form. They seem to say ad infinitum, This is a novel about writing a novel about. . . . Sensing the fragility as well as the fascination of that theme, Proust held it off until the very end of his work. Marcel, we are repeatedly told, will never be a writer. Yet when at the end, against all odds and expectations, he metamorphoses into the Narrator of his own life, a whole new state of things appears. The shift takes place, of course, only if we have read the novel for ourselves and do not come armed with the interpretations of ambitious critics (inescapably, I am one) anxious to tell us what it all means. Proust's ending leads us firmly out of the *Search* as Marcel's story and across into a symmetrical mirror-novel, consisting of all the same words and incidents, giving the Narrator's story. A new circumambulation begins, this time not of living the events but of writing them.

Proust's construction of his novel could now be traced out in graphic form. The firmly established paths marking the opening and close permit almost limitless latitude in the intermediate sections. And the careful alignment of the entry with the exit, retracing the same steps in reverse order, leads us over into a second reading or interpretation of the same text as an act of narrative composition after it has first been the story of a man's life (see Diagram V).

Through the literary account B, which has the advan-

V. SHAPE AND TRAJECTORY OF THE *SEARCH*

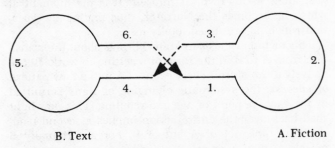

B. Text   A. Fiction

A. *Life as failure*   { 1. Three stages of *Combray* (first fifty pages)
                   2. Vagaries of Marcel's life
                   3. Three stages at the close of *Time Regained* (two hundred pages)

B. *Narrative as success*   4.⎫ The same incidents as 1, 2, and 3
                  5.⎬ seen not as Marcel's present
                  6.⎭ but as the Narrator's past.

tage over life of being transparent and temporally plastic, we look at the fictive life A, Marcel's remembered experiences as he grows up. Occasionally as we read we become aware of B, the account itself, with its cross references, stage whispers, signal flags, and demurrers. Insofar as we do pay attention to B revealing A, we accept a relation between the two as one of translation. Ideally, during an innocent first reading, the effect of the double *I* keeps one's attention generally fixed on A, Marcel's story. We watch love and friendship, social success and even art disintegrate as he reaches them. Only at the very end does the reader follow Marcel in performing a great double take on what has happened. No major new element enters the action. Chance alone intervenes in the humble form of paving stones and spoons and water pipes. Yet everything Marcel has gone through has slowly and imperceptibly shifted the odds in his favor until chance has the force of fate. He lives surrounded by signs and secrets. Suddenly, *qui perd gagne*: loser takes all. By an act of recognition which incorporates rather than rejects lived experience, Marcel sees the past anew as his own, as himself. It is the moment at which he becomes the Narrator, thus finding the vocation which he presumed totally lost.

This metamorphosis in Marcel brings about the transition from A to B in the form of a setting to work. Retroactively it transforms every event of A into a new pattern *of success*, the systematic changing of signs permitted by the vantage point of age and retelling. This new light shed back over the entire action implies a second reading, this time not of A but of B. For as originally B reveals A, now A reveals B. Ideally again, two readings are implied. Yet a skilled reader will read A and B simultaneously, even if he can take advantage only of the clues given him in the text. For example, how can Marcel's sensibility and his alertness to his own flickering states of mind (doubted and belittled in A; recorded in B) simply wither away as A keeps saying? The richness of the prose one is reading, as well as the long detour through painting and music which sustains Marcel's interest in art, imply the contrary.

It is precisely this firm construction that is lacking in Proust's earlier attempts at large-scale fiction. Having only a highly contrived beginning and no end, *Jean Santeuil* gives the effect of being all middle. The motley of texts lumped together under the awkward title, *Against Saint-Beuve* reveals Proust's impatience to find a form that would contain both events and reflections on events. The preface he drafted for that project shows how far astray Proust still was in early 1909, even though he had collected most of his essential ideas and incidents, including the resurrections. He opens the preface with three rapid pages narrating the three classic resurrections: toast dipped in tea, uneven paving stones, the clink of spoon on a plate. The incidents barely receive their due, and the exposition quickly moves on to other matters. It appears that Proust did not know what use to make of these importunings of involuntary memory and simply blurted them all out at the beginning. Within a few months, however, he had changed his scheme completely and saved the resurrections for the *end* of a story which he would eventually name *In Search of Lost Time*. In order to give the reader one clue to go on, one anticipation of the end, Proust left the tea and toast (or *madeleine*) sequence in place, near the opening. The others are transferred to the new location. Now we can see that the first pages of preface to *Against Sainte-Beuve* contain in germ both the opening and the close of the *Search*, but with no sense of a life lived in between. They read like a manifesto on memory, creating no undertow of narrative.

For the *Search*, Proust found the arrangement that allowed him to tell a story. The theme of great expectations runs very strong at the start and then diminishes, leaving us adrift on the ocean of Marcel's desultory life. The ocean seems to go on forever, until, when we have given up hope of any further movement, we find that the current is running again and has carried us back to shore—the same shore we left, now transformed by the passage of time.

This narrative line makes strict demands on the timing by which things can be divulged. The truth must not come out too soon. The limitation goes far beyond that of Marcel's age and experience. The end of the story controls all other sections. For example, in the first volume one of the guests at the Verdurins' dinners is a vulgar, ambitious, seemingly untalented painter called Monsieur Tiche or Biche. In later volumes the dedicated artist Elstir initiates Marcel to the genuine rewards of painting. Toward the end of *Within a Budding Grove*, Marcel discovers that Tiche and Elstir are the same man. While revising *Sodom and Gomorrah*, Proust decided that this discovery comes much too soon and made an urgent note for himself.

> *Nota Bene*. Don't say in this volume that Mme Verdurin called him Monsieur Tiche, nor, secondly, that I [i.e., Marcel] understand it's the same man whose life I learned about earlier. Keep the first for the Goncourt passage, and the second for the last chapter (II, 1200).

He never had time to make the necessary changes, but the sense of narrative shape he was aiming at is clear.

At the same time Proust could not abandon his readers entirely to Marcel's shrinking world of false scents and disappointments. At intervals along the spiral stairway of the narrative, we come upon a narrow window from which we can see a fleck of the countryside that later we will see in its full expanse from the top. These anticipatory glimpses do not fit together into a single picture, but they encourage our climbing. The first such window occurs early when Marcel flees from the scene in which his great-aunt exasperated his grandmother by urging his grandfather to drink more than he should.

Alas! I didn't know that, much more grievously than these little weaknesses of her husband, my lack of will power, my delicate health, and the uncertainty they shed over my future, preoccupied my grandmother as she incessantly paced about morning and evening (I, 12).

Narrative has its own form of preterition. Proust's "I didn't know" is a fairly crude way of smuggling a fragment of contraband information into the text. He can do better. The concert of Elstir's septet, occurring two thirds of the way through the novel, is a subtle and ambitious extension of the same hortatory device. When both the reader and Marcel need it badly, the scene anticipates esthetic rewards still to come.

Aside from these brief remissions to keep us moving along, the *Search* flows powerfully within the confines of its double loop. Marcel and the Narrator attain their respective goals, the one of finding and assuming his full identity, the other of writing an account of that achievement. As Diagram V seems to say in its very appearance, this circular construction does not appeal beyond life fully lived to any higher domain—a world of eternal verities, a divine being, or the historic destiny of man. Proust's story of self-rehabilitation makes a very human and earth-bound document. It does not hesitate to invoke any resource men have tried in order to sustain their faith, including the transmigration of souls and the legend of *le peuple éternel*. However, they are transient appeals. The reflexive architecture of the novel informs us that memory and art will lead us not out of life but back to it.

MEMORY

To endure, to keep the faith entails some form of continuity with the past. Men have ritual, ideology, and institutions to serve the purpose. When Scott Moncrieff translated *A la recherche du temps perdu* as *Remem-*

brance of Things Past (after Shakespeare's Sonnet 30), he was being clumsily explicit about expressing the special form of continuity explored in this case history: memory. So many different affective processes hide behind that simple word that I must begin by distinguishing them.

The *Search* follows a rough chronological order of stages in Marcel's life that corresponds to an emerging intellectual order of significance and reward. At the start the most vivid segment of Marcel's world is made up of *impressions.* They are isolated perceptions of the natural world, which discover an indefinable yet almost palpable aura of significance in the ordinary objects and places that provoke them. Such moments bring Marcel a feeling of happiness and a heightened sense of reality; they seem to ask for some kind of response. Yet the response usually aborts, and the moment passes. It is worth looking at a specific instance of these impressions.

Marcel, not yet in his teens, is taking one of his customary autumn walks "out Swann's way" after a morning's reading. Both the landscape and the windy weather seem to answer his need for animated motion after a sedentary morning. Every feeling in him seeks immediate release. The whole tradition of the promenade, from Petrarch to Rousseau to Rimbaud, hovers over this carefully constructed page. Proust frames the sensuous description of the scene between accounts of two human discrepancies: the inadequacy of our actions and words to express our feelings, and the contrast between the feelings of different people reacting to the same situation. Those discrepancies cause deep frustration in Marcel at the time. For he perceives a delicate pattern of elements that gives the scene, for his sensibility and possibly for no one else's, a wondrous beauty. In the first two sentences, the Narrator is speaking; then he dissolves into Marcel in a perfect case of the double *I.* I quote the scene in full:

When we attempt to translate our feelings into expression, we usually do no more than relieve ourselves of them by letting them escape in an indistinct form which tells us nothing about them. When I try to reckon up all that I owe to the "Méséglise way," all the humble discoveries of which it was either the accidental setting or the direct inspiration and cause, I am reminded that it was that same autumn, on one of those walks near the bushy slope that overlooks Montjouvain, that I was struck for the first time by this lack of harmony between our impressions and their normal forms of expression. After an hour of rain and wind, against which I had put up a brisk fight, as I came to the edge of the Montjouvain pond and reached a little hut, roofed with tiles, in which M. Vinteuil's gardener kept his tools, the sun shone out again, and its golden rays, washed clean by the shower, gleamed once more in the sky, on the trees, on the wall of the hut, and on the still wet tiles of the roof, where a chicken was walking along the ridge. The wind pulled out sideways the wild grass that grew in the wall as well as the chicken's downy feathers, both of which floated out to their full length in the wind's breath with the unresisting submissiveness of flimsy lifeless things. The tiled roof showed in the pond, whose reflections were now clear again in the sunlight, as a pink marbled area such as I had never noticed before. And, when I saw both on the water and on the surface of the wall a pale smile answering the smile in the sky, I cried aloud in my enthusiasm and excitement while brandishing my furled umbrella, "Gosh, gosh, gosh, gosh."

And it was at that moment too—thanks to a peasant who went by, apparently in a bad enough humor already, but who became even more so when he nearly got a poke in the face from my umbrella, and who barely replied to my "What a fine day! Good to be out walking!"—that I learned that identical emotions do not arise in the hearts of all men simultaneously according to a pre-established order (I, 155).

Movement, light, and texture compose a landscape as unified as a Corot painting. Marcel recognizes it as such. The Narrator describes it in an accelerating paragraph that seeks to follow the rapid motion of Marcel's glance. The dynamics of light and wind are forceful enough to connect all elements of roof, pond, and sky within Marcel's sensibility as a set of Baudelairean correspondences. For a moment the "border" of consciousness is lifted. Then come the umbrella flourishing and the childish exclamations to passing peasants. Inevitably, the Narrator brings out the comic side of Marcel's frustration before so great beauty. After this, the Narrator drops the scene as if it were an unattached detail, a fortuitous moment of delight, transitory because it fits into no established sequence and leads nowhere. A few pages later, he explains.

> It was certainly not impressions of this kind that could restore the hope I had lost of succeeding one day in becoming an author and a poet, for each of them was associated with some material object devoid of any intellectual value, and suggesting no abstract truth (I, 179).

Though they continue to provoke a deep personal response in him, Marcel turns his back on his impressions. Only later does he realize that they are the very stuff of reality and have prepared him for the two later stages of memory: *resurrection-reminiscence* (Proust uses the Christian and the Greek terms interchangeably; I shall do likewise), and *art*.

An impression re-encountered after a sufficient interval for forgetting may provoke a resurrection, a close relative of *déjà vu*. A resurrection may or may not lead to recognition of the original impression or memory trace. When it does, a revelation ensues which is even more gratifying then the simple impression. In the *madeleine* passage near the opening of the *Search*, Proust depicts reminiscence as an overpowering recollection of the Narrator's past in all its "form and solidity" (I, 48). At the end of the novel, resurrections are assigned the even greater power of affording us a glimpse of "the essences of things." Without being explicit, Proust implies that the mental functions that permit reminiscences to occur exist at least potentially in all men, and that we have probably experienced them without paying much attention. They are a form of true spiritual experience, without reliance on a divine being or on the miraculous. They signify the existence of a realm of awareness beyond the ordinary. Marcel's resurrections are usually accompanied by his exhortations to himself to "go beyond the moment," to "get to the bottom of" ("*approfondir*") the experience. From his friends' accounts we know that Proust's own reminiscences were so acute as to constitute a form of hyperesthesia. By attributing this condition to Marcel, he made it crucial to the novel.

The most condensed explanation of involuntary memory can be found in a scene where the process fails to occur. Late in life Marcel revisits Combray.

> I found the Vivonne narrow and ugly along the towpath. Not that I noticed particularly great inaccuracies in what I remembered. But, separated by a whole lifetime from places I now happened to pass through again, there did not exist between them and me that contiguity out of which is born, before one even notices it, the immediate, delicious, and total flaming up [*déflagration*] of memory (III, 692).[11]

Though he switches terms disconcertingly, Proust here does not depart from the principles by which Hume, and

[11] As we know from several other passages on successful resurrections, what Proust refers to in the above passage as "contiguity" really means *similarity* between a material object in the present and one in a past impression. The real Vivonne does not resemble his childhood impression of it. He probably says contiguity here because similarity is felt subjectively as a closeness, a near relation.

after him Bergson, deal with the association of states of consciousness. Hume recognized the relations of *contiguity* (in the temporal aspects of simultaneity or close succession and the spatial aspect of proximity) and *similarity*, and devoted much of his career to an attempt to reduce a third principle, causation, to a special case of succession. In his second book, *Matter and Memory* (1896), Bergson picks up Hume's terms. He even puts forward a capsule version of Gestalt theory by insisting that our first perceptions come in "an aggregate of contiguous parts" and that the primary mental process is one of dissociation from "the undivided unity of perception." Usually our psychological life oscillates between similarity and contiguity. Yet in one key passage Bergson suggests that the two processes may work together. ". . . once the memory trace has been connected [by similarity] to the present perception, a multitude of events contiguous to the memory trace immediately attach themselves to the perception."

In passages of phenomenological description whose ideas and introspective tone anticipate Proust's writing, Bergson argues that pure or spontaneous memory is "independent of our will." Both men describe how a tiny link of similarity between present and past can provoke a sudden spreading of recollection to all contiguous elements—Proust's "deflagration." The power of involuntary memory lies in combining two associative principles.[12] Similarity triggers contiguity, and the explosion blasts a whole segment of contiguous past events into the present. The force of this explosion stops Marcel in

---

[12] Gérard Genette has written a penetrating article on this subject: "Métonymie chez Proust," *Poétique*, no. 2, 1970. He borrows his terms from the linguist Roman Jakobson who, in an article on aphasia, equates metaphor with similarity and metonomy with contiguity. By using the rhetorical terms Genette makes a good case for the hybrid state of Proust's work as both realism and poetry. In order to comprehend the phenomenon of reminiscence in Proust, I find it wise to stay with the philosophical terms.

his tracks and elevates him to a state approaching felicity. He comes back to contingent reality only with great difficulty and reluctance.

The impressions and the reminiscences which resurrect them resemble polished gems which the rest of Proust's prose seems to set off with its lower relief. Both the psychological intensity they produce and the poetic style in which they are written attest to their special status. The drafts of the novel reveal that Proust conceived most of these passages very early, revised and perfected them through many versions, and finally did set them like precious stones in the surface of the narrative. As he states explicitly many times, he found precedent and confirmation for his experiences of memory in a number of his favorite authors: Nerval, Chateaubriand, Baudelaire, George Eliot, Ruskin. Each of them depicts a particular mode and mood by which the present comes into phase with the past. But in order to examine the nature of memory in Proust, I shall refer to two philosophers, one ancient and one modern.[13]

[13] Two sidelights on the subject of Proust and memory deserve brief mention.

The eminent Russian neurologist and psychologist A. R. Luria has written an absorbing study of the vaudeville mnemonist, S., who could memorize almost anything and never forget it. Certain aspects of his case seem to relate to Proust's, or at least to the experience of memory Proust projects in the *Search*. S.'s memory was basically nonverbal and highly synesthetic. Out of professional necessity, S. had developed a technique for remembering items, including words, by distributing them along a kind of mental walk or improvised story. Thus linked, these images "reconstructed themselves whenever he revived the original situation in which something had been registered in his memory." *The Mind of a Mnemonist*. Lynn Solotaroff, trans. (New York, 1968), p. 63. It might almost be a systematized reminiscence. The differences may be even more revealing. S. developed his memory by long training and careful attention to items given to him to remember. Proust insisted on the primacy of involuntary memory and implied that attention upsets the mechanism. Nevertheless, in the course of the novel Marcel develops

Beginning in the *Meno* Plato developed a theory of knowledge based on reminiscence. Its greatest importance was to deny the empirical origin of knowledge from sense experience. True knowledge is understood to mean true beliefs dialectically rooted in the logical reasons for their truth. And those reasons, as the *Meno* demonstrates, are found within us by *remembering*. We may remember from an earlier existence; Plato's first affirmation of the doctrine of the transmigration of souls comes in this dialogue. The theory of Ideas, developed later, is his response to the question of how the soul attains knowledge in the first place. The significant element here is that Plato discredits empirical knowledge or sense observation in favor of the recognition or recollection of logical relationships.[14] Truly to know something means reconciling past and present experience; the soul's bumpy journey through previous lives greatly extends the reservoir of past experience available to our present lives. Proust had studied Plato and was familiar with this nexus of ideas.

I have already mentioned Bergson. *Matter and Memory* appeared with great éclat when Proust was twenty-five. Its blend of phenomenological description, scientific attitude, philosophical intent, and lucid style must have been irresistible to a young author who was already

---

a kind of negative technique in which successful *forgetting* serves as the prelude to later retrieval. Marcel has to forget and later remember his grandmother's death in order to feel its reality. He even has to forget his vocation in order to find it. Proust was a mnemonist looking the other way.

In *Proust's Binoculars* (New York, 1963), pp. 148–49, I discuss Dr. Wilder Penfield's experiments in surgical stimulation of the brain under local anesthetic. His patients experienced flashes of total recall whose "reality" rivaled or surpassed that of actuality. These experiments are the nearest neurological confirmation we have of Proust's theories of memory. (See also Justin O'Brien's article in *PMLA*, March 1970.)

[14] Gregory Vlastos, "Anamnesis in the Meno," has helped me understand Plato's argument, *Dialogue*, IV, 2, 1965.

absorbed in closely related problems of subjective experience. In his second chapter, Bergson spends fifteen pages distinguishing two forms of memory. "The memory of habit" enables us to develop a series of motor responses to present reality and to learn how to cope with our environment. "Pure or spontaneous memory" occurs when a chance event disturbs the equilibrium established by habit and brings back the complete image of a past moment still stamped with "a date and a place." In the third chapter, Bergson examines the various ways in which these two forms of memory interpenetrate and tend to fuse in ordinary experience. Despite Proust's widely accepted statements to the contrary (see Appendix, page 170), the distinction between voluntary and involuntary memories is basic to Bergson's argument. For example:

> This spontaneous memory, which no doubt lurks behind acquired or habitual memory, can reveal itself in sudden flashes: but it withdraws at the tiniest movement of voluntary memory.

Bergson's steady and highly sensitive scrutiny of memory is masterful, an essential complement to the commonly cited "classic" on the subject, F. C. Bartlett's experimentally based *Remembering*.[15]

Furthermore, Bergson makes memory the central principle of his psychology, very nearly the equivalent of Freud's unconscious. Everything seems to depend on the way we deploy the two kinds of memory. The basic processes of adaptation grow out of it, as well as our mental health, our character, and our oscillation between contrasting mental states. Bergson constantly uses ideas and turns of phrase that belong to the spiritual world of Proust, even the term "resurrection." What strikes one particularly in *Matter and Memory* is Bergson's strong interest in pure or spontaneous memory.

[15] *Remembering: A Study in Experimental and Social Psychology* (New York, 1932).

Toward the end, he argues that withdrawing attention from life and abandoning oneself to spontaneous memory amounts to the state of dreaming, and "dream in every respect imitates insanity." Bergson keeps a firm hold on the *juste milieu*. But earlier passages do not hide a deep fascination with "the storehouse of memories" and the circumstances that bring them into play.[16] Proust's denials of Bergson's influence can only be termed disingenuous.

Plato, Bergson, and Proust assemble in the vicinity of the philosophical conviction that a single direct sense perception does not suffice to furnish right knowledge. Though they describe contrasting ways in which sense perceptions combine into pairs and patterns, none of them describes association taking place without the individual's interests and volition playing a crucial role. Recognition, recollection, binocular vision, stereo-reception in time—all these modes characterize our mental processes. A wholly unique sensation remains alien until assimilated by one or more of them. Consciousness in full command of its powers is double or even multiple— divided between waking and sleep (as in the opening of the *Search*), between habit and disruption by the unfamiliar (as in many of the middle sections), between past and present (toward the end). The crucial moments in the *Search* belong to composite states. Proust presents the resurrections of involuntary memory as the most complex and the most rewarding.

Proust's epistemology could be called Platonic insofar as he echoes the doctrine of reminiscence as the source

[16] Bergson occasionally even sounds like Proust. This sentence recalls one of Proust's near the opening of the novel and glows with the same sympathy for certain privileged subjective states. Bergson: "A human being who *dreamed* his life instead of living it would probably thus keep constantly in sight the infinite multitude of details of his past history." Proust: "A sleeping man keeps arrayed in a circle around him the stream of hours, the ordering of years and worlds" (I, 5).

of true knowledge, and Bergsonian insofar as he distinguishes two kinds of memory—spontaneous-involuntary and habitual-voluntary. The parts of Plato's and Bergson's thinking that he dismissed are equally significant. Though deeply tempted by reincarnation as an ancient myth and metaphor for human transcendence (e.g., I, 3 and II, 985), Proust appealed to it only in highly poetic terms and generally confined memory to the dimensions of a single human life. Though he makes frequent use of the term "essence" in conjunction with intelligence, he never posits a supreme set of entities comparable to Plato's Ideas. Proust is usually careful to cast his allusions to transcendent entities and experiences in metaphorical style. Yet he refuses to accept the strict continuity of *la durée*, the temporal mode of Bergson's intuition. In the *Search* the twinge of involuntary memory is portrayed as surmounting contingency by an act that is not continuous with *la durée* but that overleaps it. The book as a whole has a fall/redemption pattern that seems to beg for spiritual interpretation. Though Proust proposes no deity, and no direct experience that transcends human life, many critics have come to the conclusion that the basic orientation of his work is religious and that mystical experience, as described in the resurrections, provides the impetus for his novel.

R. C. Zaehner devotes a cool-headed chapter to Proust in his book, *Mysticism, Sacred and Profane*. Zaehner believes that Proust had had "the natural mystical experience." Proust does not attribute it to an apprehension of God and carefully analyzes its occurrences along lines which, according to Zaehner, approach descriptions of Zen *satori*. My own view parallels Zaehner's. I believe Proust was in search of an integration of his sense of self beyond the pure present. In spite of some slippage in vocabulary and in figures of speech, his most elevated passages are not properly speaking religious but physiological and psychological, based on the secular experience of impressions and resurrections. They concern his earthly life. Death is final; metempsychosis, however alluring and even "reasonable," remains a "Celtic belief" (I, 44). Impressions and resurrections can be considered "spiritual" in several senses of the word. Proust values them highly enough to have made them a major theme in a long novel that can indeed be read as a spiritual exercise. But the novel's fall-redemption theme grows out of the basic movement of forgetting-remembering. It should not be given religious or transcendent meaning beyond that of developing a heightened mental capacity to respond to such experiences.

From a very early age, then, Proust lived with impressions and reminiscences. These moments overflowed with psychic and spiritual significance, yet there was something missing. For years Proust could not discover a direct and essential relation between their potency and the other major country of the mind that absorbed him: art and literature.

Several passages in *Jean Santeuil* relate a struggle to grasp the origin and significance of moments of total recall or *déjà vu*. In the most striking of them, Jean wonders why the sight of Lake Geneva from his carriage one afternoon not only reminds him of the ocean in Brittany but also "raises him up out of the slavery of the present and floods [him] with the sentiment of a permanent life" (*JS*, 402). But his reflections about essence and imagination seem to be stillborn.

The notebooks of about 1908 suggest that Proust had not advanced much further. He was still swinging indecisively between a hollow social life and desultory writing. Even a newly found gift for literary pastiche did not relieve his general discouragement.

> As soon as I read an author, I perceived the melodic line which is different in every artist. . . . But I have not used that gift, and from time to time at different periods of my life, I have felt it still alive in me, like that other gift of discovering a deep-seated connection

between two ideas, two sensations. It is still alive but not strengthened, and it will soon weaken and die (*CSB*, 303).

In this instance Proust specifically associated his literary capacities with his moments of intense mnemonic association—but only to call them both failures.

The *Search* follows a parallel trajectory. The impressions and, even more intensely, the rare resurrections release great psychic force into Marcel's consciousness. But they lead nowhere and they remain transitory. They allow a glimpse of a higher, more permanent reality, but no permanent abode. In *The Captive*, Marcel finally loses confidence in the one talisman he has been carrying for many years, the experience of the *madeleine*. "Nothing assured me that the vagueness of such states was a sign of their profundity" (III, 382). His strongest insights lock him into a deeper solitude than ever. He can share these moments with no one. His inner life isolates him even more than the false scents of love and social climbing. "The universe is real for all of us, and different for each one of us" (III, 191). It is a desperately forlorn sentence. Marcel's difference, i.e., his mnemonic gift, brings him isolation as its only reward.

ART

Somewhere along the way, when he should have been coming into his own, Proust fell very low. His gifts seemed to fail him. In the novel Marcel reaches an equally dismal point. Both survived and achieved salvation through art. It had been there all along. We shall have to search through both stories again in order to discover how it happened.

In the opening chapter, I touched on the perplexities and moral insecurity of Proust's existence as he entered his late thirties. He had no job, no wife, no firm social status, no sure sense of past or future accomplishments. He had published one book of youthful fragments, about which he had ambivalent feelings, two translations of an author whose intellectual posture he had rejected, and a few semijournalistic texts. But the bulk of his writing lay buried in a stack of notebooks. By his own exacting standards he was a failure; by outward appearances he was a wealthy amateur and a social sycophant. Nevertheless, he kept trying. In the latter part of 1908, Proust announced to his friends that he was working on a new project: an essay, combined somehow with a personal narrative, on Sainte-Beuve's critical method. In the second sentence of the preface he drafted for the work, he states flatly that "past impressions" form "the only materials of Art" (*CSB*, 211). But after a brief discussion of the "resurrection" of three such impressions, he moves on into an ambivalent and unfinished discourse on the role of the intelligence in literature. *Against Sainte-Beuve*, as this project came to be called, assembles the old materials once again and tries to arrange them in a kind of circle around a half-dreaming consciousness in a bedroom. Proust put the project aside within a year—or rather he incorporated it into something significantly different. For, during the first half of 1909, Proust resolved his personal and artistic crisis and redeemed much of the writing he thought he had been producing to no purpose.

At this point Proust was traveling on two kinds of moral credit: his declining theories about the experience of involuntary memory (by now confirmed in his reading of Bergson's first two books); and the growing conviction that suffering and grief are ultimately salutary and provide a form of spiritual knowledge. Both sets of ideas turned Proust back toward his own past and encouraged him to see it with augmented relief, with depth perception in time. Both involuntary memory and the "agitations of grief" raise up out of the mind a landscape of thoughts and feelings that otherwise lies at too low a level to be seen (III, 897). In one direction these clues led backward in time toward one crucial incident that held the germ of everything to some. They took Proust to *le drame du coucher* (the goodnight scene), a play within a play enacting the ritual of desire and discontent that animates soul error. But the same forces of memory and grief also led Proust in the opposite direction, forward toward the present in its relation to the future.

What happened represented a distinct mental leap. Sometime in 1909 Proust grasped that his story was the very process of failure and rediscovery that he was going through. His book lay at his feet. He must watch and tread carefully. For his present turmoil over memory and art projected his theme, both the message and method of a novel. He reached beyond autobiography toward the transformation of his life into the shape of a story that could convey his deepest sense of self. He discovered the device, or the design, of what could be called *a play outside a play*. By seeing his personal situation from outside as if it radiated a larger, generalized narrative action of loss and recovery, he transformed his failure into potential success and his isolation into communication. Thus he discovered the unity of form fatally absent in *Jean Santeuil* and *Against Sainte-Beuve*. What the draft preface of the latter of those texts states vainly at the start, the *Search* affirms triumphantly at its close. "I understood that those materials for a literary work were my own past life" (III, 899). This insight of 1909 signifies a shift away from both autobiography and fiction (as pure invention) to *translation*, a term that keeps occurring in the final section of the *Search*. Henceforward, Proust became the author of his own life and also of a book which subsumed his life. Increasingly he gave priority to the latter, to his work, for which the former became a rehearsal subject to observation and experiment. Proust produced a work of art representing as its subject the circumstances and vagaries of its own creation and the origin of its form.

Proust detected something comparable to this *play*

outside a play effect in the work of three nineteenth-century authors. The separate books of Balzac, Hugo, and Michelet, he observes, fail to sustain the powerful schemes those authors invented later (and expressed in prefaces) to create one massive work encompassing the individual volumes.

> . . . watching themselves work as if they were both workman and judge, [these authors] drew out of that self-contemplation a new form of beauty exterior and superior to the work, imposing a retroactive unity on it, a grandeur it does not have (III, 160).

With some qualifications I accept Proust's implication that his work does have the unity and grandeur which Balzac, Hugo, and Michelet failed to achieve. Proust's expanded vision of his life as the source of his work came in time to allow him to recast his earlier work and project the vision over writings to come. His equivalent of a preface describing his "subsequent unity" (III, 161) is contained inside the novel in passages like the one just quoted.

This reorientation in Proust's writing resembles an inversion of the figure-ground relation in painting. In *Jean Santeuil* neutral stretches of lived time form the background against which Proust picks out vivid, discontinuous incidents for description. In the *Search*, the over-all movement of Marcel's life, i.e., time as he ultimately lived it, becomes the figure finally discerned. The ground against which it is gradually revealed consists of all those false scents and misconceptions—the accumulated incidents of the story. The contrast in approach and emphasis is complete, and completely significant for his art. There is another comparison that may illuminate the shift. In "The Circular Ruins" Borges tells the story of a man who discovers that his life consists of, or enacts, the dreams of another more powerful human consciousness, on which he is therefore entirely dependent. Proust "woke up" to the higher consciousness and unity of his literary vision; beside it, or within it, his own life became a dream, a play, a fiction. At this point sheer form becomes an omnivorous force, seeking to assimilate everything it encounters. At this point also, Proust adopted for keeps the ambiguous narrative *I*. He developed a first-person discourse that merges the protagonist of the incidents forming the ground (Marcel) with the retrospective witness-writer (the Narrator) who discovers the figure, the "new form of beauty" superior and exterior to them.

Proust weathered his artistic crisis in mid-career and came out on the other side of it with hopes of making good in three or four years on his big literary wager. In the end he used all fourteen years he had to live. The biography gives a clear enough picture of the outward events, yet it is extremely difficult to speak with certainty about the nature of the insight that transformed Proust's career and produced the *Search*.[17]

In the novel there are two significant differences from the biography. First, Marcel's conversion to literature as a vocation comes not in mid-career as in the case of Proust, but very late—nearly at the end of the book when Marcel is described as an old man. Thus the dramatic effect is enhanced, and the body of the book is constructed as a long decline. My remarks in the previous chapter about art as idolatry and a false scent should suggest how art conforms to that pattern in the *Search*. Painting and music keep some of their savor, but as the story goes on literature, representing Marcel's first aspiration to transcend ordinariness and isolation, withers to a dry husk. Even Marcel's long discussion with Albertine in *The Captive* about Dostoevski, Mme de Sévigné, Thomas Hardy, and Baudelaire, dangles from the troubling thought that "Vinteuil's music seemed

[17] Three powerful biographer-critics have approached the subject. In order of increasing judiciousness and mastery of the overwhelming materials, they are: George D. Painter, Henri Bonnet, and Maurice Bardèche.

to me something truer than all known books" (III, 374). These discouragements begin soon after Combray and become one of the leitmotivs of the book until close to the end.[18]

The first difference, then, between the novel and the biography is one of timing. Marcel rediscovers his literary vocation near the end of his life, not in his prime as Proust himself did. The second difference is that what the circumstances of life tend to obscure—namely, the origins and meanings of things—the novel tends to reveal. There lies its essence and its purpose as a work of art. In fact, the earliest sustained reflections on literature in the *Search* develop precisely this esthetic theory.

At the beginning of *Swann's Way* the reader comes upon several celebrated set pieces: the kaleidoscope of bedrooms in Marcel's life; the goodnight kiss withheld and granted; and the *madedeine* dipped in linden tea.

---

[18] To emphasize this downward movement, Proust wrote a somewhat contrived coda for the last pages of *Swann's Way*, the first volume to be published. The mythological Bois de Boulogne, peopled with the most elegant creatures in the world, collapses into its most paltry self, a mere woods. Six pages of romantic despair lead up to a muted allusion to Horace in the closing lines: ". . . the memory of a certain scene means nothing more than the loss of that instant; and the houses, roads, and avenues are as fleeting, alas, as time itself" (I, 427). The spinning of the story goes on, but deprived now of the hope that memory or art can transcend the flux.

Is it really so? as Proust himself would immediately have asked. In a significant letter written to Jacques Rivière just a few months after publication of *Swann's Way* in 1913, Proust states that this coda is merely "a screen to finish off the volume within the limit of 500 pages" and that the thought expressed there is "the contrary of my conclusion." But at that point in the text, the despair is convincing and authoritative. The weight of the evidence continues to bear it out, not just through a few hundred pages as Proust originally planned, but through five more volumes, before the contrary movement begins in *Time Recaptured*. It makes a prolonged and seemingly irreversible descent.

And what then? Aunt Léonie? The village church and steeple. The two ways? Each one has high definition. Yet we cannot go on endlessly dealing with a novel composed of detachable parts. The pages of "Combray" form a radial unity that it is unwise to cut up into scenes and sections. Still, one sequence stands apart because it casts everything else into doubt and jeopardy. The Combray world that displays convincing color and strong personality dims temporarily when seen from another perspective. The shift occurs when Marcel is reading in the garden (I, 84–88). This carefully reasoned yet poetic passage places us suddenly inside his world, looking out. Marcel's faith in the special world of childhood weakens briefly in the face of a competing faith— the reality of a book. Art makes the challenge. Marcel describes his long Sunday afternoons of reading as forming a single consciousness "simultaneously dappled with different states." He remains only marginally aware of the world around him.

> [For] my most intimate thought, the constantly shifting control that regulated everything else, was my belief in the philosophical richness and in the beauty of the book I was reading and my desire to appropriate them for myself (I, 84).

And we are told why. Being not opaque, material creatures but *images*, the characters of such a story are transparent and can reveal their feelings and motives to us. As images they can also concentrate the actions of a lifetime into a few hours' reading, thus making perceptible what we cannot observe at the slow pace of living. The transparent image of fiction is doubly revealing compared to life, and hence more alluring than life. Furthermore, the Narrator explains in this passage, the "prestige" of the fictional world consoles Marcel for the apparent mediocrity of his own life and releases the constant gushing forth [*jaillissement*] of his consciousness toward other things and beings. These beautiful Sunday afternoons, described as "silent, sonorous, perfumed, and limpid," transform Marcel's life and anticipate both the long stretches of soul error and the final return to art. They do not destroy Marcel's basic faith in his childhood experiences, but they shadow it.

As a reader, then, Marcel lives through a few afternoons that both transcend the magic and relieve the mediocrity of childhood. Yet like the impressions and resurrections, they do not last. Instead, they lead into the false or idolatrous attitudes toward art of Swann, Bergotte, Charlus, and Marcel himself. However this first sustained esthetic meditation presents art as a form of revelation and communication that importunes our inmost being. Like the *madeleine* sequence in the domain of memory, it remains a talisman in the domain of art.

Art is never far from the narrative line of the *Search*. Marcel lives surrounded by the mythological presences of art, in the double form of the masterpieces of Western culture and of several characters in the story who practice one of the arts. The three major artists represent a kind of progress: Bergotte, the most compromised by the world, society, and idolatry; Elstir, who seems to work directly with the phenomenon of vision rather than to render reality; and Vinteuil, depicted as a martyr-composer. It is Elstir who means most to Marcel after he has passed adolescence.

> . . . if God the Father created the things of the world by naming them, it is by depriving them of their names, or by giving them new names, that Elstir re-created the world (I, 835).

Marcel gleans lessons like this one and many more along the way. However, such insights become less frequent and more fragmentary with time. Art takes the same downward path as memory. It is not until we are well into the fifth volume that Marcel has another experience of art as intense and as carefully described as the Sunday afternoons in Combray. The fifteen pages devoted to the Vinteuil septet in *The Captive* (III, 248–265) carry Marcel through a series of stations along the path to understanding art. Taken unawares by the music, he first hears it as a description of a seascape, and then associates it with his love for Albertine. After thinking of the piece as an expression of Vinteuil's troubled life, Marcel goes on to discover in the music something "ineffable": a sense of individual being and "the communication of souls" (III, 258). Proust has written a profound meditation on music as a progressive experience engaging one's whole consciousness. The passage is less about music than about coenesthesia, the organic sensation of existence, released by a full encounter with music. Within the context of Marcel's story, however, the incident falls short of changing Marcel's life. He hears the music as a "call" away from the "emptiness" of his life. He cannot answer that call, possibly because he remains a hearer or spectator, possibly because it is a musical rather than a literary experience. Nevertheless, this scene takes so long a step toward divulging the outcome of the novel that Proust saw fit to lead us back into a swamp of misunderstanding and disappointment before the end comes. When Marcel reads the Goncourt brothers' journal (see previous chapter, page 88) he has lost his esthetic bearings so thoroughly that he all but renounces his ambitions as an artist along with his hopes of grasping the significance of past events in his life.

After so many tribulations the outcome of the novel may begin to look strained. When impressions, reminiscences, and art have lost their power to sustain Marcel, how is it that they return miraculously and more compellingly than ever in the long culminating scene? What accounts for this melodramatic turn of events? The basic reason has a sturdy simplicity about it. At long last Marcel comprehends the crucial interrelation between these three elements of his experience. Earlier, he barely associated them. The impressions faded as soon as they occurred. The reminiscences might or might not lead him back to their source among forgotten impressions, and did not reach out toward artistic creation. Art wallowed increasingly in the sloughs of prestige and idolatry. The one exception to this compartmentalization turns up fairly early in the story and is worth a look. I am referring to the scene in "Combray" when Marcel scribbles out on the spot a description of the beautiful slow dance of the Martinville steeples on the horizon as seen from Dr. Percepied's fast moving carriage (I, 178–92). Yet nothing in this carefully composed sequence encourages the reader to regard Marcel's product as a work of art. "I never thought about the page again," the Narrator says. And he ridicules the whole affair by telling us that Marcel began to carry on like "a chicken . . . that had just laid an egg." There is little here to convey any lasting faith in impressions, reminiscences, and art, or to bring them together.

No such flippancy marks the last two hundred pages of the *Search*, even though it contains the great mock-apotheosis of nonrecognition and many smaller comic touches. Five successive resurrections impel Marcel to collect the thoughts and experiences of a lifetime into a final meditation. This philosophical-poetic discourse does not reflect *on* the action at this juncture; its powerful movement of thought *is* the action. It reconstitutes every theme in the novel. Joyce seeks a similar effect in Molly Bloom's great affirmative monologue at the end of *Ulysses*. Marcel's fifty-page monologue that opens the final sequence follows a basic argument as clearly articulated as that of the passage describing the Sunday afternoon readings in Combray. The opposite of a *dénouement*, it knots together the several strands that have hung slack and barely intertwined during the central portion of the novel:

1. Though they bestow a sense of "the essence of things" and of "our true self," resurrections such as those

just experienced by Marcel are of fleeting effect (III, 866–75).

2. The only means to arrest and transfix their elevating impulse is to capture it in a work of art (876–83; 883–88 form a later insertion).

3. The writer does so by creating a metaphorical link or loop between ordinary, lived "reality" and the "vision" of a work of art. This esthetic loop encompasses the analogous loop between past impression and its resurrection in the present (889–96).

4. The understanding of art as a creative process permits Marcel to embrace his literary vocation and to see the carefully defined role literature gives to intelligence and general laws, and to suffering. He also speaks of the role and the rewards of the reader (897–917).

The last two parts of the argument, especially 3, need elucidation.

In approaching what he considers to be the essential function of a work of art, Proust relies heavily on the French word, *rapport*: relation. In the crucial paragraph of his meditation (III, 889), he describes a set of interlocking relations connecting all parts of his universe and based on the "natural" phenomenon of seeing one thing in another through association or analogy. The analogy that links past and present experiences through memory confers on them a sense of "reality," of "true life." Resurrections create a kind of relief or depth perception in time. This reality is in turn related to art through the analogy of metaphor. The transparent, accelerated image of fiction can capture what is opaque or imperceptible in life. Thus art forms a second loop in a different dimension, reaching out of reality and time, yet also flowing back toward them. When Proust describes the writer discovering the *rapport* between art and life, he does so in the context of a now familiar incident.

If I tried to analyze for myself just what takes place in us at the moment when something makes a certain impression on us—as, for example, that day when, as I crossed the bridge over the Vivonne, the shadow of a cloud on the water made me exclaim, "Gosh, gosh," as I leaped for joy . . . —I perceived that, to describe these impressions, to write that essential book, the only true book, a great writer does not need to invent it, in the current sense of the term, since it already exists in each one of us, but merely to translate it. The duty and the tasks of a writer are those of a translator (III, 890).

Involuntary memory links past the present into reality. "Translation" links that reality, focused in reminiscences and impressions, to the work of art. A little further on Proust adds a third loop: reading. The reader ultimately reads *himself* in the work of art and gains an insight into his reality by retrospection or anticipation.

In the hope of clarifying my exposition, I have constructed a diagram of the operation of Proust's literary esthetic as I comprehend it (see Diagram VI). The significant aspect of this vision of things is that every element is linked by a universal principle of analogy or relation. Literature, and by implication the other arts, play a key intermediary role between one person's reality and that of another. In fact, the word which best sums up Proust's philosophical attitude in this context, encompassing both an epistemology and an esthetic, is *communication*. In 1905, when toiling to find his way beyond Ruskin's idolatrous attitude toward art, Proust had spoken of reading as "that fecund miracle of communication in the midst of solitude" (*CSB*, 174). For social conversation distracts the mind; solitude strengthens it. Directed toward a work of art, reading brings communication without social distraction. Yet Proust went on to insist that reading constitutes an "incitement" to the true life of the mind, and not the full realization of that life (*ibid.*, 178). Part of the same train of thought reappears in *The Guermantes Way* when the Narrator passes harsh judgment on friendship,

VI. THE LOOPS OF ART

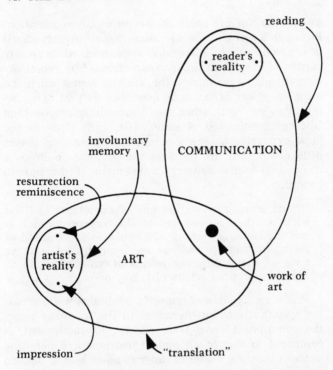

—Any person's experience may emit a field of heightened awareness: namely, *art* in its simplest meaning.

—The pattern central to the *Search* is that of a relationship between a past impression and its resurrection in the present.

—Only the gifted and dedicated artist *translates* his reality into the *work of art*.

—Through the work of art the reader may attain *communication* with others (the artist and, presumably, other readers) and an enhanced recognition of his own lot.

all of whose effort is to make us sacrifice the only part of ourselves which is real and incommunicable (except by means of art) to a superficial self which, unlike the other, finds no reward in its own being (II, 394).

The work of art holds the secret of communication. But at this point in the narrative that truth is confined in a parenthesis of suspended animation, while society carries Marcel along in its distractions. The secret declares itself again during the Vinteuil septet when the ultimate power of music is described as that of allowing us to see "with other eyes," something approaching "the communication of souls" (III, 258). One of the most expansive passages in the last meditation leaves little doubt that art provides the antidote to Proust's complaint, to the solitary confinement of the human condition.

> By art alone can we get out of ourselves, find out what another person sees of this universe which is not the same as ours. . . . Thanks to art, instead of seeing only one world, we see it multiplied, and we have as many different worlds at our disposition as there are original artists (III, 895–96).

Proust rarely allowed himself such flights when speaking specifically about literature. In the following pages the communication a book affords, its incitement, is compared to that of an optical instrument which "the author offers the reader in order to allow him to discern things which, without the book, he would possibly not have seen in himself. The reader's recognition in himself of what the book says is proof of the book's truth, and vice versa" (III, 911). True reading of a worthwhile book takes us just far enough out of ourselves and our solitude to return to them restored. Art affords this communication with our own life through self-recognition. Those admirers of art who cannot make the return trip to their own reality are harshly judged by Proust as

"*célibataires* of art" (III, 892). Their admiration has no
dynamic relation to their own lives. Permanently sensitized by Ruskin, Proust would never allow art to present
itself as a substitute for life, even for the life of the
mind, but only as the exercise of communication which
leads us back into life. When Marcel's Sunday afternoon
reading in Combray tempted him to turn away from his
existence in dissatisfaction and desire, he was misusing
art as an escape and not discerning himself through
its lens. In a boy this is natural enough. It may take the
better part of a lifetime to discover that reading can
augment rather than diminish one's own life and circumstances.

In sum, art springs from life and in turn serves it
through the interlocking *rapports* or loops of communication. Yet there remains an underlying inconsistency
between this affirmation that art belongs to life and
Proust's thoughts on solitude and society. Everything
he says about social life and friendship and snobbery
as contrasted to reading and meditation establishes the
vanity of social intercourse next to the true rewards of
solitude. To converse with a friend is "a self-abdication"
(II, 906). Marcel prefers to read and look at pictures
alone; on country walks he drops behind his friends
when he wants to commune with a hawthorn bush or a
view of the ocean. The deepest experiences of memory
and art appear to be excluded from that portion of our
lives spent with other people. Few divisions in Proust's
universe go so deep as this cleavage between the integrity of solitude, associated with memory and art, and
the distraction of society associated with superficiality
and snobbery.[19]

[19] During the *madeleine* resurrection, Marcel's mother is with
him and in fact supplies both the tea and the cake. However, the text does not indicate that she either shares the
experience or receives an account of it from her son. He
becomes totally rapt in his own mental processes and never
mentions her again even at the end of the sequence. It is
significant that during the Martinville steeples impression,

Yet the close of the book brings an unexpected shift in Marcel's attitude. Most of the dramatic developments at the end, concerning art and memory and vocation, have been anticipated many times over in earlier passages. But on the matter of society and solitude, Marcel and the Narrator have kept their secrets of state very successfully. Directly after the fifty-page meditation on the nature of art and its relation to memory and to life, Marcel is told that he can enter the salon and join the other guests. Brought back to himself and his surroundings, he seems to have found a new calm.

> But in the line of thought upon which I was embarked I was not in the least disturbed by the fact that a fashionable gathering, my return to society, might have provided me with that point of departure for a new life which I had been unable to find in solitude. There was nothing extraordinary about this fact, there was no reason why an impression with the power to resuscitate the timeless man within me should be linked to solitude rather than to society (as I had once supposed and as had perhaps once been the case, and as perhaps would still have had to be the case had I developed harmoniously instead of going through this long period of arrest which seemed only now to be coming to an end) . . . I felt that the impulse given to the intellectual life within me was so vigorous now that I would be able to pursue these thoughts just as well in the drawing room, in the midst of the guests, as alone in the library; it seemed to me that, from this point of view, even in the midst of a numerous gathering, I would be able to maintain my solitude (III, 918).

Undistracted, no longer deceived by the false prestige of noble names and celebrated faces, sustained by the sense of his own life as worth living, Marcel passes

---

the coachman, next to whom Marcel was sitting, refused to talk with him. ". . . I was obliged, for lack of any other company, to fall back on myself" (I, 180).

among the guests and watches the scene around him as if it were part of a play or a painting. Marcel here achieves the familiarity and the detachment to behold these other people without soul error, without the abdication of self that has always beset him before in a social context. His equanimity and powers of recognition allow him at last to enter into his own existence as into a work of art, briefly transcending intermittence by fusing solitude and social intercourse. Marcel can now return safely and even profitably to his old haunts. What ensues is a magnificent comic scene revealing the tenacity of general and individual human traits beneath the grotesque masquerade of age. Odette and the Prince de Guermantes and the rest are incorrigibly themselves to their last breath—which seems very near.

Presumably Marcel could now find the rewards of old age in the same social milieu that for years arrested his development. Yet it is not to be so. Marcel the writer realizes that he must devote the months remaining to him to composing the book he feels alive within him as the true fruit of his experience. Having attained an inner equilibrium of solitude and society, he will not have time to enjoy it. It is the final irony. Attended only by Françoise, Marcel must turn resolutely to his solitary work as an artist.[20]

Even though it opens a place for the reader, Proust's esthetic raises an uncomfortable question: is full salvation by art reserved for the creative artist? The three major artists in the book play the role of collective godfather to Marcel. Until he finds his own vocation, they

[20] In *Proust's Binoculars*, I consider two important aspects of Proust's esthetic which are omitted here. One is the way in which the topographical division of Combray into "two ways" resolves finally into one and becomes a metaphor for metaphor itself (pp. 125–27). The other concerns the double, twice-lived nature of life, for whose total experience literature cannot substitute. But literature can furnish one beat of that double rhythm of re-cognition and thus modify the basic economy of living (pp. 132–36).

take his vows for him and guide him on his way. Con-
versely, the gifted amateurs—Swann, Charlus, even his
grandmother—are all "bachelors of art" and often lead
him astray. When Marcel comes back to art at an advanced age, he does so not as an amateur or apprecia-
tive spectator but as a novelist. The hierarchy of functions is fully declared. Yet there are a few glints of hope
for the nonartist and ordinary citizen. The basic materials of art, meaning impressions and possibly reminiscences, exist in all of us, available for translation into
art. The true text is life itself, if only we know how to
approach it. Art is a matter of vision and revision. A
few pages later Proust develops this thought and dramatically closes the loops between life and literature.
Realism depicts only the surface of things, he states;
both and life and art lie "underneath."

> The greatness of true art . . . was to find, grasp, and
> bring out that reality which we live at a great distance
> from . . . that reality which we run the risk of dying
> without having known, and which is quite simply our
> own life. True life, life finally discovered and illumi-
> nated, is literature; that life which, in a sense, at
> every moment inhabits all men as well as the artist
> (III, 895).

"All men" does not equivocate; "in a sense" holds something back. The stuff of literature is there for all to
find and take. Few people find it; fewer still translate
it into a work of art. But it is precisely that literary work
which may help the less gifted to find their true life.
They do so not vicariously by seeking to identify with
another life, but indirectly by the reciprocating movement of literature, which propels them first toward
clearly visible beings in a novel and then back toward
their own existence insofar as they recognize themselves
in the story. But only the writer-artist has the task and
the reward of extruding a work of art out of his own
experience. According to Proust's mature esthetic,

which is also his ethic, the writer draws both on an exceptional memory (encompassing impressions and reminiscences) and on a logical-imaginative insight which related these mnemonic experiences to, and in, the work of art—process and product as one. The shape and the content of the *Search* derive from this esthetic insight. The novel depicts the artist very much in the role of the Prodigal Son, or of Ulysses. After a long journey and many trials, a joyful homecoming. It is primarily the obbligato motifs of suffering and work in the artist's life that keep the conclusion from sounding prideful. Within that obbligato, furthermore, one detects the soft but unmistakable suggestion that each one of us is potentially the artist of his own life.

APPENDIX

In the fall of 1912 Proust thought he had virtually finished his novel. Half of it was in typescript, half still in manuscript. After submitting the first half to the publisher Fasquelle, he decided that he might do better with the new house set up by the *Nouvelle Revue Française*. Through friends he sent another copy of the typescript to Jacques Copeau, André Gide, and Jean Schlumberger, the *NRF* editors, accompanied by a long statement explaining the purpose and methods of his novel. Principally on the basis of Gide's hasty judgment, they turned him down a month later in a now famous decision they soon came to regret.

A few days before Grasset finally published *Swann's Way* in November 1913, Proust arranged for *Le Temps* to run an interview with him. Elie-Joseph Bois, the journalist who visited Proust for the purpose, received a copy of the statement originally written for the *NRF* editors the year before. He reproduced it virtually unchanged, adding his own comments as an opening. Thus the interview contains both one of the earliest published descriptions of Proust's living conditions and his most coherent and cogent declaration of artistic faith at that period. Many of its themes and phrases are borrowed directly from portions of the novel that would not appear for several years.

The complete text has not previously been translated into English.

In Search of Lost Time
—Elie-Joseph Bois

This is the enigmatic title of a novel the first volume of which has just appeared and has provoked much curiosity. A few pages of it have already passed from hand to hand, and those privileged readers speak of the book with great enthusiasm. Such premature success is often an advantage, and sometimes a hidden danger. I do not know how public opinion will react in this case, whether it will consecrate as a masterpiece, as some have already called it, this self-contained opening volume entitled *Swann's Way*. But I run no risk in predicting that it will leave no reader indifferent. It will probably disconcert many readers. *Swann's Way* is not a book to read on the train, skipping over the pages with one eye on the landscape; it is a book of true originality and profundity to the point of strangeness, claiming the reader's full attention and even seizing it forcibly. Its clutch takes you by surprise; it confuses and overwhelms. As for plot—plot in the sense of what we rely on in most novels to carry us along in some state of expectation through a series of adventures to the necessary resolution—there just is no such thing here. There is an action of sorts, but its threads seem to be covered over with an exaggerated concern for discretion, and it is up to us to find our own way through, breathing heavily, absorbed in the development of characters which the author etches pitilessly in successive situations. A novel of analysis, yes; but I know of few novels in which the analysis penetrates so deep. At times you want to cry out, "Enough!" as to a surgeon who spares no detail in describing an operation. Yet you never say it. You keep on turning the pages feverishly in order to see further into the souls of these creatures. What you see is a certain Swann in love with Odette de Crécy, and how his love changes into an anxious, suspicious, unhealthy passion tormented by the most atrocious jealousy. You probably know the kind. It happens in every novel, in every play, on every street corner. But in this case we aren't kept on the outside of things; willy-nilly we are thrust into the mind and heart and body of that man. An impassive guide leads us on and forces us to look, to read each thought, to live each emotion, from the joy of spreading happiness to the pangs of jealousy that rack the heart and leave one's head in a whirl. The same thing happens with a child's love for his mother, and with a boy's puppy love for one of his playmates, and with all the characters' feelings in *Swann's Way*.

Mr. Marcel Proust is the author of this disturbing book.

The translator and critic of Ruskin is by no means unknown to the reading public. Mr. Anatole France, toward whom he feels deep gratitude, wrote the preface for *Pleasures and Days*, a charming work whose extreme indecency Mr. Proust regrets (the word is his own) but does not disavow. The older author characterized him as a depraved Bernardin de Saint-Pierre and an innocent Petronius. Mr. Edouard Rod found in him an affinity to La Bruyère. Mr. Albert Sorel gave an account of his first book in this newspaper. After that, except for an occasional article, Mr. Proust withdrew within himself, or rather illness forced him to withdraw. It is no new writer, then, who comes along today to offer us *Swann's Way*. In *Pleasures and Days* there's already a preliminary version, called *Jealousy's End*, of the most striking chapter in the new novel. In the preface to his translation of *Sesame and Lilies*, you will find the embryo of another chapter. But the writer has undergone a great change, His horizons have broadened, and at the same time his sensibility has matured to the point where he can say: "There's not a single adjective in my new work that's not fully felt." Like plants which grow best in a hothouse, Mr. Marcel Proust, intent upon himself, has drawn out of his own suffering a creative energy demonstrated in his novel. He set himself a task. But what task? He can describe it better than I can.

Mr. Marcel Proust is lying down in a bedroom whose shutters are almost permanently closed. Electric light accentuates the dull color of his face, but two fine eyes burning with life and fever gleam below the hair that falls over his forehead. Mr. Marcel Proust is still the slave of his illness, but that person disappears when the writer, invited to comment on his work, comes to life and begins to talk.

"I'm publishing only one volume, *Swann's Way*, of a multivolume novel which will have the general title, *In Search of Lost Time*. I would have liked to publish the whole work together, but these days editors won't bring out several volumes at a time. I feel like someone with a tapestry too large for any of his rooms and who has to cut it up into sections.

"Many young writers, with whom I'm on good terms, favor the opposite course: short action, few characters. That's not my conception of the novel. I'll try to explain why. As you know we have both plane and solid geometry—geometry in two-dimensional and in three-dimensional space. Well, for me the novel means not just plane (or plain) psychology but psychology in time. It is this invisible substance of time that I have tried to isolate, and it meant that the experiment had to last over a long period. I hope that at the end of my book certain unimportant social events, like the marriage between two characters who in the first volume belonged to totally different social worlds, will imply that time has passed and will take on the kind of beauty and patina you can see on the statues at Versailles which time has gradually coated with an emerald sheath.

"Then, like a city which, from a train following its winding track, appears first on one side of the car and then on the other, the various situations in which one character will have been seen by another—to the point of seeming to be different and successive characters instead of the same one—will give, and for that very reason, the sensation of time elapsed. Some characters will turn out later quite different from what they are in the present volume, different from what we think they are, as it happens in life."

Mr. Proust told us that it is not just certain characters that will reappear with modifications, as in cycles of Balzac's novels. Certain profound, almost unconscious impressions will recur in the same person. And he went on.

"From this point of view, my book might be seen as an attempt at a series of 'novels of the unconscious.' I would not be ashamed to say 'Bergsonian novels' if I believed it, for in every age literature tries to find a link—after the fact, of course—to the reigning philosophy. But the term would be inaccurate, for my work is based on the distinction between involuntary and voluntary memory, a distinction which not only does not appear in Mr. Bergson's philosophy, but is even contradicted by it."

"How do you make this distinction?"

"To my way of thinking, voluntary memory, which belongs above all to the intelligence and the eyes, offers us only untruthful aspects of the past; but if an odor or a taste, re-encountered in totally different circumstances, unexpectedly reawakens the past in us, then we can sense how different this past was from what we thought we could remember, from what voluntary memory offered us, like a painter working with false colors. Already, in the first volume, you will see the character who tells the story, and who says 'I' (he's not me), suddenly rediscover forgotten times, forgotten gardens and people, in the taste of a sip of tea with a *madeleine* cake soaked in it. Probably he could remember these things, but without any vividness or attraction; I was able to have him say that, as in the Japanese trick of dropping into a bowl of water tiny bits of paper which then unfurl and fill out into flowers and people, all the flowers in his garden, and the Vivonne water lilies, and the good folk of the village along with their houses and their church, and the whole of Combray and its environs, all that, with its shape and solidity restored, comes forth, town and gardens, from his cup of tea.

"So you see, I believe that the writer should expect involuntary memory to furnish almost all the raw material of his work. First of all, precisely because such memories are involuntary, because they take shape of their own accord out of the attraction of one moment for another, they alone carry the seal of authenticity. Second, they bring things back in the right proportion of memory and forgetfulness. Finally, since they let us experience the same sensation in a totally different setting, they liberate it from all contingency and give us its extratemporal essence, the essence which becomes the content of meaningful style, the general and necessary truth which beauty of style alone can express.

"I'm talking this way about my book," Mr. Proust went on, "because I have in no way written a work of reasoning, because all its elements have been furnished by my sensibility, because I first perceived them deep within me without understanding them, and have had as much difficulty putting them into intelligible form as if they were alien to the intelligence, like a musical theme. You may think I'm talking about extreme subleties. Not at all, believe me, but about realities. Anything we have not had to elucidate ourselves, anything that was clear before we came along (logical ideas, for example), does not really belong to us, we don't even know if it's real. We choose arbitrarily from 'the possible.' Anyway, you know, you can see all this in the style.

"Style has nothing to do with embellishment, as some people think; it's not even a matter of technique. Like the color sense in some painters, it's a quality of vision, the revelation of the particular universe that each of us sees and that no one else sees. The pleasure an artist offers us is to convey another universe to us."

In that case, we ask, how is it that some writers claim to have no style at all? Mr. Proust cannot understand them and insists:

"They could say that only if they have given up trying to get to the bottom of their impressions."

Mr. Proust has dedicated *Swann's Way* "To Mr. Gaston Calmette, as an expression of deep and affectionate gratitude."

"I may have older debts," Mr. Proust told us, "toward masters to whom I have dedicated works written before this one but which will appear after it—first of all to Anatole France, who treated me practically like a son. Thanks to Mr. Calmette, I experienced the joy of a young man who reads his first published article.

"And also," Mr. Proust added with a note of melancholy, "since publication of my articles in his newspaper gave me a way of visiting certain people I found it hard to do without, he helped me make the change from a social to a solitary life . . ."

And the gesture made by this ailing author brought me back to the darkened room with its closed shutters, where the sun never enters. But his look shows no sadness. If the invalid has reason to complain, the writer has reason to be proud. The latter has consoled the former.

Le Temps
13 November, 1913

ACKNOWLEDGMENTS

A travel grant from the American Philosophical Society, Philadelphia, Pennsylvania, permitted me to consult the collection of Proust manuscripts in the Bibliothèque Nationale, Paris.

Some materials in this book were originally presented in a series of three lectures during November 1971 at the University of Wisconsin, Madison, as part of a symposium celebrating the Proust centenary and sponsored by the Department of Romance Languages; and in the John Hamilton Fulton Memorial Lecture at Middlebury College, Vermont, in January 1973.

A modified version of a section from Chapter IV is included in the essay "This Must Be the Place: from Wordsworth to Proust," in *Romanticism: Vistas, Distances, Continuities*, eds. David Thorburn and Geoffrey Hartman. Ithaca: Cornell University Press, 1973.

R. S.

SHORT BIBLIOGRAPHY

See page vii for the standard edition in French of Proust's works and for the editions in English of *In Search of Lost Time* (published title: *Remembrance of Things Past*).

Proust's correspondence, originally collected in six volumes during the 1930s and supplemented in numerous separate collections since then, is now being consolidated and re-edited by Philip Kolb. The first two volumes have appeared (Paris: Plon, 1970, 1973).

I. ENGLISH TRANSLATIONS OF WORKS OTHER THAN *In Search of Lost Time*

Marcel Proust: A selection from His Miscellaneous Writings. Trans. Gerard Hopkins. London: Allan Wingate, 1948.

The Maxims of Marcel Proust. Ed. and trans. Justin O'Brien. New York: Columbia University Press, 1948.

Letters of Marcel Proust. Selected and trans. Minna Curtiss. New York: Random House, 1949.

Jean Santeuil. Trans. Gerard Hopkins. New York: Simon & Schuster, 1956.

Pleasures and Days and Other Writings. Trans. Louise Varèse, Gerard Hopkins, and Barbara Dupee; ed. F. W. Dupee. Garden City, N. Y.: Anchor Books, 1957.

Marcel Proust: Letters to His Mother. Trans. George D. Painter. New York: Citadel Press, 1957.

Marcel Proust on Art and Literature, 1896–1919. Trans. Sylvia Townsend Warner. New York: Meridian, 1958. (Contains *Against Sainte-Beuve* in the extended text published by Gallimard in 1954.)

On Reading. Trans. Jean Autret and William Burford. New York: Macmillan, 1971. A bilingual edition of Proust's Preface to his own translation, published in 1906, of Ruskin's *Sesame and Lilies.*

II. ON PROUST AND HIS WORK

In the lists below an asterisk indicates a work containing a useful bibliography.

a. Books of a general nature and biographies

Barker, Richard H. *Marcel Proust: a Biography.* New York: Criterion, 1958.

*Bersani, Jacques, ed. *Les Critiques de notre temps et Proust.* Paris: Garnier, 1971.

*Brée, Germaine. *The World of Marcel Proust.* Boston: Houghton Mifflin, 1966.

*Fowlie, Wallace. *A Reading of Proust.* Garden City, N. Y.: Anchor Books, 1964.

Hindus, Milton. *The Proustian Vision.* New York: Columbia University Press, 1954.

Levin, Harry. *The Gates of Horn: A Study of Five French Realists.* New York: Oxford University Press, 1963. (Chapter VII is on Proust.)

*Maurois, André. *A la recherche de Marcel Proust.* Paris: Hachette, 1949. (*Proust, Portrait of a Genius.* Gerard Hopkins, trans. New York: Harper, 1950.)

*Painter, George D. *Proust: the Early Years* and *Proust: the Later Years.* 2 vols. Boston: Atlantic-Little Brown, 1959, 1965.

Poulet, Georges. *Etudes sur le temps humain.* Paris: Plon, 1949. (Chapter on Proust.) (*Studies in Human Time.* Elliot Coleman, trans. Baltimore: Johns Hopkins University Press, 1956.)

*Tadié, J.-Y. ed. *Lectures de Proust.* Paris: Armand Colin, 1971.

b. Other works mentioned in the text

Bardèche, Maurice. *Proust romancier.* 2 vols. Paris: Les Sept Couleurs, 1971.

Béhar, Serge. *L'Univers médical de Proust* (Cahiers Marcel Proust, nouvelle série, I). Paris: Gallimard, 1970.

Bersani, Leo. *Marcel Proust: the Fictions of Life and of Art.* New York: Oxford University Press, 1965.

Brée, Germaine. *Du temps perdu au temps retrouvé*. Paris: Les Belles Lettres, 1950. (*Marcel Proust and Deliverance from Time*. C. J. Richards and A. D. Truitt, trans. New Brunswick, N.J.: Rutgers University Press, 1955.)

*Bonnet, Henri. *Marcel Proust de 1907 à 1914*. Paris: Nizet, 1971.

Deleuze, Gilles. *Proust et les signes*. 2ᵉ ed. Paris: P. U. F., 1970. (*Proust and Signs*. Richard Howard, trans. Paperback. New York: George Braziller, 1972.)

Fernandez, Dominique. *L'Arbre jusqu'aux racines*. Paris: Grasset, 1972.

Frank, Joseph. *The Widening Gyre*. New Brunswick: Rutgers University Press, 1963.

Genette, Gérard. *Figures I, II, III*. Paris: Seuil, 1966, 1969, 1973.

Girard, René. *Mensonge romantique et vérité romanesque*. Paris: Grasset, 1961. (*Deceit, Desire, and the Novel: Self and Other in Literary Structure*. Y. Freccero, trans. Baltimore: Johns Hopkins University Press, 1966.)

Muller, Marcel. *Les Voix narratives dans "A la recherche du temps perdu."* Geneva: Droz, 1965.

Picon, Gaëtan. *Lecture de Proust*. Paris: Mercure de France, 1963.

Pierre-Quint, Léon. *Marcel Proust*. Paris: Sagittaire, 1935.

Pinter, Harold. *The Proust Screenplay*. New York: Grove Press, 1977.

Poulet, Georges. *L'Espace proustien*. Paris: Gallimard, 1963.

Revel, J.-F. *Sur Proust*. Paris: Julliard, 1960. (*On Proust*. Martin Turnell, trans. Paperback. LaSalle, Ill.: Open Court, 1973.)

Rousset, Jean. *Forme et signification*. Paris: Corti, 1962.

Shattuck, Roger. *Proust's Binoculars*. New York: Random House, 1963.

Stambolian, George. *Marcel Proust and the Creative Encounter*. Chicago: University of Chicago Press, 1972.

Wilson, Edmund. *Axel's Castle*. New York: Scribner's, 1931.

Zaehner, R. C. *Mysticism, Sacred and Profane*. New York: Oxford University Press, 1957.

Valuable essays on Proust have been written by Roland Barthes, Samuel Beckett, Walter Benjamin, Maurice Blanchot, Michel Butor, Ernst Robert Curtius, José Ortega y Gasset, Jacques Rivière, Jean-Paul Sartre, Leo Spitzer, and Paul Valéry.

INDEX

LILLIAN HELLMAN

MODERN LITERATURE MONOGRAPHS

GENERAL EDITOR: Lina Mainiero

In the same series:

S. Y. AGNON   *Harold Fisch*
SHERWOOD ANDERSON   *Welford Dunaway Taylor*
LEONID ANDREYEV   *Josephine M. Newcombe*
ISAAC BABEL   *R. W. Hallett*
SIMONE DE BEAUVOIR   *Robert Cottrell*
SAUL BELLOW   *Brigitte Scheer-Schäzler*
BERTOLT BRECHT   *Willy Haas*
ALBERT CAMUS   *Carol Petersen*
WILLA CATHER   *Dorothy Tuck McFarland*
JOHN CHEEVER   *Samuel T. Coale*
COLETTE   *Robert Cottrell*
JOSEPH CONRAD   *Martin Tucker*
JULIO CORTÁZAR   *Evelyn Picon Garfield*
JOHN DOS PASSOS   *George J. Becker*
THEODORE DREISER   *James Lundquist*
FRIEDRICH DÜRRENMATT   *Armin Arnold*
T. S. ELIOT   *Joachim Seyppel*
WILLIAM FAULKNER   *Joachim Seyppel*
F. SCOTT FITZGERALD   *Rose Adrienne Gallo*
FORD MADOX FORD   *Sondra J. Stang*
JOHN FOWLES   *Barry N. Olshen*
MAX FRISCH   *Carol Petersen*
ROBERT FROST   *Elaine Barry*
GABRIEL GARCÍA MÁRQUEZ   *George R. McMurray*
MAKSIM GORKI   *Gerhard Habermann*
GÜNTER GRASS   *Kurt Lothar Tank*
PETER HANDKE   *Nicholas Hern*
LILLIAN HELLMAN   *Doris V. Falk*
ERNEST HEMINGWAY   *Samuel Shaw*
HERMANN HESSE   *Franz Baumer*
CHESTER HIMES   *James Lundquist*
HUGO VON HOFMANNSTHAL   *Lowell W. Bangerter*
UWE JOHNSON   *Mark Boulby*
JAMES JOYCE   *Armin Arnold*
FRANZ KAFKA   *Franz Baumer*
SINCLAIR LEWIS   *James Lundquist*
GEORG LUKÁCS   *Ehrhard Bahr and Ruth Goldschmidt Kunzer*
NORMAN MAILER   *Philip H. Bufithis*
ANDRÉ MALRAUX   *James Robert Hewitt*
THOMAS MANN   *Arnold Bauer*
CARSON McCULLERS   *Richard M. Cook*
ALBERTO MORAVIA   *Jane E. Cottrell*
VLADIMIR NABOKOV   *Donald E. Morton*
ANAÏS NIN   *Bettina L. Knapp*
(continued on page 182)

LILLIAN HELLMAN

Doris V. Falk

FREDERICK UNGAR PUBLISHING CO.

NEW YORK

Library of Congress Cataloging in Publication Data

Falk, Doris V
  Lillian Hellman.

  Bibliography: p.
  Includes index.
  1.   Hellman, Lillian, 1905–   —Criticism and inter-
pretation.   I.   Title.
PS3515.E343Z67   812'.5'2   78-4299
ISBN 0-8044-2194-3
ISBN 0-8044-6144-9 pbk.

Contents

Chronology

1905   On June 20, Lillian Hellman is born in New Or-
        leans, Louisiana, to Max Bernard Hellman and
        Julia Newhouse Hellman.

1912–24 The family moves to New York and Lillian spends
        six months of each year in New Orleans, attending
        school in both cities. In 1922 to 1924, she is en-
        rolled at New York University.

1924–32 Works as manuscript reader at Horace Liveright,
        Inc., publisher. Marries Arthur Kober (1925). She
        writes book reviews for the New York *Herald
        Tribune*, publicity for Broadway shows, and be-
        comes a theatrical play reader. Her husband's work
        takes them to Europe and Hollywood. In Europe
        she writes amateurish short stories for the Paris
        Comet; goes to Germany (1929) and considers
        enrolling in the university at Bonn, experiences
        antisemitism, and returns to the U.S. and Holly-
        wood. Becomes a reader of scenarios for Metro-
        Goldwyn-Mayer in Hollywood, and of play scripts
        for Herman Shumlin in New York. In Hollywood
        she meets Dashiell Hammett. She and Kober are
        divorced in 1932, and she begins life with Ham-
        mett.

1934   In January, Hammett's last and most famous novel,
        The Thin Man, is published and dedicated to Lil-
        lian Hellman. Her first play, *The Children's Hour*,
        opens in May to a long successful run and is dedi-
        cated to Hammett.

1935   Her mother dies. She writes the screenplay for *These Three*, an adaptation of *The Children's Hour*.

1936   *Days to Come* opens and closes after a brief run.

1937   Hellman travels to Europe with Dorothy Parker and her husband, Alan Campbell. She is to attend a theater festival in Moscow. After Moscow, she goes to Spain to witness the Spanish civil war.

1939   *The Little Foxes* is produced with great success. Hellman buys an estate later known as Hardscrabble Farm in Pleasantville, New York.

1941   *Watch on the Rhine* is produced and wins the New York Drama Critics Circle Award.

1942–44 Her activities on behalf of antifascist causes, begun in the 1930s, continue, including publication of a limited edition of *Watch on the Rhine* for the benefit of the Joint Anti-Fascist Refugee Committee. Hammett goes in the army. Hellman negotiates to do films about Russia; writes *The North Star*. She goes to Russia as cultural emissary and visits the fighting front. Continues in psychoanalysis with Gregory Zilboorg, begun some years earlier. *The Searching Wind* is produced (1944).

1946   *Another Part of the Forest*, directed by Hellman herself, is produced.

1948   She campaigns for Henry Wallace.

1949   Helps to chair the opening dinner of the Cultural and Scientific Conference for World Peace. Writes and directs the adaptation of Emmanuel Roblès' play, *Montserrat*.

1951   *The Autumn Garden* is produced. Hammett is jailed for contempt of Congress.

1952   Appears before the House Un-American Activities Committee. Is released without charges, but has been blacklisted by Hollywood. Is compelled to sell the farm at Pleasantville. *The Children's Hour* is revived, now with political implications.

1955   Buys a summer home at Vineyard Haven, Mass. Edits *The Selected Letters of Anton Chekhov*.

Completes the adaptation of Anouilh's *The Lark* and writes the book for the musical, *Candide*.

1960   Her last original play to date, *Toys in the Attic*, wins the New York Drama Critics Circle Award.

1961–68 Begins a long teaching career with a seminar at Harvard. Hammett dies. Wins many honors and awards, including the Gold Medal for Drama of the American Academy of Arts and Letters and the National Institute of Arts and Letters. (Was elected to the Academy in 1963, after serving as vice-president of the National Institute in 1962.) Awards and honorary degrees from major universities begin to pour in.

1969   *An Unfinished Woman* is published and wins the National Book Award as the best book of the year in the category of Arts and Letters.

1973   *Pentimento*, the second volume of memoirs, is published and becomes a Book-of-the-Month Club selection.

1976   *Scoundrel Time* is published and stays on the best seller list for twenty-three weeks, setting off a continuing political controversy. Receives the Edward MacDowell Medal for her contribution to literature.

1977   The episode, "Julia," from *Pentimento* is made into a film which receives mixed reviews, but which keeps the persona of Lillian Hellman still before us.

I

Hellman in Her Time:
A Biographical Preface

BACKGROUNDS AND BEGINNINGS—1905-1934

Lillian Hellman is an American phenomenon. By birth she is a southerner, a Jew, and female; by profession a playwright, memoirist, essayist, and teacher; by political persuasion a liberal, and a controversial one. She is an often angry, ironic, and witty commentator on her time, and is not fond of biographers. What she wants the public to know about her life she has told in the memoirs, where, as she says, she has tried to make sense out of experience. But to do that obviously requires an imaginative interpretation of that experience; much more than a chronology of dates and facts.

For these she refers the biographer to *Who's Who in America*—but even that source, according to Hellman, cannot always be trusted. For one thing, *Who's Who* is always getting her age wrong.[1] Wrong or right, *Who's Who* and some other secondary sources indicate a certain inconsistency in this matter. Before 1967, Hellman's birth date (in *Who's Who*) is given as 1905; after that, as 1907. *Contemporary Authors* gives it as 1906. The date we shall accept here is 1905, since that was the date given by Hellman herself, in her now-famous testimony before the House Un-American Activities Committee.[2]

Many of the facts in this preface are drawn from standard reference sources: *Who's Who in America, Con-*

3

temporary Authors, Contemporary Playwrights, Current Biography, Twentieth Century Authors, and others. For the most recent accounts of Hellman's achievements and awards, I have relied on newspaper and magazine interviews and feature stories. The two most useful book-length sources devoted exclusively to Hellman are Richard Moody's *Lillian Hellman, Playwright* and the catalogue, with comments, of the collection of Hellman manuscripts, typescripts, and other papers at the University of Texas. (*The Lillian Hellman Collection at the University of Texas*, compiled by Manfred Triesch, Austin: The University of Texas Press, 1966).

But the primary sources of information on Lillian Hellman as a human being are her own autobiographical writings—fact or artifact—the three volumes of memoirs.

Hellman was born in New Orleans, Louisiana, the only child of Max and Julia Newhouse Hellman. Her father was born in New Orleans, into a family that had emigrated from Germany in the 1840s. Her mother had spent her childhood in Demopolis, Alabama, and the Newhouse family moved to New York City when Lillian was a child. When Max Hellman suffered business reverses (costing much of Julia's considerable dowry) he and his wife and daughter moved to New York City. His two sisters, Hannah and Jenny, who became important influences on their niece, remained in New Orleans.

From the age of six to early adulthood, Lillian lived in two separate cultures, spending half of each year in New York City, and half in New Orleans. The New York relatives were wealthy, and often condescending toward Lillian and her parents. (Hellman was to get even, later, when the Newhouses are portrayed as the Hubbards in *The Little Foxes* and *Another Part of the Forest*, and as themselves in the memoirs).

The southern interlude—when Lillian stayed with her two Hellman aunts in the boardinghouse they ran in New Orleans—that was homecoming. That was to be the remembered ambience of her childhood and growing up, and the source of lifelong emotional ties. Anchors in her life were always to be the humorous, practical likable aunts, and the much-loved Sophronia, the black woman who cared for Lillian through infancy and childhood. We meet all of these people in the memoirs, and we also see some of the unique conflicts taking place in a southern girl-child, who could be happy with a simple life in the pastoral south but felt the need to "make it" in the complex, affluent north. A southern lady, brought up to be a "lily"—but with a yen to climb trees and fish and hunt —would eventually have to reconcile femininity and aggression, in her own consciousness as well as in the public image. Even now, when Hellman is in her seventies, the image she projects is both ladylike and tough: clothes-conscious to the point of occasional vanity; "difficult" to the point of occasional ferocity.

To be Jewish in the old south posed another problem of identity, especially if the family were an old one and not orthodox. Many young southern Jews were not aware of semitism—pro or anti—during their childhood. And when they became aware, they realized very slowly, and sometimes painfully, that their self-concepts as Americans, or Louisianians, or New Yorkers, were not the whole story. Whether they liked it or not, the rest of the world thought of them as an ethnic, not a religious, group. This identity came home to many for the first time during the Hitler holocaust. Hellman, in *Scoundrel Time*, remarks that her own awareness of antisemitism dated from a visit to Bonn, Germany, where she intended to enroll at the university: "Then for the first time in my life I thought about being a Jew." She was twenty-four.

Hellman's formal education in grammar school and high school was split, as were her living arrangements, between New Orleans and New York. The widely differing standards and the broken-up semesters made schooling a matter of boredom in the south and fear of failure in

the north. From 1922 through 1924, she attended New
York University, but that milieu was not hers, even
though she remembers being introduced to the philos-
ophies of Kant, Hegel, Marx, and Engels. Later she took
courses at Columbia and was deeply impressed by readings in Dostoevsky, Dante, Melville, and even Lewis
Carroll. But on the whole, the university approach to
writing and to literature was not for Hellman—not until
about forty years later when she herself became a member of the academic establishment. At eighteen, as a
junior, she left college. At nineteen she had her first job,
reading manuscripts for the publishing house of Horace
Liveright.

This was an exciting introduction to the literary mar-
ketplace, and may have set the direction of Hellman's
future more than she knew. In *An Unfinished Woman* she
emphasized the "party" atmosphere at the publishers'
(although even that had serious overtones). But as she
said, "A job with any publishing house was a plum, but
a job with Horace Liveright was a bag of plums." Among
the writers "they discovered, or persuaded over . . ." were
"Faulkner, Freud, Hemingway, O'Neill, Hart Crane,
Sherwood Anderson, Dreiser, E. E. Cummings, and many
other less talented but remarkable people. . . ."

But Hellman remembers this as a period of social
and sexual, rather than literary, exploration. She went to
the constant parties, was as casual about sex as most of
her generation, had an abortion and then in 1925 married
the man who was responsible for her pregnancy, Arthur
Kober. Kober at that time was a theatrical press agent,
but was later to become a successful and popular writer
and humorist, author of some thirty films, and two long-
running Broadway shows, *Having a Wonderful Time*
(1937) and *Wish You Were Here* (1952).

During the years of her marriage, Hellman played at
being a housewife, a part-time student, and European

tourist, but was always casting around for something constructive to do. She wrote what she calls a couple of "lady-writer" stories, which were published in *The Paris Comet*, a magazine for which Kober worked. For a time she wrote theatrical publicity and book reviews, reading plays for a group that was eventually to be headed by Herman Shumlin, later the producer of her own first five plays. She even demonstrated her sense of what would go in the theater by spotting the manuscript of Shumlin's spectacular long-run play, later to be a movie, "Grand Hotel."

But Hellman's future really began to take shape in 1929 after the trip to Germany when she became aware of antisemitism, and when, upon her return, she and Kober moved to Hollywood. There she read and wrote reports on manuscripts for Metro-Goldwyn-Mayer. The job was drudgery. She detested the shoddy Hollywood setting and the long terrifying drives in throughway traffic—but she was gaining skills and making contacts that were to last a lifetime. The links were close between Hollywood and Broadway; in those pretelevision days, the film industry was hungry for material, and some of our best writers and playwrights also worked in Hollywood. Hellman met many of them. Her closest friends at that time were the humorist, S. J. Perelman, and his wife; the novelist, Nathanael West (Mrs. Perelman's brother); and the writer of detective fiction—and former Pinkerton detective—Dashiell Hammett.

Lillian Hellman and Hammett—known to her and their friends as Dash—were to live together (on and off) for the next thirty-one years. Her marriage to Arthur Kober had long been deteriorating, and ended with an amicable divorce in 1932. Hammett was thirteen years older than Hellman, a successful writer and film scenarist, the possessor of a quiet, ironic sense of humor and an idealistic commitment to political radicalism. He was to become her home base—friend, companion, critic, disciplinarian, mentor—even in the times when he suffered from alcoholism, illness, and neurosis.

Hammett was at this time hard at work on what was to be his best-known book—and later film—*The Thin Man*. The character of Nora Charles in that book was modeled on Lillian Hellman. She, in turn, began to understand the difficult demands of professional writing, and set to work in earnest. She published two "short-short stories" in the *American Spectator* (September, 1933; January, 1934). She also collaborated with Louis Kronenberger on a farce called *The Dear Queen* (copyrighted in 1932), which almost, but—mercifully—not quite, reached the stage in 1934.

More importantly, she had begun work, with Hammett's encouragement and criticism, on her first serious play, *The Children's Hour*. Herman Shumlin, her friend and former boss, read the play and decided to produce it, even before he had finished the first reading. The play was an immediate and long-running hit.

In the 1930s the plot of *The Children's Hour* made it a succès de scandale: two young headmistresses of a girls' school are accused by a vindictive schoolgirl of having a lesbian relationship. The rumor results in the social ruin of both teachers and, ultimately, the suicide of one. In 1952, the play was successfully revived; then it spoke to the audience about the events of those times—the ruin of careers and lives by the "McCarthy" technique of the smear, the blacklist, and the "big lie." But between the two productions of *The Children's Hour*, the tumult of world events had changed more meanings than just those of this play. The world had seen the rise of Hitler, the Nazi holocaust, and World War II; the founding of the state of Israel; the increasing power of Russia and communism, and, in the 1950s, the Korean "military action." History, and the commitments of her friends, were to turn Hellman into a political as well as a literary figure, whether she wanted it that way or not.

In the early 1930s the world had already divided into ideological and political camps, rumbling toward world conflict. American attitudes toward communism were confused by the facts of American allegiance: the Russian revolution of 1917 had been followed, eventually, by American recognition of the Soviet Union in 1934; then, with the Nazi-Soviet pact in 1939, Russia had become a villain and potential enemy; a few years later she was to be our heroic ally in World War II. Concern with the great depression and unemployment, as well as fears of involvement in another war, kept most Americans from acknowledging the threat of events in Germany, Spain, and Italy. Lillian Hellman had been made aware of that threat in 1929 in Germany. On subsequent trips to Europe, especially those in 1934 and 1937, she was to know first-hand the destruction of human life and freedom left in the wake of fascism.

She tells the story in *An Unfinished Woman* and in the "Julia" chapter of *Pentimento*. I do not know how literally we can take the story of "Julia" as biography, but certainly its outlines must be factual.* The protagonist was Lillian's close friend in childhood and youth. She was the daughter of a wealthy American family, and, according to the memoir, studied in Europe, first at Oxford and later as a student of Freud's in Vienna. By 1934, Julia had become a socialist, active in the anti-Nazi underground. While Hellman was in Europe that year, Julia

---

* Miss Hellman is so determined to keep the identity of the real Julia a secret, that she creates deliberate confusion for the reader between the characters of "Alice," "Marie-Louise," and "Marie-Louise's" brother, "Hal," in *An Unfinished Woman* and those of "Julia," "Anne-Marie," and *her* brother, "Sammy," in *Pentimento*.

was badly injured in the Floridsdorf battle between socialist workers and Austrian troops and cooperating Nazis.
Hellman visited her in the hospital in Vienna, tried to
help, but Julia disappeared. None of Hellman's efforts to
find her friend succeeded, and she returned to the United
States. The following year, Hellman heard from Julia and
learned that she was still active in the anti-Nazi underground.

Two years later, in 1937, Hellman planned another
European tour, using as an excuse an invitation to attend
a theater festival in Moscow. The itinerary was indefinite,
until she talked on the telephone from Paris to Julia in
Vienna. The upshot of that conversation was that Hellman
found herself smuggling $50,000 from Paris, across the
German border, into Berlin. In Berlin, Hellman was to
change trains and proceed to Moscow—always with the
danger of being found out by the Nazis. With the help
of a carefully contrived escort system, she completed the
mission. In the short period between trains she was taken
to Julia in Berlin. As Hellman feared, Julia had been
mutilated—had lost a leg—in the 1934 Austrian Civil
War. The money Hellman had carried was Julia's, and
was to be used for the relief of both Jewish and non-
Jewish antifascists.

Shaken by the Berlin encounter, Hellman went on
to Moscow, only to discover later that she had narrowly
escaped arrest. Her trunk arrived two weeks late, thoroughly ransacked. She could not know then that a year
later Julia was to be murdered by the Nazis, and that
only Hellman would care enough to bring the body home
for cremation, unclaimed by Julia's family.

It is no wonder that after the Berlin episode Hellman
found the 1937 Moscow theater festival a bore and her
meetings at that time with Russian officialdom inconse-
quential. (She did not even know that this was the time
of one of the most severe of the Soviet purges.) She re-

turned to Paris and there made the decision to go to Spain.

The republican government of Spain had been established in 1931, following the overthrow of the dictator, Primo de Rivera, and the exile of King Alphonso XIII. The Republic was controlled by a coalition of many factions, largely leftist, and these initiated social reforms designed to improve the conditions of the poor. In 1936, Spain was invaded by a reactionary rebel force soon to be under the leadership of General Francisco Franco. This army represented the interests of the military, high clergy, land-owning aristocracy, and big industry. Franco's purpose was to overthrow the legally constituted Republic, and to establish a dictatorship on the Fascist model.

The only major-power support for the Republic came from Soviet Russia, and that was largely token. (Stalin did not consider the communist factions in Spain useful to his own purposes). The democracies could not, because of noninterventionist policies, come officially to the aid of the Republic, although Franco was receiving aid from Germany and Italy. To many Americans and citizens of other democracies, the Spanish Republic seemed to represent the last hope for individual liberty in Europe, and the lineup of forces in that war became symbolic. The choice to support the republic had to be made, regardless of the imperfections and confusions of the Spanish republicans, and regardless of their support by many various communist ideologies. As it turned out, none of these was unified or strong enough to overcome Franco's forces, and in 1939, when Russia withdrew its support, the republic fell.

It was the European and American communists and socialists who organized the military resistance to Franco in the form of the International Brigade and the Abraham Lincoln Brigade. While the brigades originated with the Comintern, the members were not all communists, or even socialists. Many were believers in Jeffersonian democracy, in the opposition to tyranny; all felt angry, guilty, and frustrated that their own governments were, in effect, appeasing the fascist powers. As Hellman said, "Never before, and never since, in my lifetime, were liberals, radicals, intellectuals, and educated middle-class to come together in single, forceful alliance."

Hellman's trip to Spain in 1937 had not been really planned—but then it was not entirely unpremeditated either. Earlier that same year she had agreed to make a documentary film about Spain with Archibald MacLeish, Ernest Hemingway, and the film director Joris Ivens. Because of illness she had been unable to complete the assignment, and Hemingway and Ivens had produced, without her, the very moving film entitled *The Spanish Earth*.

So, in Paris in 1937 when, at dinner, Otto Simon suggested that she should go to Spain, Hellman readily agreed. Simon was a communist, author of *The Brown Book of the Hitler Terror*, and at this time, according to Hellman, "a kind of press chief for the Spanish Republican Government." (He had been born in Prague, fled the Nazis, and was finally executed by them in Prague.) As Hellman wrote, "It didn't take much persuasion [for her to go to Spain]: I had strong convictions about the Spanish War, about Fascism-Nazism, strong enough to push just below the surface my fear of the danger of war."

She encountered that danger first in Valencia that October when the city was under fire by both sides. She went through air raids; saw the damage done by Italian bombs. She scrambled over the rubble and witnessed the suffering of the victims. She visited the hospital of the International Brigade in Benicasin—escorted by Gustav Regler, a well-known anti-Nazi German novelist, who had become a leader of the Brigade. There was not much Hellman could do in Valencia except to record her impressions and her admiration for the soldiers in the Bri-

gade, whom she described as "noble"—a word not easy
for her to use. In Madrid, in the company of Hemingway
and other involved foreigners, Hellman was able to take
a more active part in the struggle. She made speeches to
the International Brigade, did recordings to be translated,
made a radio broadcast to Paris, and visited hospitals and
a nursery.

In *An Unfinished Woman*, Hellman describes the
aftermath of that 1937 journey as "the root-time of my
turning toward the radical movements of the late thirties."
Then she adds that she was late, and was never completely committed. But for her, as for many liberals who
turned toward radicalism because there seemed no place
else to turn, the consequences in later life were to be
serious.

The years between the brief Russian visit of 1937 and
the second "mission to Moscow" in 1944, were taken up
largely with playwriting, but saw also some participation
in liberal activism—which Hellman is inclined to dismiss
in the memoirs as "idle lady stuff . . . speeches at rallies
for this or that, bundles for something or other. . . ." Her
growing political education consisted of reading leftist
philosophers with Hammett who was, of course, dedicated
to his own version of Marxism and was probably a communist party member.

In 1936, Hellman had written an unsuccessful play
about unions and strikebreaking, *Days to Come*. Although
Hellman said the play was not intended to portray the
class struggle, but rather that between individuals, audiences saw it as highly political. Then came *The Little
Foxes* produced in 1939, *Watch on the Rhine* in 1941;
a film about Russia, *The North Star*, in 1943, and *The
Searching Wind* in 1944.

The Little Foxes drew on Hellman's knowledge of the
American south and her own family. *Watch on the Rhine*
and *The Searching Wind* were both concerned with the
struggle against fascism and the response (or lack of it)

of middle-class Americans to the issues of World War II. The sentiments of *The North Star* and the last two plays were obvious. But even *The Little Foxes*, with its attack on exploitive southern merchants and class speculation, earned its author the label of "leftwinger" or "fellow-traveler" among conservatives, to whom antifascist (especially if not spelled out as anti-Nazi) meant pro-communist.

Most of Hellman's prewar "bundles for something or other" activities were connected with organizations or causes also tarred with the red brush. She had solicited contributions to the Emergency Anti-Fascist Refugee Fund and had allowed the Joint Anti-Fascist Refugee Committee (destined to be high on McCarthy's list of communist-front organizations) to publish for its benefit an expensive limited edition of *Watch on the Rhine*, with a dedication by Hellman's long-time friend, Dorothy Parker, herself active in antifascist causes.

There was also a much-aired battle with Tallulah Bankhead, then playing Regina in *The Little Foxes*. Apparently Bankhead had refused to do a benefit performance for Spanish refugees at Hellman's request, and Hellman refused to do one for Finnish refugees from Russia at Bankhead's request. Hellman felt that Finland was actually pro-Nazi. There are several conflicting versions of this row, but the upshot for Hellman was that she was again labeled as procommunist.

America had gone to war in December 1941. In 1942, Hammett enlisted, and Hellman felt that she must participate more actively in the war. Early in 1942 she had agreed to do a documentary film, with William Wyler, about the war in Russia, but the project never matured. She did begin work, however, on the semidocumentary, *The North Star*, but, after much rewriting by the director, Lewis Milestone, the film had become such Hollywood hokum that Hellman bought back her Goldwyn contract.[3] One version, presumably Hellman's original, has been pub-

lished under her name, however, with an introduction by
Louis Kronenberger and an "author's note" by Hellman
explaining the cinematic terminology.[4] Serious critics,
American and Russian, did not think much of *The North
Star*, but Russian audiences liked it. That may have been
one reason that Hellman (with the approval of both
Moscow and Washington) was invited on a cultural-
exchange mission to Russia in 1944. The diaries of that
visit formed the basis of a magazine article, and later,
of important chapters in *An Unfinished Woman*.

On her return to the United States, Miss Hellman
continued the activities which were to lead to the events
of spring 1952. With her usual genius for espousing the
most conspicuous of liberal causes, she joined, in 1946,
the Independent Citizen's Committee for the Arts, Sciences, and Professions, known also as ICCASP, or ICC
for short. This was truly a "star-studded" organization,
including such illustrious representatives of their various
fields as Einstein and Oppenheimer, Orson Welles and
Frank Sinatra. But, as one writer described it, ICC was
also "the major political arm of the Russophile left."[5]

Along with other liberal political action committees,
the ICC placed its hopes for important reforms (full employment, minimum wage, friendship with Russia, aboli-
tion of HUAC, etc.) in a third party which could operate
outside the platforms of the Republicans or Democrats.
The strongest candidate for President seemed to be
Henry A. Wallace, one-time Secretary of Agriculture and
Vice President under Roosevelt, and Secretary of Com-
merce under Truman. Wallace was running on the ticket of
the Progressive Party. Hellman campaigned for him in
1948, but in *Scoundrel Time*, describes the doubts she
soon developed about his qualifications. Publicly at the
time, however, she gave Wallace her strongest support,
even praising him to Marshal Tito of Yugoslavia.

For in October of that same election year Hellman
accepted a writing assignment for the New York *Star*

(successor to *PM*) that took her to Prague, Belgrade, and Paris. Her prime goal was the interview with Tito, but she was warmly greeted by both high officials and ordinary people in Czechoslovakia as well as Yugoslavia. In her articles in the *Star* she pleaded for tolerance and understanding of the Communists on the part of the western nations. As was to be her custom, Hellman based her political convictions on her intuition and personal experience. The Communists whom she had met had always been nice to her, and she returned the compliment.

Between writing her adaptation of *Montserrat* (a historical drama by the French playwright Roblès) and running her farm in Pleasantville, New York, Hellman helped to chair a stormy dinner at the Waldorf hotel marking the opening of the Cultural and Scientific Conference for World Peace, sponsored by the National Council of the Arts, Sciences and Professions. (This was an offshoot of, or successor to, the ICC; many of the participants belonged to that organization.) The storm over the conference had been rising ever since its inception, and since the first Russian delegation—appointed by the Soviet government—had accepted their invitations. The state department (along with hundreds of well-known intellectuals who withdrew from or questioned the conference) was convinced that the conference table would be used as a sounding board for Soviet propaganda. At one time the state department alleged that some of the delegates were members of the Russian secret police— an allegation strongly denied. The department refused to grant visas to delegates from France, Italy, Rumania, and Hungary, and to three of the four Britons invited, on the grounds that these were not official representatives of their countries.

When one looks at the information available to the public at this time, it is no wonder that such animosity should have been turned upon a "world peace" conference. This came not only from some liberal intellectuals who refused to attend or who challenged delegates on the floor. Five thousand people planned to picket (2,000 were permitted by police). The pickets included paraplegic veterans in wheelchairs, Gold Star Mothers and other kneeling and praying women, and even members of the musicians' union, who had invited the Russian composer, Shostakovich, to defect and join them. The confusion, disillusion, and panic are predictable when one reads even the most respectable newspapers and popular news magazines of March 1949—the month of the conference.

The last signers were just joining NATO, the North Atlantic Treaty Organization, which was under fire by the Russians, including those at the Waldorf conference. Russia had been withdrawing personnel from the United Nations, and there were fears in all quarters that the cold war might become hot. Spies seemed to be everywhere. Just two weeks before the conference, Judith Coplon had been arrested in the act of handing documents to a Russian spy. On March 2, the American Communist Party had announced that in case of war with the Soviet Union, the party would not support the United States, and, at the very least, would sabotage the war effort.

Then on the front page of the *New York Times* for March 24, literally side by side with the story on the conference, was an account of the trial of the eleven communists charged with conspiracy to overthrow the U.S. government by violence. And in that story Fordham Professor Louis F. Budenz (an ex-communist who became a professional anticommunist witness) testified that the American Communist Party did, indeed, demand that its members pay first allegiance to Stalin. It had been the knowledge of Stalin's ruthless purges and imprisonment of their counterparts in Russia that led a faction of intellectuals to oppose the conference, through their own organization, Americans for Intellectual Freedom.

I go into this much detail about this one event, only because it epitomized the rift in the American intellectual left that gave rise to the *Scoundrel Time* controversy and that still continues. Garry Wills's vitriolic view of the period in his introduction to *Scoundrel Time*, plus Hellman's own comments on the intellectuals of the anticommunist left, have turned this dinner party of almost thirty years ago into an historical confrontation. Hellman's chief supporters now are younger than she—they were children at that time. Her opponents are her contemporaries who were there, many of whom vigorously survive today to challenge her.[6]

Miss Hellman had heard rumors as early as 1948 that she was on a secret Hollywood blacklist of film employees—actors, writers, directors, editors—who were not to be employed in the industry because of suspected communist affiliation or procommunist sympathies. Then, in 1949, her name appeared on a list of alleged procommunists—"fellow travelers"—investigated by a committee headed by California State Senator Jack Tenney. Hellman was in famous company: Charles Chaplin, Pearl Buck, Katherine Hepburn, Danny Kaye, and of course, Dashiell Hammett, among others, were also on that list. In 1951, Hammett would be sentenced to six months in jail for contempt, having refused to name contributors to the bail-bond fund of the Civil Rights Congress, a fund set up to supply bail for jailed communists. This was one of the organizations on the Attorney General's list of communist fronts. In *An Unfinished Woman* Hellman says that Hammett had never been in the office of the Congress and did not know the name of a single contributor, but he went to jail rather than break silence. And that same year, 1951, an ex-communist screen writer named Martin Berkeley placed Hellman's name on a list of one hundred Hollywood "members at large" of the Communist Party and identified her as one of those attending a meeting of the party at his home in 1937. (In *Scoundrel Time* she denies both allegations.) She was not surprised, then, when she was summoned to appear before the House Un-American Activities Committee in May of 1952.

This congressional committee had begun its activities as far back as 1938 when it was known as the Dies Committee, named for its chairman, Martin Dies, Jr., Democrat of Texas. The committee had blossomed in the 1940s, during World War II and after, in response to popular fears of both fascist and communist subversion of democracy from within, rather than to threats of dictatorship from without. (The armed services and intelligence agencies could take care of that).

After World War II, the concern focused on communist rather than Fascist activity. The House Un-American Activities Committee searched out communist influences on the arts, sciences, and professions, while Senator Joseph McCarthy[7] played upon fears that communists were making or influencing policy within the State Department, the Army, and other official agencies of government.

In 1947, under the chairmanship of J. Parnell Thomas (himself shortly to be convicted of defrauding the government), HUAC had aimed its guns at "Communist infiltration of the Motion Picture Industry." The investigations revealed that indeed some film people had—like many liberals—turned toward communism at one time in their lives. Some had bought the party line and continued to follow it, jockeying for position in the Screen Writer's Guild. Of the nineteen witnesses called before the committee in its most spectacular hearings, the Hollywood Ten were avowed communists who aggressively challenged the constitutionality of HUAC itself and its questioning of witnesses. The courts upheld the right of Congress to work through such a committee, and the Hollywood Ten were found guilty of contempt.

But before the verdict was handed down, fifty executives of the film industry met secretly and drew up a resolution to the effect that the unfriendly ten would be discharged or suspended, and that "unrepenting Communists would no longer be considered suitable for employment in the movies."[8]

The threat of loss of income and professional standing made some leftists quickly "repentant"; others had already become sincerely disillusioned. Among these latter were the idealistic Marxists who were shocked by the ruthless separation of ends from means in the actual workings of the party. As "friendly witnesses" to HUAC, any who confessed, or who testified freely about their own actions, were often obliged to implicate others. For if a witness answered a given question, he could then be required to answer related questions. "Disclosure of a fact waives the privilege as to details." Thus, for example, if the witness admitted to having attended a meeting, he might then be asked to affirm or deny a list of names of others who attended that meeting. If he refused, he could, in the judgment of the Committee, be cited for contempt; and in the event that a court of law upheld the Committee's decision, could be convicted and sentenced. The maximum penalty would be one year in prison and a thousand dollar fine.

Hellman's full account of her appearance before HUAC is the subject of *Scoundrel Time*. Suffice it to say here that in a letter to the Committee she expressed her willingness to discuss her own activities, but not to answer questions about those of anyone else: not to "bring bad trouble to people who in my past association with them, were completely innocent of any talk or any action that was disloyal or subversive." Obviously, however, according to the law, the only way she could avoid answering such questions was to plead the privilege of the Fifth Amendment: to refuse to testify about her own activities on the grounds of self-incrimination. This refusal might make her look guilty in the eyes of the Committee and the public, but such was the chance that she and other "unfriendly" witnesses had to take in order to protect their friends and to avoid a possible conviction.

Although she did have to take the fifth, the letter was an effective statement read into the record. It expressed not only Hellman's own code of honor, but that of others in the same position. She escaped citation for contempt, but not the Hollywood blacklist nor the coincidental discovery by the IRS that an expensive error had been made on her tax returns. The loss of employment for both her and Hammett, and the enormous tax payments due for both, necessitated selling the farm in Pleasantville, which Hellman had owned and loved since 1939. Not until the 1960s was she permitted to work openly for Hollywood again.

In late 1952 and early 1953 the time was certainly ripe for the revival of *The Children's Hour* as a political play. McCarthy was riding high, and his technique of the blatant lie or rumored suspicion had caused the same devastation in many lives that took place in that play. The new *Children's Hour* was a success, but the proceeds went chiefly to the Internal Revenue Service.

That summer of 1953 Hellman went to Rome to work on a movie for Alexander Korda, at one-fifth of her pre-blacklisting salary. But even that contract fizzled because of the producer's own financial troubles. In the meantime, however, Hellman had experienced passport difficulties, a planted news story that she had been subpoenaed by the McCarthy committee, and being shadowed by an agent of the CIA. (We are told all about this in *Scoundrel Time*). When she returned to the U.S., it was to straitened circumstances—hard times. For a while, she was even forced to take a part-time job in a department store, under a pseudonym. But about six months later she came into an inheritance from one of her New Orleans aunts, and gradually began to write again.

A testimonial to Hellman's tremendous energy is her productivity throughout those stormy years of political activity. After the overnight success of *The Children's Hour*, followed by the depressing failure of *Days to Come* two years later, Hellman turned her hand to screen-writing: she collaborated on *Dark Angel* (United Artists, 1935) ; wrote a screen version of *The Children's Hour* called *These Three* (United Artists, 1936) ; and wrote the film script for Sidney Kingsley's *Dead End* (United Artists, 1936). Then in 1939 she completed what is prob-ably her most famous play, *The Little Foxes*. Its success enabled her to buy the farm in Pleasantville, where she and Hammett spent so many productive years. By that time, she had written seven of her eight original plays; had shuttled between New York and Hollywood to work on six films, had made her eventful journeys to Europe, and still had time to play her part in politics and to make Hardscrabble Farm not only a writer's haven for herself, Hammett, and friends, but a going agricultural concern. Life there was to provide important material for the memoirs.

For all her public visibility, Hellman is essentially a private person. In the memoirs we learn what she wants us to know about the significant events and relationships in her life during these years—her psychoanalysis, the death of her parents, her lifelong friendships and con-tacts. In 1955, she bought a house in Martha's Vineyard and since then has divided her year between that island off the coast of Massachusetts, and New York City.

Hellman's memoirs tell us little about her develop-ment as a playwright; for changes in interests and style, we must look to the plays themselves. They fall roughly into two groups: the early melodramas of active villainy, and the later, more discursive plays about characters whose participation in life is essentially passive. Nineteen fifty-one had seen the production of *The Autumn Garden*, a play about middle-aged characters whose lives have simply happened to them—or not happened.

After *The Autumn Garden*, Hellman experimented with adaptations of plays, or plots for plays, by others. She selected congenial material: the originals were all concerned, in one way or another, with an individual's freedom of choice in a milieu alien or hostile to him. But none of the adaptations achieved anything like the success of her own *Toys in the Attic* (1960). For this, her last original play—to date—Hellman returned to the real or imagined past of her own family, or of one remarkably like it. She was moving in the direction of the memoirs.

On her way there, however, (*An Unfinished Woman* was published in 1969) she traveled, wrote magazine articles, collected honors and honorary degrees, and entered academe as a teacher of creative writing and literature. Some of her plays had already won prizes: The Pulitzer went to *The Little Foxes*; the New York Drama Critics Circle Award, to *Watch on the Rhine* and *Toys in the Attic*. Among other honors, between 1960 and 1965, she was elected to the American Academy of Arts and Sciences; the National Institute of Arts and Letters elected her vice-president; and the institute's parent organization, the American Academy of Arts and Letters, invited her to become one of its fifty members. Then the Academy-Institute awarded her its gold medal. Her university awards and honorary degrees included the Brandeis University Creative Arts Award (a medal and $1500), the Achievement Award of the women's division of the Albert Einstein College of Medicine of Yeshiva University, and advanced honorary degrees from Tufts, Wheaton College, Douglass College of Rutgers University, and Brandeis. Later she acquired honorary degrees from (among others) Smith, Holyoke, New York University and Yale.

In 1961, after the triumph of *Toys in the Attic*,

Hellman began teaching at Harvard. That was a sad year for her personally, since Hammett died in January. Professionally, however, this was the beginning of some fifteen years of teaching at prestigious universities including Yale, Massachusetts Institute of Technology, the University of California at Berkeley, and most recently, Hunter College in New York. Her reputation as a teacher, as might be expected, was that of an eclectic scholar and a tough critic of student writing. She was, of course, sympathetic with the rebellious students during the years of unrest and rioting in the late 1960s. In 1968 she was completing work on the first memoir while teaching at Harvard. In 1969 she spoke in defense of the student rioters there—and was later, in the late 1970s, disappointed in the apathy that took the place of the former rebelliousness.

It is not surprising that after the success of *An Unfinished Woman* in 1969, which won the National Book Award in the category of Arts and Letters, Hellman continued to express herself politically. She saw a straight line of descent between the repression of individual rights as she had experienced it at the hands of government through the HUAC, and the attempts of the authorities to stifle the dissent of students and others not only through the police, but through federal agencies such as the FBI and the CIA. The Watergate coverups, to Hellman, only masked a larger conspiracy of secrecy on the part of a government that involved its citizens in a war they did not believe in, and the full extent of which they did not know.

In 1970 Hellman took the lead in founding the Committee for Public Justice. Her idea was "to create an early-warning system that would detect violations of constitutional rights and then alert citizens, the media, and legislators about them."[9] The organization has been doing this and more: has held and published the proceedings of two major conferences[10] and initiated publication of a newsletter called *Justice Department Watch*. Many abuses brought to public attention only recently were revealed long ago by CPJ. Hellman has lent her influence to raising money for the organization and currently serves as its cochairman.

Pentimento, the second volume of memoirs, appeared in 1973, and *Scoundrel Time* in 1976. Both were best sellers, and both have kept Hellman in the public eye. *Scoundrel Time* not only recounted Hellman's experiences before the HUAC in that time of scoundrels, but also castigated those of her liberal acquaintances who, according to Hellman, did not oppose McCarthy or come to the rescue of his victims. She blamed attitudes of the anticommunist liberal intellectuals for the sequence of events from McCarthyism to Vietnam and Watergate. The original reception of *Scoundrel Time* was as enthusiastic as that of the other two memoirs. In recent months, however, both the anticommunist left and the conservatives (as well as some middle-of-the-roaders) have counterattacked, and Hellman has become a controversial figure.

The movie, *Julia*, from the episode of that title in *Pentimento*, had its New York première with much fanfare. Hellman's instinct for timeliness has made *Julia* one of the new "woman-flicks" portraying women not as competing man-traps, but as loyal, loving friends and political idealists. While Hellman supports the new feminism, she has never felt the need, herself, to be liberated from the chauvinist male put-down. The real goal of the movement, she says, should be economic equality. Still, she is irritated at so frequently being called a "woman playwright" (even "America's greatest") and has no use for the "lady writers" of what was once characterized as women's magazine fiction. Oddly enough, some of her most devoted followers now are readers of those magazines—educated upper-middle-class matrons who see in Hellman's career what might have been for them. Other worshipers are the young feminist writers and artists who consider her an inspiration and a role model.

Hellman has also become a grande dame of the literary establishment in America. She may not be universally liked and admired, but she is known as a presence to be reckoned with. As a playwright she was a major contributor to American theater; now she has become an innovator in the literary form of the memoir.

II

The Plays

1

Hellman's Dramatic Mode—
"The Theater Is a Trick . . ."

Lillian Hellman wrote eight original plays, four adaptations of plays or stories by others, and wrote or collaborated on more than seven screenplays. The original plays fall into two principal groups, based on Hellman's view of human action and motivation—a highly moral view, interpreting both action and the failure to act in terms of good and evil.

The first two plays became signposts, marking the directions to be taken by the later plays. *The Children's Hour* concerned active evil—here the ruin of two women by the spreading of a malicious lie. The drama pointed the way toward the three plays whose chief characters are despoilers—those who exploit or destroy others for their own purposes. Hellman's second play, *Days to Come*, was not so much about the despoilers—the evildoers themselves—as about those characters who, well-meaning or not, stand by and allow the despoilers to accomplish their destructive aims. Often these bystanders may be the victims of their own naiveté or lack of self-knowledge.

The despoiler plays are *The Little Foxes*, *Another Part of the Forest*, and *Watch on the Rhine*. Each is a tightly constructed drama, leading to a violent climax that is the result of evildoing. Most of the characters are clearly defined as evil or good, harmful or harmless. But the so-called bystander plays—*The Searching Wind*, *The Autumn Garden*, and *Toys in the Attic*—are as different

29

from the despoilers in structure as they are in theme. The
action is slower, the plot more discursive and low-keyed,
moving more within the characters and the events that
befall them, than through their actions. For most of
these people are unable to act positively or with conviction. They let things happen and they become the passive victims of the despoilers and themselves. Despoilers
and bystanders appear in some form in all the plays, but
Hellman clearly differentiates between evil as a positive,
rapacious force in the first group, and evil as the negative
failure of good in the second.

Hellman's plays are written in the realistic mode, as
distinguished from "theatricalist." In the history of theater, realism is a fairly recent phenomenon, dating from
the late nineteenth century. The drama of earlier centuries, from the Greeks to the English Restoration, had
been mainly theatrical: that is, it assumed that the theater
was its own small world or microcosm, and that drama
was a unique art form with its own accepted conventions.
The microcosm of the stage reflected the ultimate macrocosm—the universe. The audience expected the actors to
be larger than life (or smaller and cruder, if they were
comic) and to speak with exaggerated tones and gestures.
The actor could address the audience directly in solilo-
quies and asides, or he could drop the part he was playing and speak in his own voice.

By the nineteenth century, theatricalism had produced a theater devoted chiefly to diversion, entertainment, and thrills. The rising demand for verisimilitude in
all the arts seemed urgently necessary in the theater.
Henrik Ibsen in Norway, and August Strindberg in Swe-
den, led the way in the 1870s and 1880s, and were soon
followed by Anton Chekhov and George Bernard Shaw.
The drama of the period became (as it had previously
been with the great theatricalism of the Greeks and
Shakespeare) a serious art form, now concerned with
examining and representing the lives and problems of

real, i.e. contemporary, human beings. Sets became complicated facsimiles of real places, and actors were expected to use the language and gestures typical of real people. Theatricalist form survived, of course, in romantic verse dramas, farces, fantasies, and in the musical theater —from grand opera, to Gilbert and Sullivan, to music-hall vaudeville.

But the new realism did not always produce quality. The assumption that art or the theater should be an imitation of life does not always lead to profundity, nor does the opposite assumption, that art or the theater exists for its own sake, lead necessarily to song-and-dance acts. Realism as a style has been dominant in both good and bad plays and novels from about 1900 to the present. In its early days, it was represented not only by the work of Ibsen and his followers but also in the comedies and melodramas of such playwrights as Dion Boucicault. For the aim of theatrical realism is ultimately to convince the audience, through skillful deception, that they are witnessing real events. The aim of many a nineteenth-century "mellerdrammer" was to make the audiences boo the villains and cheer the heroes as if they were not actors. Popular patterns were often repeated, as they are in that most realistic of modern forms, the television soap opera. Audiences did not need the grandeur of mythical or royal characters when they could identify with brave Mose, the fireman, as he climbed the ladder to save the child crying in the window of the burning house. No *deus ex machina* in *Medea* could match that horse-drawn fire engine clanging and roaring across the stage.

Realism, then, may include any form of drama, from tragedy to drawing-room comedy; it is not a genre but a style or mode. It may also avail itself of symbolic action or language. Movies and television scripts are full of visual puns and symbolic gestures that only enhance the realistic, or photographic, effect. Ordinary speech at its best is full of images and metaphors. But realism on the modern stage makes some assumptions about narrative and about communication not always shared by theatricalism. Realism assumes that there is a certain logical connection between events; that all actions have consequences, if only to disturb the air; that no matter how fragmentary or figurative the dialogue, it has some recognizable meaning to convey. Realism also assumes a clear division between subject and object, on stage and off. A speaker is a subject; a listener on the stage or in the audience is an (indirect) object; all persons are subjects compared to things, which are objects. (Things do not think or talk in realistic drama.) And all people and things are distinct units, separate from one another, and need to be so for us to perceive them clearly.

Theatricalism considers the assumptions of realism to be limitations that theatrical form should try to transcend. And, indeed, no sooner had realism become established than it began to harden into a conventional mold, with its own restricted vision, stereotyped characters, conventional plots, and stock situations. Among the first to realize the limitations of realism was Strindberg, himself, one of the movement's founders. In *The Dream Play* (1902) and *The Ghost Sonata* (1907), Strindberg turned to a form known as expressionism. The action of the play was not modeled on action in a world of concrete reality, but on what takes place in the mind, as projected in dreams or visions. Events followed each other by association, not logic. A stream of events prefigured the stream of consciousness technique in the novel; a stream of scenes—pictures or tableaus—prefigured the technique of projecting a character's thought on the film screen.

Expressionism was only one of many theatrical techniques aimed at overcoming the limitations of realism, but it was a technique that appealed to many of Hellman's immediate precursors and contemporaries. Eugene O'Neill had written expressionistic plays side by side with the realistic ones—both *Anna Christie* (realistic) and *The*

Emperor Jones (expressionistic) were written in 1920. In 1923, Elmer Rice's *The Adding Machine* became the classic example of expressionism in American theater. More recent Americans to experiment with a combination of modes include Arthur Miller, Tennessee Williams, and Edward Albee.

Modern European and American theatricalist forms of drama have gone through innumerable trends and schools, both preceding and following expressionism. Some present a fragmented, nonlogical, nonnarrative view of life, e.g., surrealism, the theater of the absurd, or the sprawling epic. Others annihilate the boundary between audience and stage, demanding audience participation and response as part of the play, i.e., the theater of cruelty, the living theater, and the guerilla theater. Still others use words or situations abstracted from the logic of meaning, words for their own sake, as in Peter Handke's *Sprechstücke*; or situations for their own sake, as in *I*, a "theatrical event only," produced by the Belgian Theatre Laboratoire Vicinal.[1]

Hellman declared for realism at the beginning of her career, and left it only in a couple of adaptations, late in that career. In the introduction to her first published collection (*Four Plays*, 1942) she stated her position. Her argument in that essay is directed at the criticism that she writes "well-made plays"*—plays depending upon the careful structuring of events to create suspense, or as she defines it: "the play whose effects are contrived, whose threads are knit tighter than the threads in life and so do not convince." This charge was leveled at much of her

---

* The term "well-made play" derives originally from the *pièce bien faite*, a form invented by the French playwright Eugene Scribe (1791–1861), and popularized by him in some five hundred plays. They are written to formula, designed by spacing effects to keep the audience expectant throughout. By the late nineteenth century, the form came to include "clear, neat, balanced, overall construction, and the appearance, at least, of verisimilitude."[2]

work, and her answer was always to the effect that drama as a form demands contrivance, and what does it matter if the play is contrived, as long as it *is* convincing? For the stage, says Hellman, is a

tight, unbending, unfluid, meager form in which to write. . . . [The author] has three walls of a theatre and he has begun his pretense with the always rather comic notion that the audience is the fourth wall. He must pretend and he must represent. And if there is something vaguely awry, for me, about the pretense of representation . . . it is not that I wish to deny to other writers their variations of the form, but that, for me, the realistic form has interested me most.

As to "well-madeness," the theater itself is a trick, according to Hellman, and demands that the playwright "trick up the scene."

 This statement, written in 1942, remains definitive. It was not until many years later in the memoirs, and occasionally in interviews, that Hellman spoke again about her playwriting, and about the two men who helped launch her career. Herman Shumlin, for whom she had once read scripts, became the producer of her first five plays. Dashiell Hammett taught her the need for discipline, objectivity, and constant rewriting. This was always to be hard work for Hellman, but she felt that she had an instinct for theater: that the "second-rate form" came naturally to her, while the novel form did not. The memoirs were to be her novel, but they, too, sometimes took the form of plays or screenplays—instinctively theatrical, instinctively well-made.

2

Signposts

THE CHILDREN'S HOUR AND BROADWAY, 1934

American drama was coming of age in the 1930s. The list of famous names among playwrights began, of course, with O'Neill, and included Maxwell Anderson, Robert Sherwood, Phillip Barry, Elmer Rice, Clifford Odets, Paul Green, Marc Connelly, S. N. Behrman, Sidney Howard, Sidney Kingsley, and Thornton Wilder. There were few women: Rachel Crothers and Susan Glaspell had done most of their work in the 1920s or before; Zona Gale was primarily a novelist. Zoë Akins and Rose Franken were Hellman's only female competitors of any stature, and they were what she would call "lady writers."

The realistic mode was far and away the most popular on Broadway in 1934. One hundred and forty-five modern plays were produced in New York City in the season of 1934–1935, not counting plays in the repertories of the Abbey Theater or the Moscow Art Players. Only nine nonmusical plays of the entire season can be called nonrealistic, or theatrical, in mode. But some of the most distinguished writers were experimenting with theatricalism, and the nine plays in that style (mostly pageants or poetry, or fantasy) included work by O'Neill, Sean O'Casey, Paul Green, Marc Connelly, Maxwell Anderson, and Archibald MacLeish. Of the ten best plays of 1934–1935, as selected by Burns Mantle,[1] three were theatricalist (a high percentage considering the totals given above) and seven were realistic.

In form, then, Hellman was conventional—but her material was a different matter. She was just beginning to formulate her political philosophy and was not yet ready to make that the theme of a play. But she was ready to challenge the conventions of a society that destroys those who deviate from its mores—in this instance, sexual. And that same conventional society would award the Pulitzer Prize to a sentimental drama, *The Old Maid*, by Zoë Akins, instead of to *The Children's Hour*—the only one of the acceptable candidates to be designated as "outstanding."

The plot of *The Children's Hour* was based on the narrative of an actual trial: "Closed Doors; or The Great Drumsheugh Case," one of a collection of criminal cases entitled *Bad Companions*, by William Roughead (New York: Duffield and Green, 1931). The events in the original took place in 1810. Two headmistresses of a genteel Scottish boarding school for young ladies were accused of a lesbian attachment to each other, on the lying testimony of a pathologically vindictive sixteen-year-old schoolgirl. The girl's grandmother believed the accusation and influenced the parents of all the students to withdraw them from the school. The teachers sued for libel, and the case dragged on for ten years. Although they were finally exonerated by the House of Lords, the teachers were destroyed socially and economically. (Hellman used a few additional details from her source: the character of the ex-actress aunt of one of the teachers, a nonexistent keyhole, and the location of the rooms.)

While the theme of *The Children's Hour* was unconventional enough to cause a stir among moralists, it was hardly revolutionary on the stage, historically speaking. Homosexuality had been portrayed in the Renaissance English drama, and made its appearance on the modern American stage about 1920. The best-known play on lesbianism was *The Captive* (1926), a translation from the French of Edouard Bourdet. *The Captive* achieved notoriety when it was closed by the New York police; but it had been preceded by other plays on the subject as early as 1921. Two of these were concerned with life in a girls' boarding school—*These Days* (1928) by Katherine Clugston, and an adaptation of Christa Winsloe's German play, *Girls in Uniform*, produced just the year before *The Children's Hour*.[2]

Hellman said that *The Children's Hour* was a play about good and evil. The terms did not apply to the theme of homosexuality but to that of destructive scandal-mongering—the smear and the big lie. And, simultaneously, to the power of the old and rich to rob—to despoil —others of livelihood and life.

The machinery leading to the downfall of the two teachers, Karen Wright and Martha Dobie, is set in motion in Hellman's version by the neurotic child, and completed by the grandmother, as in the Drumsheugh case. The girl, fourteen-year-old Mary Tilford, hates the school and all authority, even the reasonable, gentle approach of the two teachers. She has learned how, by lying and flattery, to win sympathy from adults, and by bullying to make tools of her schoolmates.

We are given no reason or motivation for Mary's hostility. In her manuscript notes[3] for the play, Hellman compared Mary to Shakespeare's Iago, the villain in *Othello* who is traditionally considered to exemplify "motiveless malignancy." Hellman indicates that Mary is different from Iago only in her fear of consequences.

Although Mary is the initiating force of evil in the play, other characters, by their own pride, weakness, and gullibility, execute her purposes. Most important, of course, is her wealthy grandmother—rigidly self-righteous and status-conscious. But there is also Martha's Aunt Lilly Mortar, a vain ex-actress, dependent upon Martha and envious of her success. For their own reasons, both these

women are receptive to Mary's lies. Mary's schoolmates
are terrified of her. The terror of one child, Rosalie (who,
Mary knows, has stolen another girl's bracelet), accounts
for Mary's success, through blackmail and intimidation.

Mrs. Mortar is a nuisance at the school, undermining
discipline and irritating the teachers. For respite from
her, they offer Mrs. Mortar a trip to England. In her
anger at this plan, the aunt accuses her niece of opposing
Karen's impending marriage to Dr. Joseph Cardin. This
is a sore point for Martha, because there is some truth
in it: she is afraid of loneliness—in spite of Karen's re-
assurance that the three of them will be together and that
Martha and she will continue to run the school. The
aunt's accusation is explicit:

MRS. MORTAR: I know what I know. Every time that man
    comes into this house, you have a fit. It seems like you
    just can't stand the idea of them being together. God
    knows what you'll do when they get married. You're
    jealous of him, that's what it is.

MARTHA: I'm very fond of Joe, and you know it.

MRS. MORTAR: You're fonder of Karen, and I know that.
    And it's unnatural, just as unnatural as it can be. You
    don't like their being together. You were always like
    that even as a child. If you had a little girl friend, you
    always got mad when she liked anybody else. Well, you'd
    better get a beau of your own now—a woman of your
    age.

Two of the schoolgirls overhear this conversation,
and Mary Tilford bullies them into telling her what was
said. Armed with this information, and the memory of
some passages she has read from *Mademoiselle de Maupin*
(Gautier's titillating novel describing some varieties of
sexual experience—including inversion) Mary runs away
to her grandmother's.

She tries to convince Mrs. Tilford that she is being
persecuted at the school, but her lies are so transparent

that the grandmother sees through them. Even after Mary's wheedling flattery, "I love you, grandma," etc., the old lady still insists that the child return to school. Then, when nothing else works, Mary plays her ace: she tells Mrs. Tilford about the overheard quarrel between Martha and Mrs. Mortar, with emphasis on the word "unnatural." Mary elaborates on the situation from her imagination and the episodes from *Mademoiselle de Maupin*, suggesting sexual goings-on between Karen and Martha in Karen's room. Mrs. Tilford panics, and telephones the parents of other girls, who promptly take their daughters out of school.

The two teachers and Joe, Karen's fiancé, confront the grandmother and Mary, and almost succeed in breaking down the child's story: she said that she had seen "things" through a keyhole in Karen's door, and heard things through the wall in Martha's room. But, as in the Drumsheugh case, there is no keyhole in that door, and Martha's room (which she shares with her aunt) is on a different level, at a far end of the building. But as the grandmother begins to waver, Mary claims that she got the story from Rosalie, and Rosalie, afraid that her "borrowing" of another girl's bracelet will be revealed, confesses falsely that she had seen and reported the damaging evidence to Mary.

The teachers bring a libel suit against Mrs. Tilford, but lose because of the absence of Mrs. Mortar, who refuses to return from her trip to testify. (An absent "bystander," she is afraid of being involved in a scandal.) The teachers become social outcasts, unable even to leave the house. The school is ruined, and distrust has even tainted Karen's engagement to Joe—his protestations to the contrary. Joe departs, at Karen's insistence that their marriage would never work and that his suspicions would never be laid to rest. When Martha hears this, she suddenly admits to Karen—and herself—that she, Martha, has indeed loved Karen "that way," and that in fact,

the aunt's accusation was true; but Martha herself was
not conscious of her feelings until all the trouble.

> "It's funny, it's all mixed up. There's something in you,
> and you don't know it and you don't do anything about
> it. Suddenly a child gets bored and lies—and there you
> are, seeing it for the first time. . . . It all seems to come
> back to *me*. In some way I've ruined your life. I've
> ruined my own. I didn't even *know*. . . ."

Karen is shaken by the confession, weeps, and unconsciously—in the Shakespearian manner—suggests
Martha's fate: "Go and lie down, Martha. You'll feel
better." Martha goes, and a few minutes later a shot is
heard; she has committed suicide. Shortly afterward,
when Karen and the aunt have discovered Martha's body,
Mrs. Tilford arrives. She is old and broken; the black
maid, Agatha, persuades Karen to see her. The bracelet
has been found in Rosalie's room, and the truth about
Mary's blackmail is out. Mrs. Tilford wants to make whatever amends she can, mostly financial. Karen is not interested, but there is a small note of hope at the end of the
play—she and Joe Cardin may get back together after
all.

Two major objections were raised to the play by
well-known critics—among others, Brooks Atkinson of
the *New York Times*, reviewing the 1934 production, and
Eric Bentley, reviewing the 1952 version. The two agreed,
essentially, that the play should have ended with the pistol
shot, or even before. Atkinson said, "When two people
are defeated by the malignance of an aroused public
opinion, leave them the dignity of their hatred and
despair."[4] In her introduction to *Four Plays*, Miss Hellman acknowledged that perhaps the play should have
ended with the suicide, but added: "I am a moral writer,
often too moral a writer, and I cannot avoid, it seems,
that last summing-up."

The second objection is related to this answer. Bentley was unhappy that Hellman supposedly established the premise that the two women were "innocent," and then shifted ground by making one of them "guilty."[5]

But Hellman carefully prepared her audience in act one for Martha's final revelation. Martha is portrayed as depressed and fearful at the prospect of Karen's marriage. Moreover, in Hellman's source, *Bad Companions*, the author-editor, William Roughead, had declared emphatically (his italics), "My interest in the case resides in the fact that *the charge was false*." Roughead was apologizing for handling such a distasteful subject at all, but this is just the kind of statement that would inspire Hellman to react with the opposite view. What if the charge were *not* false? What if, after all, one—or even both—women had such feelings, consciously or unconsciously? Would the "guilty" deserve destruction at the hands of society? Changing mores between 1934 and 1978, and the open treatment of homosexuality on the stage and elsewhere today, make the answer for most audiences, clearly, no. In fact, it is ironic that this most outspoken and revolutionary play in its time should now seem so old-fashioned.

The play may have lost the Pulitzer Prize because of its theme, and been banned in Boston and, for a while, in Chicago and London, but New York audiences supported it for 691 performances—an astounding record for a first play. After eighty-six weeks in New York, the play went on tour here and abroad for another year.

The Children's Hour was twice made into a motion picture. The first, 1936, was called *These Three*, and Miss Hellman herself rewrote it as a love triangle, omitting, as censorship demanded, the homosexual theme. In 1962 another version was filmed, using the original title and restoring the lesbian relationship. One can still see *These Three* on the late show on television, but the movie called *The Children's Hour* seems to have disappeared. And

probably for good reason, since most of the critics found
it clumsy and embarrassing; Hellman herself preferred
the censored movie version.

In the 1952 revival Hellman directed the play herself,
to point up the analogy between the destructive forces in
The Children's Hour and those represented by McCarthy
and the House Un-American Activities Committee. The
smear technique and the big lie now became applicable
to the witch hunt for communists, but again, the double
question was raised: What if the accused *were* communists? How bad was that? In *Scoundrel Time*, Hellman
was to say that she thought it was not nearly as bad as
being a member of the anticommunist liberal left: intellectuals who, Hellman said, gave indirect support to
McCarthy and all he represented. This argument, as we
shall see, has brought down a tempest on her head: the
gays and the straights may be reconciled in 1978, but
not the factions of the old and new political left—much
less those of the left and right.

Characterization in all Hellman's plays is trenchant,
and her characters are looked at, objectively, from the
outside; the playwright sees them but does not identify
with them. Unlike many playwrights—O'Neill is the most
obvious example—she does not use the stage to express
her innermost, personal conflicts or sufferings; she is
singularly intolerant of self-pity wherever she sees it.
With a few exceptions, her compassion and empathy were
to be saved for the memoirs, and there, too, it is highly
selective. Even the persona of herself—the "I" who remembers and the "Lillian" who acts—is sometimes mocked
in the memoirs and the plays. In a recent interview, Hellman commented on this critical attitude toward herself.
She was discussing her difficulties with psychoanalysis:
"The man who analyzed me once said I was the only
patient he'd ever had in his life who talked about herself
as if I [sic] were another person. He meant no compliment. He meant that I had too cold a view of myself."[6]

In the introduction to *Four Plays*, Hellman says that she saw some of Mary, the *enfant terrible*, in herself and her early experience: "I reached back into my own childhood and found the day *I* finished *Mlle. de Maupin*; the day *I* faked a heart attack; the day *I* saw an arm get twisted." (In fact, in *Pentimento*, Lillian herself does a bit of arm-twisting on another girl, one Christy Houghton.) "And I thought again," she added, "of the world of the half-remembered, the half-observed, the half-understood which you need so much as you begin to write."

Hellman's portraits of the two women in *The Children's Hour*, especially of Martha, seem to have been drawn also from this half-remembered world. The rebelliousness of the young Lillian in the memoirs is often rooted in jealousy—sometimes in an adolescent crush on an adult of either sex, or a close relationship to another girl, the "beloved friend," Julia, of *Pentimento*. Hellman was to be as honest and outspoken about that in the memoirs as she was about her irritability and brattishness. By 1934, whatever was sexual in the Lillian-Julia relationship had been outgrown, or suppressed or sublimated; Hellman was living with Hammett, and Julia was studying medicine in Vienna (where Dr. Joe Cardin of *The Children's Hour* also studied.) But when Julia was maimed in an explosion, and Lillian sat at her bedside, Hellman's complicated, half-understood feelings must have given her some insight into Martha Dobie—one of the few Hellman characters whose fate could be called tragic. For if the villainy of Mary was, to Hellman, like that of Iago, then the suicide of Martha, in her self-hatred for what she could not help, was like that of Othello, who could not live with what he had seen in himself. *The Children's Hour* and, possibly, *Watch on the Rhine* are the only plays that approach the definition of tragedy, in the Aristotelian sense. Miss Hellman's customary detachment from her characters is related to the genre in which she writes—not tragedy, but "serious drama" or melo-

drama. For tragedy requires a protagonist whose fall—
partly through his own fault, partly through circumstances beyond his control—can excite pity or terror in
the spectator. Detachment, objectivity, or simple dislike
or hatred rule out such emotional involvement.

Hellman never claimed to be writing classic tragedy,
but she *was* writing more than is usually meant by melodrama. Her serious plays are always about good and
evil, and evil may seem to prosper unjustly, but the
actions and the strivings of the characters have meaning
and consequence. Violence is there for a purpose, not just
for sensational effect. In the introduction to *Four Plays*,
Hellman makes this distinction:

I think the word melodrama, in our time, has come to be
used in an almost illiterate manner. By definition it is a violent dramatic piece, with a happy ending. But I think we can
add that it uses its violence for no purpose, to point no moral,
to say nothing in say-nothing's worst sense. . . . But when
violence is actually the needed stuff of the work and comes
toward a large enough end, it has been and always will be
in the good writer's field. . . . There is a needed return to the
correct use of the word melodrama. It is only then the critic
will be able to find out whether a writer justifies his use of
violence, and to scale him against those who have used it.

Melodrama, as Hellman used the term, was a logical
outcome of realism in drama. For in tragedy, some mysterious, often supernatural force, hovers over the action,
partly, at least, controlling human destiny. In the mode
called naturalism the forces of destruction are also beyond human control, but they are not mysterious. Naturalism depicts life as predetermined by social, economic, or
biological forces. Realism, however, assumes that life is
seldom mysterious, seldom predetermined. When, in most
of Hellman's plays, human beings fail or are destroyed,
the powers of destruction are in human hands; they are
not functions of a higher necessity or fate, or of natural-

istic forces. One reason that *The Children's Hour* is closer
to tragedy than most of Hellman's plays is that the evil
motivation of Mary, and the psychological drives of
Martha, are both outside immediate logical human understanding or control. But it is clear enough that these
forces are allowed to triumph by human machination and
human weakness. Mary is the first of the despoilers—the
foxes who "spoil our vines"—and her accomplices in
evil are the self-righteousness in Mrs. Tilford and cow-
ardice in Mrs. Mortar.

In summary, then, *The Children's Hour* has many
of the qualities of Hellman's later plays. Its mode and
setting are realistic; its characters, strongly etched; its
theme, serious; and its tone, indignant. The object of
that indignation was both social and individual—a society
made up of a group of individuals so bound by their own
mores and conventions as to feel compelled, for the pres-
ervation of that society, to punish those who deviated
from it. But this "society" is general and diffused, not
limited to any one class: the blue-collar Archie Bunkers
are just as intolerant of deviation from the sexual norm
as are the uppercrust Mrs. Tilfords.

It is not until the curtain falls on *The Children's
Hour* that one realizes the irony of the opening lines,
quoted from *The Merchant of Venice*: "It is twice blest;
it blesseth him that gives and him that takes. . . ." The
reference, of course, is to mercy, singularly lacking in
those who implement the destruction of others. Mercy has
nothing to do with political persuasion or social strata:
"it droppeth as the gentle rain from heaven" and is "an
attribute of God himself." The principle is ethical, moral,
Christian—not political. But for many playwrights in the
1930s, human suffering and exploitation was political in
origin, and political reform alone could do battle with it.
In her next play, *Days to Come*, Hellman made a brief
foray into the melee of class struggle.

DAYS TO COME

No intellectual could live through the decade from 1929
to 1939, beginning with the great depression and ending
with World War II, without a concern for social action—
for the plight of the poor, the victims of the capitalistic
system, and of the oppressed, the victims of political
tyranny. Many playwrights felt that serious writing must
treat these problems. The proletarian and activist theater
became a movement, operating through both amateur and
professional groups. The amateurs might be offshoots of
the unions or other labor causes, chanting their messages
at strikes or rallies. Professional playwrights, actors, and
production staff formed groups not only for propaganda
purposes, but to set standards of high quality, to give
each other encouragement, and to provide their members
some measure of economic security. The most well-known
and effective of these (and there were many) were probably The Group Theater, The Union Theater, The Theater
Guild, and the Playwrights' Company. The Federal Theater Project, established in 1935 to provide jobs for
actors, playwrights and technicians, produced many activist plays.

Hellman might have joined any of these groups, but
did not. She stayed with the independent Broadway
theater even in the production of *Days to Come* (1936),
a play on the theme of labor unionization. Thirty-one
plays (twenty-one percent of the total) on Broadway
that season—1935–1936—were on social or political
themes.[7] The most famous of the leftist, pro-labor battle
cries was Clifford Odets's immensely popular *Waiting
for Lefty* (1935).

In her later work, Hellman was to be drawn to causes
only indirectly related to labor or the proletariat: the
ruthless decadence of the southern capitalist in *The Little
Foxes* and *Another Part of the Forest*, and the atrocities

of fascism in *Watch on the Rhine* and *The Searching Wind*. Most of the social action plays on the Broadway stage in the 1930s had a generally liberal or populist orientation. They were not only realistic in form but theatricalist also, from the lighthearted labor-union musical, *Pins and Needles*, to heavy verse tragedy (Maxwell Anderson's *Winterset*), historical drama (Robert Sherwood's *Abe Lincoln in Illinois*), or fantasy (Paul Green's *Johnny Johnson*). *Days to Come*, however, took Hellman's characteristic form—realistic melodrama. The play was a failure, partly because as Hellman said, she tried to say too much about the people in it. The labor cause was not enough to unify the action; Hellman had to explore the individual characters who were themselves often confused about their own motives. There were plot confusions, too —"accidental judgments, casual slaughters . . . purposes mistook" that did not necessarily, as in *Hamlet*, fall on "the inventors' heads," but on everybody's.

The play is set in a small town in Ohio, in which workers are reluctantly striking against their paternalistic employer, Andrew Rodman, part owner of a brush factory, a family business inherited from his father. Hard times have forced Rodman to cut the workers' wages below the poverty level. Some of the less paternalistic stockholders—Henry Ellicott, the family's lawyer, and Rodman's sister, Cora—have persuaded Rodman to break the strike by importing professional strikebreakers, who are mobsters and jailbirds.

The union organizer, Leo Whalen, warns his men not to allow themselves to be provoked by the strikebreakers into rioting or other violence. A long stand-off results, and the gang leader plants the dead body of one of his men, killed in a gambling quarrel, at Union Headquarters. The workers and Whalen are made to look guilty of the murder, and a pretext is established for the strikebreakers to attack the workers. In the ensuing violence, the child of the foreman, Firth, an old friend of the Rodman family, is killed. The town is torn apart with shooting, the workers are hungry and tired, and they agree to call off the strike. They go back to work and Whalen gives up the attempt to organize a union.

The plot of the play as a whole is as abortive as Whalen's efforts. It is crowded with loosely related elements, including blackmail, adultery, and broadly satirical sketches of the rich. Rodman, the benevolent manufacturer and reluctant oppressor, turns out to be a well-meaning but unbelievably naive cuckold. His wife's ex-lover is Henry Ellicott, the foxiest of little foxes, and the wife now has a yen for Whalen. Cora, Rodman's sister and co-owner of the factory, is portrayed as a frustrated spinster, and as a caricature of the snobbish, greedy, idle rich. Hellman said in the introduction to *Four Plays* that she had known prototypes of these characters—had hated the sister, Cora, pitied the wife, Julie, and respected Leo Whalen. She "had been raised with the Ellicotts of this world," presumably the Newhouses, whom we will meet again in *The Little Foxes.*

All these characters, good and bad, are ineffectual; and their efforts, along with the plot, just peter out. The hired thugs accomplish the villainous purpose for which they are—finally—paid, and leave town. The strike fails, the unionization fails, the company will probably go broke, and the marriage of the well-meaning Rodman is bankrupt. His wife's adulterous affair with Ellicott has gone sour, and her mawkish attraction to Whalen comes to nothing. The workers have gone back to their tedious, underpaid jobs, and the Rodmans go back to their tedious, trapped, unsatisfying lives. The application of the title *Days to Come* to the play is vague. It may have been intended, like much of the book of Ecclesiastes from which it was quoted, as a comment on labor and reward.[8] However, it is a sharper comment on the fate of the characters in the play: "For there is no remembrance of the wise more than of the fool forever; seeing that which is

in the days to come shall all be forgotten. And how dieth
the wise man? As the fool." (Ecclesiastes 2:16)

Days to Come lasted only seven performances, but it
was a harbinger of Hellman plays to come. The war between forces of good and evil, with evil the victor, in
The Children's Hour, had made for a tightly constructed
series of conflicts, crises, and resolutions. But Hellman
said that *Days to Come* was about evil "in the hands of
those who don't understand it," and in Hellman's scheme,
ignorance is no excuse—sad, regrettable, but weak, and
ultimately destructive. A play based on this proposition
must be comparatively discursive and undramatic. The
forces of good have no direction except muddle and
neglect, and the only reward of such failure is a dim self-
insight, when it is too late to reform. "And how dieth the
wise man? As the fool."

As Hellman grew older, the more her misanthropy
became like that of the preacher in Ecclesiastes, cynical
and sad, rather than angry and rebellious. The anger that
she had turned against the Tilfords of this world—Mary
and her grandmother in *The Children's Hour*—rages
through *The Little Foxes* and *Watch on the Rhine*, and
flares up again, but almost as parody, in *Another Part of
the Forest*. But in *The Searching Wind*, *The Autumn
Garden*, and *Toys in the Attic*, Hellman is looking at the
Rodmans of the world: the ineffectual ones who let evil
and decay attack and destroy the lives of others, as it
consumes their own vitality.

3

OOOOOOOOOOOOOOO OOOOOOOOOOOOOOOOOOOOOO OOOOOOOOOOOOOO

Despoilers

THE LITTLE FOXES

Badly shaken by the failure of *Days to Come*, Hellman took great care with the preparation of *The Little Foxes*. She filled two notebooks with research materials on southern economics, history, and culture; then struggled through nine drafts of the play itself.[1] But it was not just fear of another failure that made her so cautious; it was the personal nature of her source—her own family background. In *Pentimento* Hellman said,

Some of the trouble came because the play has a distant connection to my mother's family and everything. . . . had formed a giant tangled time-jungle in which I could find no space to walk without tripping over old roots, hearing old voices speak about histories made long before my day.

Among the voices were those of Hellman's mother, who appears as the gentle, helpless Birdie (and as Lavinia in *Another Part of the Forest*), and of her grandmother, Sophie Newhouse, and Sophie's aggressive brother, Jake. They are imagined here as Regina and Ben, and would appear in later plays in the characters of hardheaded, shrewd, witty women, and empire-building men. Hellman meant the young girl, Alexandra, to be a "half-mockery" of herself at that age. More specific identification of the Newhouses in this and later plays must wait for later biographies. (Hellman said recently that some of her family had threatened to sue for libel after the play appeared.)

The title, suggested by Dorothy Parker, comes from the Song of Solomon 2:15. "Take us the foxes, the little foxes, that spoil the vines, for our vines have tender grapes." The "foxes" who despoil the land of the south are the Hubbard family. Hellman makes the point that they are the aggressive ones, but there had been, and would be, many others after them just as bad as they were—those who would stand by and watch them "eat the earth."

The Hubbards are Regina and her two brothers, Ben and Oscar. Their father left all his money to the two sons. Regina has married Horace Giddens, a banker, to recoup her financial losses. The Giddens have a daughter, Alexandra, sixteen. All the Hubbards have one passion—money. It is the basis of Oscar's marriage as well as of Regina's. He married the sweet but helpless Birdie, to acquire her aristocratic family's plantation for the Hubbards. He and Birdie have an amoral son, Leo, who works in Horace's bank, whom Oscar hopes to marry off to Alexandra.

The elder and more powerful of the Hubbard brothers is the bachelor, Ben; but if he is king of the clan, Regina is queen, and Horace is her consort.

The action takes place in a town in the deep south in 1900. Hellman had done her homework, as the notebooks testify, on the rise of southern industry, which was beginning at that time to compete with the industry of New England. The industrial revolution is the backdrop against which the "foxes" play their human—or inhuman —roles, much as the rise of labor unionism formed the backdrop for *Days to Come.* As in that play, audience interest is much less in what the characters have done to society than in what they have done to each other.

Hellman moves them like chessmen: first one, then the other seizes power. And since power is a function of money, to understand the moves, one has to understand the dollar figures. The family has made a deal with a Chicago industrialist, Marshall, to set up a cotton mill in the town. Marshall has put up forty-nine percent of the money, and the three Hubbards will put up the remaining fifty-one percent. Regina's, of course, will come from her banker husband, Horace. But Horace, who is being treated for a heart ailment in the hospital at Johns Hopkins, has not come up with his share of the money. The brothers threaten to cut Regina out and find another partner if the money is not forthcoming, but Regina knows that they do not want to take in a stranger. She lets them think that Horace is holding out for a larger controlling share—even though he will pay only one-third of the total—and that she will not persuade him to give the money at all unless he has twice the share promised. Ben gets her to accept forty percent, the extra seven percent of control coming from Oscar's share. To palliate Oscar, the other two agree to encourage his son, Leo, to marry Zan (Alexandra) and thus keep the extra profits at least in the family.

Regina sends Alexandra to the hospital in Baltimore to bring her father home, knowing that he will not refuse his daughter, even though he is too ill to travel. But when they arrive, Horace still refuses to contribute to the scheme, more stubbornly than ever when he learns that part of the deal is a guarantee to Marshall of cheap power and labor, obtainable only, in Horace's words, "by pounding the bones of this town."

With Leo's help, the brothers steal bonds worth $88,000 from Horace's safe-deposit box, bonds which are as negotiable as money, and Oscar takes them to Chicago to make up the missing third of the investment. They let Regina think an outsider has come up with the money. She bullies and threatens Horace, who says she will get no money for this investment from him as long as he lives. Her answer is, "I hope you die. I hope you die soon. . . . I'll be waiting for you to die."

Horace discovers the theft of the bonds, and makes sure that Leo knows. Then he tells Regina of the theft. He adds that he will not report it to the authorities, but will tell the brothers that the bonds are a loan from Regina. When he changes his will, as he plans to do, the bonds will be all she inherits. Regina is trapped; she will receive nothing from her brothers except as they choose to pay back the "loan." But the next move is hers. In the course of their quarrel she and Horace go over their past. She tells him that she has always had only contempt for him. Horace has a heart attack, reaches for his medicine, but spills it. He asks Regina to call the maid, Addie, to get the other bottle, upstairs. But Regina just looks at him. He calls Addie in panic, then tries to climb the stairs, and collapses. When she is sure that he is unconscious, she calls the servants.

The brothers arrive. Leo tells them that Horace knows about the theft. Regina tells them that she knows about it also. Now she has the upper hand: "I'm smiling, Ben. I'm smiling because you are quite safe while Horace lives. But I don't think Horace will live. And if he doesn't live I shall want seventy-five percent in exchange for the bonds. . . . And if I don't get what I want I am going to put all three of you in jail."

But Alexandra comes in to announce that Horace has died and asks her mother, "What was Papa doing on the staircase?" The implications of her question are not lost on Ben, who threatens to use them eventually against his sister. But Regina is still the queen; the princess, Alexandra, refuses to stay with her, to watch the foxes "eat the earth." The only suggestion of vulnerability in Regina now is her invitation to Alexandra to sleep in the same room with her. To which her daughter replies, "Are you afraid, Mama?" The curtain falls.

The plot of *The Little Foxes* consists of a series of crises, each one only partly resolved, so that the audience is kept waiting for the resolution to be completed, only to be surprised or shocked by a reversal, leading to a new crisis. The climax is reached in the quarrel and the death of Horace. Then comes the dénouement—the unraveling in which a few raveled strands remain. This is how well-made melodrama works. Nothing is inevitable, everything is a surprise, and every step in the plot is willed and carried out by human beings. Hellman herself made this point in a newspaper commentary a few days after the opening of *The Little Foxes*:

If you believe, as the Greeks did, that man is at the mercy of the gods he might offend and who will punish him for the offense, then you write tragedy. The end is inevitable from the beginning. But if you believe that man can solve his problems and is at nobody's mercy, then you will probably write melodrama.[2]

But even as relentless a moralist as Hellman had to admit that "man" consists of both victors and victims. In *The Little Foxes*, the fate of the weaker characters shows up the viciousness of the strong in sharp relief. Horace is not entirely a victim; he too was once a despoiler but he is now relenting of his past at the point of death. But Oscar's wife, Birdie, *is* the pathetic victim. She may be weak-willed, but she is also sensitive and musical, with longings for beauty and affection. Horace and Alexandra understand Birdie; they have some of the same longings. (Horace even cherishes a piece of his old violin in his safe-deposit box, with the bonds!)

Audiences suffered with Birdie when they saw her treatment at the hands of Oscar, and pitied her even when she confessed that she drank in private. (That confession scene has always been a cherished one for actresses.) And audiences sympathized with Alexandra, and cheered her when she broke away from the clan, refusing to stay with Regina. But Hellman, as always, had meant to be tough on weak and strong alike, and was surprised by audience reactions. In *Pentimento*, she described her intentions: "I had meant to half-mock my own youthful high-class innocence in Alexandra. . . ." Elsewhere she said, "To my great surprise, the ending of the play was taken to be a statement of faith in Alexandra. . . . I never meant it that way. She did have courage enough to leave, but she would never have the force or vigor of her mother's family."[3]

As to Birdie, "I had meant people to smile at, and to sympathize with, the sad, weak Birdie, certainly I had not meant them to cry." And as for the foxes themselves, "I had meant the audience to recognize some part of themselves in the money-dominated Hubbards; I had not meant people to think of them as villains to whom they had no connection."[4]

It is to Hellman's credit as a writer of realistic drama that audiences listened to her characters more attentively than they did to implied sermons and generalizations. They felt the power of evil in the play and the excitement of each twist of the plot. But in 1939 most critics, as opposed to the audiences, heard the play's message about social conditions in the South. George Jean Nathan's review was fairly typical. He praised Hellman as the foremost among American women playwrights:

She has a dramatic mind, an eye for character, a fundamental strength and a complete and unremitting integrity that are rare among native playwrights of her sex. . . . From first to last, "The Little Foxes" betrays not an inch of compromise, not a sliver of a sop to the comfortable acquiescence of Broadway or Piccadilly, not the slightest token that its author had anything in her purpose but writing the truest and most honest play on her theme that it was possible for her to write.[5]

In 1941, the play was made into a movie, with Bette Davis in the role of Regina, and can still be seen occasionally on television. In 1949 it became an opera, *Regina*, composed by Marc Blitzstein. Since then, *The Little Foxes* has become a standard item of American repertory, amateur and professional. Its first and most impressive professional revival took place in 1967 at Lincoln Center. Audiences were enthusiastic, and the limited engagement at the Center was so oversubscribed that the play had to be moved to a Broadway theater for an additional forty performances, before it began a successful road tour.

But the opinions of the critics in 1967 were divided, and none were neutral; they went from panegyric to panning. Even two *New York Times* critics, Clive Barnes and Walter Kerr, took opposite views of the play, although both were ecstatic over the production. Barnes thought the play was still "well-turned, machine-made" melodrama. But Kerr hailed it as valid Americana, a classic performed with such genius as to provide hope for an American National Theater, a native repertory theater that would be based at Lincoln Center. Miss Hellman repaid Barnes and Kerr, in kind, in *Pentimento* when she said, "Barnes is a 'fashion-swinger'. . . . but. . . . he can't quite find where the swing is located for the new season. Kerr is the only critic on the *Times* who learned and thrived."

The performances of the actors excited as much intense comment, pro and con, as did the play—partly because Mike Nichols, the director, had reinterpreted or updated some of the parts. As for the play as literature, it no longer seemed to carry the populist implications that it had in the 1930s, nor to be a historical record: it was just a play about the evil men do to each other. A minor controversy arose when Elizabeth Hardwick attacked *Foxes*, and Hellman's work generally, in a rather turgid essay in the *New York Review of Books*.[6] The play was poor southern history, the characters were not well-motivated, and the production was not all that interesting or important. Hardwick was immediately answered in the

Review by other critics, friends of Hellman, who came to her defense—Edmund Wilson, Richard Poirier, and Penelope Gilliat. Wilson's reply took the form of "An Open Letter to Mike Nichols"[7] in which he sang the same hymn of praise as did Walter Kerr, also hoping the production might lead the way to an American National Theater, in which *The Little Foxes* would be a classic.

And a classic it became.

ANOTHER PART OF THE FOREST

Hellman had originally intended to write a trilogy of plays about the Hubbards. *The Little Foxes* would be in the middle: *Another Part of the Forest* was to cover the Hubbards' past, and a third play was to take them up through the 1930s. But Hellman said she was tired of the Hubbards after *Another Part of the Forest*, so she never wrote the third play. Although seven years and two other plays intervened, the Hubbard plays are best described in relation to each other.

In *Another Part of the Forest*, Hellman takes the family history back only one generation to 1880. The father and mother, Marcus and Lavinia, are still alive. Marcus scorns and ridicules his wife, and will be Oscar's model for his treatment of Birdie in *The Little Foxes*. At this point, however, none of the children is married; the two boys have menial low-paying jobs in the Hubbard business, and Marcus intends to keep it that way. He lavishes his money on Regina, who spends it on expensive clothes from Chicago. The family is known to the townspeople as ruthless, bigoted, and penny-pinching, having made its money during the civil war at the expense of its own neighbors. In contrast to the Hubbards are the Bagtrys—Birdie, her mother, and her cousin, John Bagtry. They are land and cotton poor, starving on their plantation, Lionnet, and because of their aristocratic heritage and manners, a thorn in the side of the Hubbards.

Hellman's aim, she said, was not to write history, but to try to understand what lay behind the behavior of the Hubbards, "to look into their family background and to find out what it was that made them the nasty people they were." She had, then, to use a psychological approach. Hellman, herself, was in analysis at the time and dedicated the play to Gregory Zilboorg, her psychoanalyst.

The nastiness of the Hubbards begins in the play with Marcus, a brutal "primal father" of his tribe, such as Freud described in *Totem and Taboo*. The drama becomes a contest between the father and the oldest son, Ben, who crushes the father in the end and takes his place. The sibling rivalry between Ben and Oscar turns into a kind of one-sided Cain and Abel struggle, in which the older brother subdues the younger and weaker. (Oscar is not only amoral, he is also stupid.) In her father's affections, Regina has displaced her mother, Lavinia, who considers herself—as her husband does—violated and soiled by her marriage to him. The father's attachment to his daughter is given incestuous overtones, and there is more than a hint that Ben is a jealous rival of his father for Regina, as well as for his money. (Maybe this is why Ben remains a bachelor, and, in *The Little Foxes*, lives next door to his sister and the weak husband he chose for her.)

The financial tricks the Hubbards play on each other need not concern us here. Suffice it to say that they attempt to enslave and exploit each other just as they have done, and will do, to the townspeople and the Bagtrys. The only passion for any of them, outside of money, is lust, and they easily make their peace with sex when cash is the substitute. Oscar is in love—"deeply and sincerely" he keeps saying—with the town prostitute. One of the comic, or satiric, highlights of the play occurs when Oscar brings his girlfriend to meet the family. But Ben soon breaks up that affair and sets the scene for

Oscar to court Birdie Bagtry, and bring those rich cotton
fields into the family. Oscar's broken heart is soon on the
mend at the prospect of being rich.

Regina is in love, too, at the beginning of the play.
She has been having an affair with the penniless John
Bagtry, and hopes to get him to elope with her to Chicago,
since she knows that neither her father nor Ben would
ever approve a marriage. (John is, after all, only a cousin
of the Bagtrys and would not inherit the plantation.) But
John is essentially a man of honor, an officer and a gentleman, who was happy only during the war when he was
in the army.* John's affair with Regina is beginning to
pale, and all he wants now is to go to Brazil to fight in a
war brewing there. When John is, finally, out of the
picture, Regina aligns herself with the money and power;
first with her father, and at the end, with Ben.

The climax of the play and the defeat of Marcus is
brought about by Lavinia, his downtrodden wife. The
audience has the pleasure—rare in a Hellman play—of
watching virtue triumph or at least, find its own reward.
Lavinia is a bit dotty, in a religious way, but she is a
woman of courage and principle, under all her submissiveness. She has always been afraid of her husband
and Ben, too:

> "I spent a life afraid. And you know that's funny, Ben-
> jamin, because way down deep I'm a woman wasn't
> made to be afraid. . . . I'm not afraid to die. . . . and if
> you're not afraid of dying then you're not afraid of any-
> thing."

For years she has been begging Marcus to build her
a little schoolhouse in Altaloosa, where she can fulfill her
mission in life, to teach black children. (And not the
Bible, either. They are too young to read about what goes

---

* Hellman said that Dashiell Hammett was the first man she had
ever known who flourished in military service. Such honorable
soldiers, or would-be soldiers, appear in several of her plays.

on in that book!) Lavinia's only friendship and support
have come from the blacks and their churches, and she
and Coralee, her maid, share the secret that destroys
Marcus. When he has refused, year after year, to listen
to her plea, and has threatened to send her away to a
mental hospital, Lavinia makes up her mind to escape.
Ben is leaving, and she demands that he take her with
him as far as Altaloosa.

Ben is reluctant until his mother gradually gives
him the information about his father's past that could
hang Marcus if it became known in the town. The townspeople already hate him for exploiting them during the
civil war; selling badly needed salt, smuggled through
the blockade, for extortionary black-market prices. Moreover, the townspeople have suspected that he led the
Union troops to a camp where southern boys—sons and
brothers of the local folks—were training, and where the
Yankees slaughtered twenty-seven boys, including John
Bagtry's twin. Marcus has always had an alibi to protect
him from the charge, but Lavinia has the proof that his
alibi is false. It is written in her Bible,* along with her
own and Coralee's eyewitness account of Marcus's where-
abouts on the night of the massacre. Lavinia's knowledge
buys her her freedom: she is not above a little blackmail
herself, but in the cause of justice. Ben promises, in
exchange for her information, to finance her school and
take care of Coralee. And just in case he should change
his mind, Lavinia keeps a tight hold on the Bible, the
repository of the evidence. As she departs on her journey
to her new life—not the insane asylum, but to do her

---

* That Bible has been too melodramatic for most critics to take
seriously—but Hellman uses it ironically. Lavinia's particular
"insanity" is supposed to be religious; religion put her in Marcus's power to have her declared insane. Now the Bible—her religion—has put him in Lavinia's power. Not only is the Bible too
dirty a book for her black children to read, it is also the instrument
of blackmail.

work in this world—she plays her own version of the Ophelia mad scene in *Hamlet*: to each of the others she gives a memento—a pin to Regina, her prayer book to Oscar, her father's watch to Ben, and her wedding ring (back) to Marcus. Of course they all want the Bible, but she is keeping that.

I have devoted this disproportionate amount of space to Lavinia because her character adds a new dimension to the Hubbard saga. She is neither a crazy woman nor a saintly one, although she has a touch of each, and her presence in the play means that some good blood has been brought into the Hubbard clan. That the character of Lavinia, modeled on Hellman's mother, as she tells us in the memoirs, should be the only bearer of good blood, is significant. It was Hellman's way of setting things to rights with the ghost of her own eccentric, misunderstood mother, who had been a source of irritation and embarrassment at times to her daughter.

After Lavinia's revelation, Ben becomes the tribal chief. He forces his father, to escape hanging, to sell him the family business for one dollar. He gives Birdie Bagtry a promised loan on Lionnet and insures that the plantation will come eventually to the Hubbards by clearing the way for Oscar to court Birdie. John Bagtry is out of the way, too, for the money will enable him to go to Brazil. Regina knows now where her bread is buttered. In the final moments of the play, Marcus, now stripped of power, goes to sit by his daughter:

MARCUS (*softly*): Pour me a cup of coffee, darling. *Regina looks at him, gets up, crosses to the table, pours coffee, brings it to him. Marcus pulls forward the chair next to him. Regina ignores the movement, crosses to chair near Ben, sits down.*

Curtain

Some critics applauded the play, others were not so kind, and reading it one can see why. The melodrama (in the ordinary sense of the word) does get out of hand. Hellman had an exchange on the subject with Brooks Atkinson, who thought the play as a whole was a "witch's brew of blackmail, insanity, cruelty, theft, torture, insult, drunkenness, with a trace of incest thrown in for good measure." But he congratulated her on some "scenes of great theatrical intensity. . . ." and added, "What you may find yourself wondering about is how an author who overwrites a gaudy melodrama can write individual scenes like Birdie's pathetic farewell in the second act with such sure, piercing economy."[8] Hellman answered him a short time later, at the invitation of the *Times*, but mainly to the effect that since Atkinson didn't like action or violence on the stage the two of them would never agree. He would continue to "frown down" upon her, and she would go on writing in her own way.[9]

But Hellman made a more enlightening comment on the play in *Pentimento*. As she went into the past of the Hubbards, she says,

I believed that I could now make clear that I had meant the first play [*The Little Foxes*] as a kind of satire. I tried to do that in *Another Part of the Forest*, but what I thought funny or outrageous, the critics thought straight stuff; what I thought was bite they thought sad, touching, or plotty and melodramatic. Perhaps, as one critic said, I blow a stage to pieces without knowing it.

Part, at least, of the satire was aimed at some dramatic forms as well as at the types of characters in this play. The phrase, "another part of the forest," is, of course, a commonplace stage direction in Renaissance drama, including the plays of Shakespeare. One far-fetched hypothesis is that Hellman may have been alluding to the use of the phrase in *Titus Andronicus*,[10] an early play of Shakespeare's in the exaggerated theatrical mode of the tragedy of blood. Except for the names, Marcus and Lavinia, there is no real evidence that Hellman meant

to refer to *Titus Andronicus*, but she certainly knew the
genre and caught the spirit of it in both *The Little Foxes*
and this play.

But there are further hints of satire and parody:
Marcus is fond of the style Hellman calls "Greek Southern"—not only in architecture but in his taste for Aris-
totle and his other affectations; he sees himself as a sort
of Marcus Aurelius—the beneficent Roman emperor called
"the Philosopher." And if, as Hellman says, *The Little
Foxes* was also intended to be satirical, then certainly one
of the objects of the satire was Eugene O'Neill's trilogy,
Mourning Becomes Electra, a civil-war tragedy in the
Greek Freudian manner, modeled on the Greek *Oresteia*
of Aeschylus. The Electra character there, morbidly attached first to her father, then her brother, is called
Lavinia. In *Mourning Becomes Electra* Lavinia's mother
is the Clytemnestra figure who kills her husband, a civil-
war general, in a way so similar to the death of Horace
at the hands of Regina, as to have been confusing critics
(especially this one) ever since.[11]

But Hellman was also parodying herself and *The
Little Foxes* in this play, and that may have caused the
confusion and mixed reactions among critics. While she
reiterates in the memoirs that she often makes fun of
herself, the adjective most frequently used by others to
describe Hellman is "formidable." One thinks twice before laughing at her, or determining whether or not she
is laughing at herself. And she *did* direct *Another Part
of the Forest* because she thought no one else could do it.

WATCH ON THE RHINE

Of *Watch on the Rhine*, Hellman said in *Pentimento*,
"There are plays that, whatever their worth, come along
at the right time, and the right time is the essence of the
theater and the cinema." This instinct for timing, as well

as for drama, has served her well in the plays, the
memoirs, and her new film, *Julia*. But none of her works
was ever more timely than *Watch on the Rhine*. It opened
on April 1, 1941. The war in Europe, and the question
of our imminent involvement, haunted the minds of
Americans. Not only Poland and Czechoslovakia but now
Holland, Norway, Belgium, and most of France had
fallen to Hitler. Britain was undergoing the worst bombing of the war. In March Congress had passed the Lend-
Lease Act permitting the president to send war material
to those countries that were soon—after Pearl Harbor,
on December 7 of that same year—to be our fighting
allies.

If the play had not been concerned with such a
deadly earnest theme, it might have been a comedy of
manners. American and European characters are thrown
together in order to say something about their differing
values and customs—not only about good and evil. In
looking back at her old diaries, Hellman was surprised
to discover that she had had Henry James's two novels
on this subject, *The American* and *The Europeans*, in the
back of her mind at the time of writing *Watch on the
Rhine*.

In construction, the first act is such a cliché of
well-made drawing-room drama, as to be redeemed only
by the wit and broad humor of the characterizations and
actions. In the plush setting of a mansion in suburban
Washington, one group of characters—including a black
butler, French housekeeper, wealthy dowager "mistress
of the house," and her son—are anxiously awaiting the
arrival of another group of characters. In expressing
anticipation and anxiety they provide the audience with
details about the new arrivals. (This is the typical "exposition" of the well-made play.) When the guests arrive,
we have a fine family "recognition scene" of the good
people—after twenty years—full of happy surprises and
further information. This is followed by an ominous

scene of suspected recognition between two old enemies. The act concludes with evil just about to get the upper hand over good, before the intermission in which the audience can relish its suspense. This mechanical structure continues in the subsequent act, through a series of confrontations, crises, and resolutions between various characters, ending in a climactic confrontation and final dénouement. . . . catastrophic, but on a lofty note.

But the characterization in the play is interesting enough to overcome our awareness of its mechanical structure. The wealthy dowager, Fanny Farrelly, is the widow of a liberal judge and diplomat, to whose memory she constantly refers and whose portrait hangs on the living room wall throughout the play. Fanny has been an arbitrary dictator over her son, David, and would have been one also over her daughter, Sara, if Sara had not declared her independence twenty years before by marrying a German, Kurt Müller. Fanny, resisting all the way, will soon be educated and "liberalized" by Kurt and his children as the play progresses. As bossy as she is, Fanny's wit gives her charm. Part of her function in life is to find out the local gossip and improve on it—"wit it up"—and the rest is to keep her family in order, according to her own upperclass lights.

The primary story is that of the Müllers (spelled "Mueller" in earlier versions of the play). Kurt is an antifascist who has fought in Spain, as well as in Germany. He is not Jewish.

He is modeled on "Julia," as Hellman acknowledges in *Pentimento*, and in early manuscript drafts of the play (now in the Texas Collection) was a radical revolutionary socialist. Hellman dropped that complication in the final draft, with its suggestion that Kurt was a Communist, except for a few general comments about the inequalities of wealth and poverty. Kurt's family arrives hungry and ill-clothed at the Farrellys' mansion. Kurt carries the marks of torture by the fascists—scars and broken hands. He has finally managed to bring his wife and children to visit her mother and brother, where the family can rest for a while. But Kurt himself is on a mission—he is carrying $23,000 in cash, collected from "the pennies of the poor who do not like Fascism." He will soon have to leave his family in Washington and take the money back to Europe, where it is needed to free other anti-Nazi prisoners.

Staying with the Farrellys when the Müllers arrive are a different group and breed of Europeans, Romanian Count Teck de Brancovis and his wife Marthe. Teck is a Nazi sympathizer and gambler—a professional Romanian aristocrat." (Hellman modeled him on a Romanian Prince whom she had met and played poker with in London in 1936.) Marthe has lived in Europe most of her life and dislikes Nazis. The couple is visiting Fanny because Marthe's mother and she were friends.

The marriage of Teck and Marthe has disintegrated. They are in debt, living on credit. What little money they have is being lost through Teck's gambling with his Nazi friends at the German embassy in Washington. Marthe is falling in love with David Farrelly, Fanny's thirty-nine year old son, and is trying to find a way to leave her husband. Kurt knows Teck's identity and his past, and Teck is suspicious of Kurt's.

When the news breaks that three prominent anti-fascists have been caught, imprisoned, and tortured by the Nazis, Teck discovers that they are all close friends of Kurt, and that he is a missing fourth on the Nazi's wanted list. Teck threatens to turn Kurt in to the Nazi embassy unless Kurt will give him $10,000 of the $23,000 he is carrying. Kurt refuses—the money is not his. Fanny offers to give Teck $4,000 in cash, which she has in the house, and a check for the remainder, dated a month in advance, to give Kurt time to get back to Europe before it is cashed. Kurt pretends to acquiesce in this blackmail, but he knows that it is a trap: Teck will betray him and his imprisoned friends anyway, in exchange for a hard-to-get German visa. When Fanny leaves the room to get the money, Kurt faces Teck with this knowledge. Before Teck can answer, Kurt attacks him and knocks him unconscious. With gun in hand, Kurt carries Teck out to the garden, where he shoots him.

Sara knows what is happening and that it is inevitable. She calls the airline and reserves a seat for Kurt, under another name, on the next plane to Texas, where he will cross over to Mexico and then to Europe. When Kurt returns from the garden, they explain to Fanny and David, who come to understand that Kurt has done what he had to do. The killing of Teck was an act of war, except that "when you kill in a war, it is not so lonely." Kurt will take Teck's body in the car with him, and leave it there when he hides the car. After two days the family will report the two of them missing. By that time Kurt will have escaped.

Fanny and David give Kurt their support. The children and Sara will stay with them there, with little hope that Kurt will ever return. There is a touching farewell scene; Kurt leaves, and Sara goes upstairs to comfort the children. Fanny and David prepare to face what trouble may come. Fanny says, "Well, here we are. We are shaken out of the magnolias, eh?" Hellman said in *Pentimento* that this was her purpose—"to write a play about nice, liberal Americans whose lives would be shaken up by Europeans, by a world the new Fascists had won because the old values had long been dead." In the play, Fanny and David see those old values of culture, honor, and dignity in Kurt.

Quantitatively, there is more comic and romantic byplay in *Watch on the Rhine* than there is tense melodrama. The children provide some of the comedy in their relationship with their gruff, basically sentimental, grandmother. The warmth between members of the Müller family, and the budding romance (we never quite see it flower) between Marthe and David give the audience hope that youth—or romantic middle age—and love will prevail over decadence and hate. This comedy of manners fills most of the first two acts; in spite of its "well-made" devices, the play is not tightly constructed. Some critics thought the first half dragged or consisted of over-emotional padding, but most described it as "pleasantly discursive" or "spontaneous" and witty. Most agreed that, melodramatic or not, the characters and the European-American contrast were skillfully drawn.

Watch on the Rhine won the New York Drama Critics Circle Award for 1941. This was no small honor, for the major playwrights of the day all had war dramas running concurrently, or almost so, with *Watch on the Rhine*. (These included Maxwell Anderson's *Key Largo*, Ernest Hemingway's *Fifth Column*, Robert Sherwood's *There Shall Be No Night*, Elmer Rice's *Flight to the West*, Philip Barry's *Liberty Jones*, S. N. Behrman's *The Talley Method*, and F. H. Brennan's *The Wookey*.) The most often cited was Sherwood's, but most critics agreed that Sherwood depended somewhat too heavily on sermonizing. As Wolcott Gibbs said (and he was not always kind to Hellman) ". . . for the first time, as far as I am concerned (and I'm not forgetting *There Shall Be No Night*) the fundamental issue of our time has been treated with the dignity, insight, and sound theatrical intelligence that it demands."[12]

Hellman's activities on behalf of antifascist causes were in the limelight at this time, especially her money-raising efforts for the Joint Anti-Fascist Refugee Committee. This fact was not lost on some of the critics, both of the right and the left. She was both praised and damned by the communist press. In general, they praised her for being antifascist, but thought she should have been more positively procommunist. Some conservatives thought she should have called the play anti-Nazi instead of anti-

Fascist, unless she meant it to be interpreted as pro-Communist.

Hellman had taken voluminous notes on the history and background of events in Europe to prepare herself to write *Watch on the Rhine*. In addition to the notebooks and drafts of the play now to be found in the University of Texas Collection, Hellman made 400 to 500 more pages of factual notes—typewritten, single-spaced.[13] She must have drawn on this material for her next play about the war and American wartime attitudes—*The Searching Wind*.

4

OOOOOOOOOOOOOOOOOOOOOOOOOOOOOOOOOOOOOOO OOOOOOOOOOOOOOO

Bystanders

THE SEARCHING WIND

Like *Watch on the Rhine*, *The Searching Wind* sets off the microcosm of manners against the macrocosm of world events. When the two worlds impinged on each other in *Watch on the Rhine*, liberal upperclass Americans were "shaken out of the magnolias." In *The Searching Wind*, the magnolias are shaking, but the liberals hardly notice until too late. *Watch on the Rhine* was a play about action in crisis. This is a play about the inaction of bystanders, a cardinal sin in Hellman's morality. The inaction takes the form of appeasement and compromises, in love and war—in the private and the public world.

The play was baffling to many of the audiences; an explanation of the title might have helped. It was a quotation from Hellman's black cook and housekeeper, Helen, and is explained in *An Unfinished Woman*—"It takes a searching wind to find the tree you sit in." The sentence means, in effect, "Who can tell what side you are on if you don't know your own mind?" In the memoir the sentence applied to upperclass liberal attitudes toward racism, which to Helen seemed confused and unformulated. In these two war plays, some well-meaning, affluent Americans were shaken out of the manorial tree by the events of World War II—but the searching wind could not even find the tree that many others sat in.

In this play a "liberal" turns out to be one who cannot believe in villainy, and who in the name of caution, and keeping an open mind, made compromises with evil— i.e., with fascism, at the cost of lives of future generations. Three scenes take place in the present—1944—the year in which the action begins and ends. Three scenes take place in the past—1922, 1923, 1938. The flashbacks represent three political and personal crises in the lives of the three major characters. These are Alex Hazen, a career diplomat; his wealthy wife, Emily; and "the other woman," Catherine (Cassie) Bowman. At each crisis, Alex appeases the fascists, and his wife appeases her rival—her ex-best friend. Alex tries to appease both women, and to keep them both.

Outside the trio (as commentators on the action) are the old man—Moses Taney, Emily's father—and the young man—his grandson, Sam Hazen. Hellman often uses this arrangement of characters along an age spectrum —the old at one end, the young at the other, affecting or commenting on the action of the characters in between; e.g., Mary and Mrs. Tilford in *The Children's Hour*, Fanny and Bodo in *Watch on the Rhine*, Mrs. Ellis and Sophie in *The Autumn Garden*. Moses (who might have led the children of Israel to freedom, but did not) is a charming but disillusioned fighting liberal, retired editor of a once great newspaper. He has withdrawn from political decision-making himself, but comments bitterly on other people's diplomatic compromises. The grandson, Sam, is one of Hellman's soldier-boys who has finally found a purposeful life in the army, only to lose his best friend, his respect for his parents, and his ability to make war in the process.

The framework of present time opens and closes with the conflict between Emily Hazen and Cas Bowman. Hellman created curiosity, and no small amount of befuddlement, in her audience by having Emily invite Cas to hers and Alex's home in Washington—nobody knows why.

Then, through the subsequent flashbacks into the past we
are still unsure, until in the final scene, at the house a few
hours after scene one, we learn Emily's purpose. Let us
look at the flashbacks as a series of double crisis-confron-
tations.

Crisis one. 1922. Moses, his daughter Emily, and her
best friend, Cas, along with the Taney maid, Sophronia,
are visiting in Rome, where Alex Hazen is a young
diplomat in the American embassy. Mussolini is marching
on Rome, and Cassie is marching on Alex, whom Emily
expects to marry. Mussolini takes over. Alex agrees with
his boss, the American ambassador, that open opposition
to the fascists would be intervention in Italian internal
affairs. His failure to take a strong political stand pre-
cipitates a quarrel with Cassie. Though this is not known
to Emily they have been lovers and have thought of marriage. Now Cassie decides to return to her teaching job
in America for a year to think it over. Emily's response
to Cas and her challenge is that of passive resistance—
to stay in Rome where Alex is. (It works, and she
catches him.)

Crisis two. Berlin, 1923. It is the time of the first
organized antisemitic riots. Emily is married to Alex, and
Cas has made it a habit to follow them (and to see Alex)
when she is on vacation in Europe. The scene takes place
in a Berlin restaurant where Alex is waiting for Emily,
and (unknowingly) being watched by Cas at another
table. The noises of riot and threats against Jews are
heard outside the restaurant. Emily comes in shocked by
the spectacle she has just witnessed of German ex-soldiers
beating up old Jews. Alex's response to the crisis is to
calm down the people in the restaurant and to blame the
riot on the negligence of the police. He is refusing to face
the complicity of the police in the antisemitism.*

---

* In an earlier draft of the play, Hellman had included another
character, a German captain of the Freikorps, an illegal fascist

Emily sees Cas and is polite. Cas takes the offensive and accuses Emily of having stolen Alex from her. Emily claims not guilty—Cas and Alex had already quarreled. Emily offers friendship—reconciliation, appeasement.

Crisis three. The third double confrontation takes place in Paris in 1938, when the Munich agreement—the archexample of appeasement of Hitler by Britain and France—is about to take place. Alex must send his recommendation to the United States government. Again, he refuses to believe in evil and corruption, even when a Nazi attempts to pressure him into trying to keep France and Britain out of war with Germany. He holds out hope that Hitler may keep his promise not to annex more territory after the Sudetenland, and supports Chamberlain's efforts to keep "peace in our time."

Emily also wants peace at any price, now in politics as well as love. She does not want to send her son to war. She and Alex quarrel—then make peace—about her hobnobbing with pro-Nazi European socialites, including the banker with whom she has deposited some of her money. (The money is a sore point with Alex, who does not like to think of himself as rich or as subject to the influences of wealth and position.)

But Cas, at Emily's invitation, has been to see Alex. Before Emily arrives, they have arranged a rendezvous. Alex has decided that he loves Emily but is "in love with" Cas. When Emily comes, she tells Alex that as she entered she saw Cas in the lobby, but was afraid to confront her. And thus, she leaves Alex in the hands of the enemy, as Chamberlain—and Alex—left Europe.

In the last scene, which takes up the 1944 action again, Hellman brings all the confrontations together, the women, the war, the generations. It turns out that

---

army of ex-soldiers. He challenges Alex, and Alex throws him out of the restaurant. Hellman dropped this scene, probably because it showed Alex in too belligerent a light.[1]

Emily had invited Cas to the house in act one in order
to have it out with her once and for all, to accuse her
directly of husband-stealing. Now Cas breaks down and
tells Emily that the accusation is true: she had been out
to get Alex away from Emily and to punish Emily for
marrying him. Alex agrees to let Cas go—without a struggle, and he relaxes with his wife.

The major confrontation, however, is between Sam
and his elders. This, too, has been hanging fire since the
opening scene. We learned there that Sam had been
wounded; now we find he must lose his leg. In spite of
his grandfather's efforts to educate him, Sam is not an
intellectual—he trusts action and sincere human relations,
not words. He had felt at home in the army with fighting
men, and especially with his friend, Leck, who was killed
in the same battle in which Sam was wounded. His war
experiences have made him ashamed of his family of
"bystanders" and now he tells them why.

He is ashamed of his grandfather, the great liberal,
who now just sits back and watches; of his father who
went along with Munich; and of his mother with her
rich pro-Nazi friends. Then with an almost apologetic
patriotism, Sam accuses his parents of damaging the
country which he loves:

> "I don't want any more of Father's mistakes, for any
> reason, good or bad, or yours, Mother, because I think
> they do [the country] harm. . . . I am ashamed of both
> of you, and that's the truth. . . . I don't like losing my
> leg . . . but everybody's welcome to it as long as it
> means a little something and helps to bring us out some-
> place. All right. I've said enough. Let's have a drink."

The public did not seem to be troubled by the implied impotence in that speech, and its final "let's have
a drink." The play ran for 318 performances, almost as
long as *Watch on the Rhine*. Most people could respond
to Sam's commitment to his country, unlike his father's

vacillation, signified by his sacrifice in the service. But a brave gesture and denunciation of his elders hardly provides a solution to the problem those elders faced.

The critics, on the whole, were not kind to the play. They had good reason. Neither the theme, nor the plot structure, nor the characters ever came completely clear on the stage—and they take considerable analyzing even on the printed page. The theme of compromise was simplistic; some critics thought Hellman was too hard on Hazen. One questioned why she believed that there was "a moral difference. . . . between Chamberlain's attempt to turn Hitler East and Stalin's attempt to turn him West."[2]

Most critics thought the love triangle silly and trivial—not worth all the mystery about it—and I tend to agree. The characters of the women are never clear—that's part of the mystery: which is the bad one? Cas is intelligent, and idealistic in her insistence that Alex take a firm stand: John Gassner called her "high-minded,"[3] but her actions are certainly not high-minded as she herself confesses. But since the obscurity of the play may partly be the result of private images and allusions, such as the title, the clue to Cas Bowman's character may be in her last name. In the memoirs Bowman is the name of some wealthy cousins whom Hellman disliked. (Sophronia, the name of Hellman's black nurse in New Orleans also appears in the play, and no doubt there are other significant names.)

In the 1960s Hellman told an interviewer that she hated "theme" plays. She apparently decided to abandon them after this one—if not in adaptations, at least in her original work. Her political activity in liberal or left-wing causes became separate from her playwriting. *Another Part of the Forest* followed *The Searching Wind*. Then came an adaptation from the French of Emmanuel Roblès, *Montserrat*, another play about compromise and

the heroism of those who are willing to die for their convictions. But Hellman's next original play, *The Autumn
Garden*, concerned itself with individual persons, bystanders who try to come to terms with what they have
made, or failed to make, of their own private lives.

THE AUTUMN GARDEN

It is customary for critics of Hellman's later plays to call
them Chekhovian, and to distinguish between the realism
of Ibsen and that of Chekhov. Any direct influence of
Chekhov on Hellman is hard to ascertain—her edition of
Chekhov's letters was not published until four years after
The Autumn Garden was completed. But "influence" or
not, the distinction between Ibsen and Chekhov is interesting because it roughly parallels that between the "despoiler" and the "bystander" plays.

Ibsen's realistic plays are strongly plotted around an
idea or social problem. His characters oppose or react to
each other in a series of confrontations, building toward
a climax.

Chekhov, on the other hand, emphasizes mood, not
plot. As a critic of *The Autumn Garden* said, "He did
not reveal his people. He invited them to be self-revealing.
Their plight did not raise ethical questions. His characters were victims of themselves; wandering egos, frustrated and despairing, who lived in a constant state of
spiritual cross-ventilation. . . ."[4]

Any summation of the "plot" of *The Autumn Garden* is a summation of the characters, those slightly faded
flowers clustering together for protection in a boarding
house—a summer resort, modeled on one Hellman had
visited. It is also reminiscent of the boarding house that
had been run by her aunts, Hannah and Jenny. (In an
early draft of the play, two sisters were the innkeepers.)

Hellman, unlike Chekhov, has more scorn than pity

for these passive characters. The only two in the play who have any vitality are a tough-minded old woman who will never wither until she dies, and an equally tough young girl, who knows what she wants and gets it when she hears the loud knock of opportunity.

When the curtain rises, representatives of all the major clusters, except one, are on stage. Of course, they are waiting for the missing set to arrive. At the Tuckerman house now are Constance Tuckerman, the owner, a plucky but romantic southern lady who was left impoverished by her supposedly wealthy parents, and converted the family summer home into the boardinghouse. One of her most faithful summer boarders is Edward Crossman, a middle-aged intellectual who was once in love with Constance, and who now finds his chief solace in alcohol. Constance has a young niece, Sophie, daughter of her brother and his French wife. Sophie's father died during the war and Constance thought it her duty to rescue Sophie from poverty in a French village. Now Sophie helps her aunt with the work at the boardinghouse.

Sophie is engaged to Frederick Ellis, a young man who is staying at the Tuckerman house with his grandmother and his mother. The grandmother, Mrs. Mary Ellis, holds the family purse strings and knows the power of her wealth. She dominates her daughter, Carrie, who in turn dominates her son, Frederick. The engagement of Frederick and Sophie is acknowledged between them to be a matter of convenience. Frederick will give Sophie financial security, and she will give him a home and respectability. Carrie approves since she feels instinctively that Sophie is no rival. Frederick's real emotional interest, however, is in Payson, a male writer whose work he is editing, and who has a dubious reputation. Some critics have called Frederick a "passive-dependent" mother's boy, who is latently homosexual. But nobody in the play, except possibly his mother, considers the inclination to be latent. The Ellises—Grandmother, Mother, and Frederick

—are planning a trip to Europe, without Sophie. Frederick is determined to invite Payson to go as his guest.

The other regular summer boarders are General Benjamin Griggs and his wife, Rose. Rose is a comic character, pathetic but childish and silly. Her husband wants a divorce, and plans to leave her whether she divorces him or not. Griggs has his own Oedipal hangups: he had always wanted love from a serious woman like his mother. To get even, Rose boasts of a love affair she had when the general was away during the war. But Griggs is beyond caring; he just wants out.

Into this garden comes the serpent, Nick—the old Nick—Denery and his rich ninny of a wife, Nina.* Nick is to be the *deus* (or *diabolus*) *ex machina* whose meddling in the lives of others "shakes them out of their magnolias." He goes from group to group making trouble. His only motive is to display his charm and use his power to manipulate others. He flirts with all the women, but when they begin to respond, protects himself against any commitment. He has been doing this for years to his wife who sees through it, is sick of his meddling and philandering, but cannot make up her mind to leave him.

Nick's first victim is Constance Tuckerman, who was once so in love with him that she rejected Ned Crossman. Twenty-three years before, Nick, an artist of sorts, had painted Constance's portrait. Now he cruelly persuades her to let him paint her again. His plan is to retrieve from her the original portrait and exhibit the two together. Nick dresses Constance in rags, and in the portrait, paints her as a sad, povertystricken old woman. (A reading of Henry James's short story, "The Liar," reveals some inter-

---

* The name, Denery, appeared in *An Unfinished Woman*, attached to a boy who had hit Lillian (about age 12) in a tug of war, and whom she repaid by a blow on the head with a porcelain coffeepot. There are other suggested connections between characters from the memoirs and those in *The Autumn Garden*, but they will have to be identified by future Hellman biographers.

esting parallels.) All the time he keeps up a lie to Constance that he, Nick, really loved her when he married Nina, and still does, but that Ned Crossman still loves her too and wants to marry her. Nick will not allow Constance to look at the new portrait of herself; now he encourages her to fantasize about Crossman.

Nick then turns his beneficent attention to the Ellises. He informs Carrie that he had seen Fred in the travel agency, booking passage to Europe for Payson. Nick warns Carrie that Payson was involved in "a filthy little scandal in Rome." Carrie thanks him for the information (which could be false scandal-mongering) and faces Frederick with it. He still insists on taking Payson with him. But his grandmother forces Carrie to tell Frederick that he can leave on the trip with Payson, but must "make clear to his guest that his ten thousand a year ends today and will not begin again." The threat works. Payson backs out of the trip if he has to pay his own way. Frederick is heartbroken.

Nick's wife, Nina, has been through this type of thing often before. He can never leave things alone. She says to him, "I can smell it: it's all around us. The flower-like odor right before it becomes faded and heavy. It travels ahead of you, Nick, whenever you get most helpful, most loving, and most lovable." And she threatens to leave him as she has done before.

Nick has tampered also with the Griggs's marriage. He comforts Rose by flirting with her. For his trouble he gains her confidence and the promise of a $5000 commission to paint a portrait of her homely niece. Rose is ill, is beginning to feel amorous toward Nick, and asks for his advice. He suggests that she go to a doctor—not to be cured, but to be certified that she is truly ill so that her husband will not leave her.

It is Nick's philandering, plus alcohol, that brings the plot to a climax, and the characters to their senses. Nick has been drinking throughout act two. He makes advances to Sophie, who is trying to get to sleep on the living-room sofa, then passes out on the couch before anything can happen. Sophie simply leaves him there and spends the night in a chair across the room. There is an uproar when the two are discovered by Mrs. Ellis and others in the morning. Hellman works hard to convince us that this is a catastrophe. Everyone in that little town will hear the gossip and think that Nick has seduced Sophie. Sophie makes use of her advantage, and in so doing, indirectly returns all the others to the reality of their situations.

Nick, himself, is out of the action. Now that he is in disgrace, Nina comes back to him and the truth about her is revealed. She needs to punish and be punished. Nick tells her, "You needed to look down on me, darling. . . . You like to—demean yourself." (In *An Unfinished Woman*, Hellman gives this characteristic to Dorothy Parker.)

The Ellises try to persuade Sophie to go to Europe with them, but she refuses. Frederick has stopped moping about Payson, but Sophie knows, as does old Mrs. Ellis, that Frederick will always be his mother's boy. Sophie also knows that she must have another source of income now. From Nina she demands $5000. Otherwise she will spread the word that Nick seduced her. With the money she will be free to go back to Europe to help her mother.

Nick was right about Rose and Ben Griggs. When Ben knows that she is ill, he gives in to Rose's appeal that he take care of her. For Ben escape is not possible; it is too late. His speech of self-insight was written by Dashiell Hammett, and Hellman said that it summarized the philosophy of the play. (And it does sound like what John Mason Brown called the "spiritual cross-ventilation" of Chekhov's characters.)

"There are no big moments you can reach unless you've a pile of smaller moments to stand on. That big hour of

decision, the turning point in your life, the someday
you've counted on when you'd suddenly wipe out your
past mistakes, do the work you'd never done, think the
way you'd never thought, have what you'd never had—it
just doesn't come suddenly. You've trained yourself for
it while you waited—or you've let it all run past you
and frittered yourself away. I've frittered myself away,
Crossman."

Now it is Ned Crossman's and Constance's turn for
self-knowledge. Ned faces the fact that he has wasted
himself—has become a drunk, living in a room and passing the day until night when the bars open. This is not
because Constance turned him down, as he once persuaded
himself, but because he "wanted it that way."

Constance has decided that she wasted herself, too,
waiting for Nick when she really wanted Ned Crossman
all the time. She asks him to marry her but it is too late.
He is sorry that he had deluded her and himself into
thinking he was in love with her. The curtain falls on his
declaration:

CROSSMAN: . . . Sorry I fooled you and sorry I fooled myself.
And I've never liked liars—least of all those who lie to
themselves.

CONSTANCE: Never mind. Most of us lie to ourselves. Never
mind.

The only two characters in the play who have not
lied to themselves are the young and old realists who have
acknowledged the value of money, Sophie and Mrs. Ellis.
Sophie is building her future by taking action in the
present; the old lady built a triumphant past in the same
way.

The Autumn Garden had mixed reviews and ran for
102 performances. It was revived in the winter of
1976 at the Long Wharf Theater in New Haven, Con-
necticut. Walter Kerr, who had some faults to find with
the original production, was fulsome in his praise of this

one. He pointed out that the emphasis had changed somewhat in the two productions. In 1951 Sophie's blackmail
had seemed melodramatic, but in the new production it
becomes (as it is in the script) a way for Sophie to keep
her dignity. She will not accept charity. She insists that
she be credited with blackmail.

A few critics, especially among literary scholars,
have seen optimism and compassion in this play. As for
the optimism, Hellman said in a newspaper interview
that the characters in the play led empty lives, but that
"the play isn't meant to say that people can't do anything about such emptiness. It is meant to say the opposite—they can do a great deal with their lives."[5]
That is, if they start soon enough. But she emphasized
that at middle age "if you have wasted what you had in
you, it is too late to do much about it."[6] So one can be
optimistic about life if one is *not* like the people in the
play; if one takes hold of some clear commitment and
works toward it.

The problems of the characters in *The Autumn
Garden* are individual and personal. There is no cosmic
background of war or politics, no ethical decisions to
make as in *The Searching Wind*. The concerns of these
people are all of the kind that Cassie Bowman called
"frivolous," and Hellman seems to agree with her. Harold
Clurman, who directed the original *Autumn Garden*,
speaks of Hellman's "feelings about most of us of the
educated near-upper class. We are earnest, we yearn, but
we are not serious, we have no clear purpose. We have
no binding commitments to ourselves or to others; we
are attached to nothing."[7] And Clurman added that Hellman's attitude toward her characters was almost cruel
compared to Chekhov's feeling for his. "The blunderers
in Chekhov are brothers in our nobility even as in our
abjectness. The characters in *The Autumn Garden* are
our equals only in what we do not respect about ourselves."[8]

Hellman has always been a doer—impatient with
thinkers or perceivers or flounderers. Her old anger
against evil and injustice in the early plays seems now
to have become a general irritability and petulance toward human inadequacy. She deplores failure through
lack of direction, self-discipline, or energy—"wasting
time." At the end of *An Unfinished Woman* she explains
what she meant by the title: "All I mean is that I left too
much of me unfinished because I wasted too much time.
However. . . ." Most readers, of course, thought what
Hellman wanted them to—if *she* wasted time, how about
me? In any case, the time-wasting characters of these two
plays, *The Searching Wind* and *The Autumn Garden*,
have been given their implied "however" too, but that
is the extent of Hellman's compassion.

In the years between *The Autumn Garden*, 1951, and
her next and last original play, *Toys in the Attic*, 1960,
Hellman tried her hand at adaptations[9] of plays in a less
realistic mode than her own. These were difficult years
for her—the House Un-American Activities Committee
hearings, Hammett's jail sentence and subsequent illness
and decline, the loss of the farm, the Hollywood black-
listing. In 1954 she edited the collection of Chekhov's
letters.[10] Her introductory essay and the three brief prefaces to groups of the letters are warmly admiring of the
Russian dramatist.

Hellman's adaptation of *The Lark*, a play about Joan
of Arc by the French playwright, Jean Anouilh, was completed and performed in 1955. *The Lark* had been translated by the British poet-playwright Christopher Fry
and performed in London earlier that same year with
moderate success. Fry's version was more literary and
philosophical than it was dramatic. Hellman worked with
other translations, tightened the action, simplified the
language, and turned the play into exciting theater, with
a first-rate part for Julie Harris as Joan. Like *Montserrat*,

the play appealed to Hellman's love of a good fight and her admiration of the honorable professional soldier. She saw Joan more as a modern career woman than as either saint or peasant. *The Lark* was Hellman's most successful adaptation; it ran for 229 performances.

The following year saw the production of *Candide*, subtitled "a comic operetta based upon Voltaire's satire." Hellman wrote the book for this elaborate musical; Leonard Bernstein did the music and Richard Wilbur, a talented and distinguished poet, wrote the lyrics. Other geniuses who had a hand in the production were John Latouche, Dorothy Parker, and the director, Tyrone Guthrie. Hellman spent a year of hard work on *Candide*, testified to by the many manuscripts, including twelve complete versions, in the University of Texas library. Ultimately, however, there were too many chefs to produce a *chef d'oeuvre*. Hellman's narrative line gradually diminished in importance, but when *Candide* closed after seventy-three performances, and nobody could fault the music, lyrics, dancing, etc., they blamed the failure on what was left of Hellman's book.

If musical comedy was alien to Hellman's talent, so was her final adaptation. It was an off-beat, zany, satirical comedy about middle-class Jews, called *My Mother, My Father, and Me*, and based on the novel, *How Much?* by Burt Blechman.[11] The play failed, but before the fiasco, Hellman had already begun to draw on her own life for materials, rather than on other people's work. By 1960 the imaginative use of memory, which was eventually to lead to her second career, had contributed to the success of *Toys in the Attic*.

TOYS IN THE ATTIC

Toys in the Attic is Hellman's last original play to date and her most textured and complex. The texture is not

simply a result of intricate plotting, but of many-layered,
often ambiguous characterization. Still, the play is less
Chekhovian than *The Autumn Garden*, and more like the
old Hellman, full of mystery and melodrama.* The characters muddle their way toward a kind of self-insight,
like those in *The Autumn Garden*, but the truth about
them turns out to be bizarre and the plot ends with a
violent climax. In contrast to Hellman's active villains
like the Hubbards or heroes like Kurt Müller, these characters are what I have called bystanders. They do not
intend evil or opposition to evil; they are hungry only for
love, and their need for it, sometimes confused with the
need for money, accomplishes their fate.

The idea for the play had been suggested to Hellman
by Dashiell Hammett, as she tells us in *Pentimento*. The
play was to center on a man—"Other people, people who
say they love him, want him to make good, be rich." He
does, and then discovers that they really don't like him
rich. He thwarts his own success and ends up worse than
he was at the start. Hellman tried to develop the idea, but
found that she could do it only if she could write it about
the women around such a man—the people who thought
they wanted him to succeed but actually needed him to
fail.

The man in question is Julian Berniers, thirty-four, a
good-looking ne'er-do-well who has been raised by his two
doting older sisters, Anna and Carrie, in the family house
in New Orleans. After several business failures, Julian
marries Lily Prine, a rich young girl whose mother,
Albertine Prine, has given them $10,000 as a wedding
present. The couple moves to Chicago, and Julian invests
the money in a shoe factory, which, like his previous

---

* One critic, Jacob H. Adler, alleged that Miss Hellman had
modeled the characters in *Toys in the Attic* on those in Chekhov's
Three Sisters.[12] According to Moody, however, Miss Hellman said
that the idea "had never crossed her mind."[13]

ventures, fails. But he returns to New Orleans mysteriously wealthy, carrying $150,000 on his person. He and Lily arrive at the sisters' home laden with gifts. Julian is now in command; he has bought his sisters the things that he and they always thought they wanted: tickets to Europe, fancy clothes, a new piano, a new refrigerator, and a deed to the house. (He has paid the mortgage.) Julian has even taken it upon himself to write letters of resignation to his sisters' employers. (There is something of the meddling do-gooder in him, like Nick Denery of *The Autumn Garden*—another weak man married to a rich wife.)

Julian's money, with his new independence, threatens to undermine the lives of all the women who claim to love him. His two sisters had complained of their lot, but now that they can sell the house that they have always hated, and travel, as they have always wanted, they feel lost. Anna, the more sensible and honest of the two, faces the fact that they have always lived for Julian, have always needed him to be dependent upon them. She has seen also that Carrie's possessiveness of Julian has masked an incestuous longing for him.

Lily, Julian's wife, adores him, but her love is also destructive, of both Julian and herself. She is a child, chronologically twenty-one, but mentally and emotionally about twelve. She is torn between satisfaction in the knowledge that her money had originally made Julian dependent on her, and fear that he might have wanted *only* her money. The thought that her mother might have sold her to Julian to get rid of her is intolerable, second only to her fear of losing him. Lily is in a state of near-hysteria throughout the play, never knowing where she stands with either her mother or her husband. Her terror and her fanatical attempt to discover what she calls "truth" accidentally bring about the catastrophe at the end of the play.

Although Albertine, Lily's mother, has always found her daughter a nuisance, she did not pay Julian to marry

her—he was in love with Lily. Hellman explained Albertine in an interview, while she was still in the process of
writing the play: "She's a very rich lady. She's always
wanted to get rid of her daughter. . . . So the marriage
has delighted her, and she's the only one who feels sort
of sorry for this poor bastard [Julian] and she'd like to
see him keep the money and keep the girl for that matter,
too."[14] Albertine's lover is her mulatto chauffeur, Henry
Simpson, whom Lily hates as a rival for her mother's
affection. Henry understands the situation, and does what
he can to help the mother and daughter communicate.

Most of acts one and two are taken up with unanswered questions to keep the audience guessing: Why
do the characters behave as they do? Who is a mysterious
woman whom Julian has been seeing, and who calls him
at the house? Where did Julian's wealth come from? The
end of act two provides most of the answers. Julian made
the money in a real-estate deal financed by his ex-mistress,
Charlotte Warkins, the "mystery woman." He had been
her lover long ago, and now they are friends. Charlotte
needs money to escape from the husband she has long
hated. She has put up the cash for Julian to buy two
cheap parcels of swampland, which she knew would be
indispensable to her husband, Cyrus, in a business venture. When the play opens, Julian has sold him the lots
for the hold-up price of $150,000, a share of which will
go to Charlotte. We discover that Charlotte is part black,
a fact unknown to her husband.

The knowledge of Julian's past sexual relationship
with Charlotte Warkins throws Carrie into a frenzy, and
heightens Lily's hysteria. Carrie's feelings turn into hatred
for her sister when Anna makes Carrie face the truth of
her incestuous love for Julian: "You want to sleep with
him and always have." Lily's wild jealousy is intensified
by the fact that Julian has been impotent since they have
been in his sisters' house. Whatever the clinical cause—
the emasculating presence of his sisters in the house, or

as Anna alleges, his unconscious awareness of Carrie's tabooed "lust"—Julian thinks of the condition as temporary. He loves Lily, who had never threatened his manhood, and thinks that all will be well when he and Lily have gone away together, the house has been sold, and his sisters dispatched abroad. He goes happily off to wind up the transaction—to meet Charlotte and give her her share of the money.

The women left behind are apprehensive—Lily that Julian may not come back to her at all, and Carrie that he will leave with Lily. Anna has determined that she will go to Europe without Carrie, and makes her exit to pack. (This is the most vital exit in the play. Without it the catastrophe could not take place.) In the tense scene that follows, Carrie satisfies her jealousy by allowing Lily to believe—without actually saying so—that Julian married her for her money and will now leave her for Charlotte. With pathetic, childlike reasoning, Lily decides to beg Charlotte to give her one more year with Julian, and if he still loves Charlotte after that she can have him. Carrie stands by while Lily telephones Cyrus Warkins to ask him to give her message to Charlotte. Lily reveals the whole story, including the fact that Charlotte is of mixed blood. Carrie is silent, except to supply the crucial information that Julian and Charlotte are now meeting at Sailor's Lane near the depot. Warkins sends his men there, and they beat and slash the couple.

Julian limps home in a state of collapse. All his new-found confidence is gone: he cannot understand how he could have "assed up" this simple deal. Lily's mother finally listens to her when Lily confesses, "Mama, I did it." Albertine—still sympathetic to Julian—begs Lily to keep the secret to herself, not to "kill him with the truth." Julian seems defeated now, for good, even when he says, "Got to start again." The sisters hover over him; Carrie is now the smiling decision-maker, the boss, even though Anna—apparently—will stay. The child bride stays, too, with a promise from Albertine that if Julian discovers the truth, Lily can always go home to mother.

I have given only the bare bones of the plot and the barest sketch of the characters, whom Hellman identifies with many interesting "tags": Anna has headaches, Carrie likes to visit the cemetery, Lily walks around in her underwear and speaks a kind of inarticulate baby-talk. The really complex action of the play is not so much in the plot, as in the shifting relationships between the characters, and the morality—or lack of it—that seems to guide them. The destruction of Julian is accomplished in the name of "love," but that love represents a compulsion that neither Carrie nor Lily can control, and that Anna, finally, cannot resist or escape. Carrie, of course, knew exactly what she was doing when she let Lily make that telephone call; the defeated Julian and Lily would henceforth be in Carrie's power. Nevertheless, she too is a victim. Alan S. Downer, critic and historian of the stage, put it this way: "She is what evil must always be, the other side of good, tragic because she cannot know of her enslavement, because she can never have the opportunity to escape."[15]

Hellman places the burden of evil on Lily, as well as on Carrie, just as she does on all of the moral weaklings in her plays, and later, the memoirs. Her judgment is summed up in the speech that Albertine calls her "goodbye present" to Lily: "The pure and the innocent often bring harm to themselves and those they love and, when they do, for some reason that I do not know, the injury is very great."

To a theater audience, as to a first-time reader, the characters in *Toys in the Attic* keep about them an air of mystery as, no doubt, Hellman intended. Some of the mystery can be cleared up, however, by reading the early drafts of the play, and by relating these to the materials now available in Hellman's memoirs. This is *not* to say that any character, or group of characters, in the play is drawn literally from life, or that the memoirs "tell all." But some puzzles are clarified, particularly that of the relationship between the two sisters, and of the peculiar behavior of Lily and her relationship to her mother.

In the play, the older of the two sisters, Anna, is the more intelligent, the more independent and humorous. Carrie, the younger, is prettier and more feminine—in a fluttery way—but she takes control in the end. The two women appear to the reader or audience to be entirely different, but in the play, Albertine says that she confuses them: "Strange. Sometimes I can't tell which of you is speaking. . . . It is as if you had exchanged faces, back and forth, back and forth."

In an early draft of the play Anna had been called Hannah. Any reader of the memoirs will see a superficial resemblance—without hint of abnormality, however —between Hellman's two aunts and her father, and the sisters and Julian. The two aunts seem clearly differentiated from each other in the memoirs; but Hellman noticed in them their similarity, as well as the same inexplicable turnabout in supremacy that takes place between Anna and Carrie. In *Pentimento*, there is this revealing paragraph:

I suppose all women living together take on what we think of as male and female roles, but my aunts had made a rather puzzling mix-about. Jenny, who was the prettier, the softer in face and manner, had assumed a confidence she didn't have, and had taken on, demanded, I think, the practical, less pleasant duties. Hannah, who had once upon a time been more intelligent than Jenny, had somewhere given over, and although she held the official job. . . . it was Jenny who called the tunes for their life together. I don't think this changeabout of roles ever fooled my father, or that he paid much attention to it, but then he had grown up with them and knew about whatever it was that happened to their lives.

Toys in the Attic plays imaginatively with the notion of what *might* have happened to similar lives.

The memoirs contain other hints about characters and situations in *Toys*—after all, many of them started out as toys in Hellman's own attic. Sometimes, she said, they appeared in the plays without her conscious knowledge: she had not realized, for example, until it was pointed out to her, that her great-aunt Lily, whose mulatto chauffeur had been her lover, had provided the "seed" of the character of Albertine Prine. Hellman's surprise at this realization may sound a bit disingenuous, but except for the lover, there is little similarity between Aunt Lily of the memoirs and Albertine. (There may be more of grandmother Sophie Newhouse in Albertine, and something of Hellman's mother in Lily—a rich girl who was afraid of her mother and married to a poor man.)

Probably the most puzzling and incredible of the characters in *Toys* is Lily—but there she is in *An Unfinished Woman*, as twelve-year-old "Lillian." The panic-stricken jealousy—the fear of losing love; the ambivalence toward money and its power; the simplistic, fanatical allegiance to what she called "truth"—all were stages in Hellman's own adolescence. She, too, became incoherent under stress, and prone to self-injury. While the incident of the seance and the "knife of truth" in the play does not appear in the memoirs, it is typical of the kind of adventure young Lillian had in her pursuit of truth in New Orleans.

Toys in the Attic is both troubling and fascinating to read, and was a great success on the stage. As literature, however, it seems to need the memoirs too much—it is too incomplete and elliptical on its own. Characters that are mysterious or improbable in the context of the play become clear and credible only in the memoirs. And of course, contemporary critics lacked this tool for reference. Their judgments of the play were often contradictory—what one critic liked, another deplored. Some thought the first two acts were overplotted, others thought they dragged, and nothing happened until act three. But on the whole the critics welcomed the professionalism of a Hellman play, and considered *Toys in the Attic* to be one of her best. So, also, did the audiences; the play ran for 556 performances, second only in popularity to *The Children's Hour*. It won the Drama Critics Circle Award for the best American play of the season.

In looking back at Hellman's work as a playwright, it is tempting to try to reduce all her plots and characters to repeated formulas and types. Such an exercise can be performed, of course, on any writer's body of work, but the demands of the stage and of her favorite genre, the realistic well-made melodrama, make Hellman's plays particularly vulnerable to this kind of analysis. I have already pointed to some similarities in structure and character-ization in the plays, but more interesting is the moral point of view that unifies both the plays and the memoirs. This is her concept of both active and passive evil, the sins produced by both commission and omission.

Herman Melville, whose work Hellman had read and taught, must have seemed a kindred soul to her in his portrayal of evil in *Moby Dick*. Like Melville, Hell-man watches evil fulfill itself not only through the de-moniac—through the mad avenging Ahab—but also through the "mere unaided virtue" of the first mate, Starbuck, and the good-humored ignorance and medioc-rity of the Stubbs and Flasks of this world.

The characters who endure in Hellman's world, are those who live their lives according to inner rules of decent behavior—of not making trouble for other people and of facing the truth when others are deluded. They are an often helpless minority, but they tacitly affirm the existence of goodness in the face of evil. In *Moby Dick* the lone survivor is the outcast, Ishmael. But he owed his life and that "survival," with all its connotations, to his friendship with the noble savage, Queequeg. The equiv-alent of Queequeg in Hellman's work are the blacks, the servants who are really the masters and mistresses because they can withstand hardship, and because they see the truth under appearances.

These characters began with Agatha in *The Children's Hour*, appeared in some form in *every* play, ending with probably the most minor character of them all, Gus, the black iceman in *Toys in the Attic*. When he advises the sisters to get themselves a nice cat, now that Julian is gone, he has spoken more truth and wisdom than ever entered the heads of the other characters. This kind of earthy insight was to be the touchstone of value in the memoirs, where it came to Hellman through two black women, Sophronia and Helen.

III

The Memoirs

5

Form and Theme—
"Through This Time
and That Time . . ."

Hellman's interest in the theater and playwriting waned
in the early 1960s. She had begun to establish herself as
a teacher of creative writing and literature and to explore
the materials and forms that would shape the memoirs.
The process had already begun, of course, when she
dipped into those materials for *Toys in the Attic*, her last
original play (to date).

As each volume of the memoirs appeared, it was
heralded by previews—excerpts published as articles—
and by much promotional fanfare. New work by Hellman
was front-page material for the Sunday *New York Times
Book Review* and major journals and newspapers throughout the country. All three volumes became bestsellers,
commanding the attention (if not always the approval)
of the critical as well as the popular readership. *An Unfinished Woman* (1969) won the National Book Award
in the category of Arts and Letters. *Pentimento* (1973)
became a Book-of-the-Month Club selection, and *Scoundrel Time*, after twenty-three weeks on the best-seller list,
set off a controversy that lingered for months in newspapers and literary journals. Hellman's achievement
brought her a multiplicity of new awards and honorary
degrees. Scheduled to appear soon was the film based on
"Julia," a chapter in *Pentimento*; Hellman had been
offered over a half million dollars for the film rights to
the series.[1]

Most readers responded to the books not as great literature, which reviewers sometimes made them out to be, but as a group of entertaining stories, some about well-known people and past events, but most of them about a person—or "persona"—named Lillian: a neurotic, rebellious character who stumbled from turned ankle to turned ankle in the general direction of heroism. But Hellman's memoirs have a deeper dimension, and so, of course, do the portraits of herself and others.

An Unfinished Woman is subtitled "a memoir" and *Pentimento* "a book of portraits." But the differences in mechanical structure are more apparent than real. The first book is built as a narrative, not strictly chronological, but still chiefly linear in movement from past to present and back again, relating events and persons to time and to each other. The second, *Pentimento*, is constructed as a series of portraits, each a unit, including group portraits and landscapes. But *An Unfinished Woman* also contains portraits—the last three chapters are the essays on Dorothy Parker, Helen (Hellman's cook and friend), and Dashiell Hammett. And the portraits in *Pentimento* are strung together in a loose chronological sequence, over the same time span as *An Unfinished Woman*.

Differences in the forms of the separate chapters or portraits are also deceptive. At first glance they seem to fall into three categories: the cluster of anecdotes or brief reminiscences grouped around a period or a subject; the diaries; and the dramatic tales—short stories told dramatically, like plays or film scripts. But a closer look reveals that the anecdotes may be clustered to illustrate a theme, and a diary may turn out to be a mysterious quest or a dramatic tale.

More interesting than the way Hellman organizes her materials is the way she sees them. The books are memoirs, rather than autobiographies, because their concentration seems, at least, to be upon the ambience of the writer rather than upon the writer herself. True, they reveal the author, but in carefully selected times, places, and company. Even in the anecdotes and diaries she is both narrator and protagonist, in a series of short, self-contained dramas.

As speaker and actress, Hellman is the principal unifier of the memoirs, but recurrent settings and characters also help to unify the books as they did her life. The bayou and the city of New Orleans, the sea near Cape Cod, the farm in Pleasantville, New York—any or all of these may surface to memory as she records an event that takes place in New York City or Hollywood or Moscow or Spain. Hellman's parents, her New Orleans aunts, her black nurse, Sophronia, and her cook, Helen, and always, of course, Dashiell Hammett, are somewhere in the background even when the immediate story is not theirs.

Hellman's professional life in the theater and in Hollywood is given relatively little attention in her memoirs. Most of the expected backstage gossip and theatrical name-dropping is confined to one chapter in *Pentimento* with some incidental references where they are relevant. For Hellman's books do not belong in the stream of theatrical memoirs that flows from Fanny Kemble to Tallulah Bankhead, any more than they do to the sensational confessions of Tennessee Williams. Her work is much more in the tradition of the autobiographical writings of such literary artists as Stendhal, in *The Life of Henry Brulard*, W. B. Yeats in his *Autobiography*, and Henry James in *A Small Boy and Others* and *Notes of a Son and Brother*.[2]

Central to these memoirs, as to Hellman's, is the concept of the writer as portrait painter, seeing himself and others in shifting lights, from varied angles. The act of remembering is inevitably selective, and the result, for whatever reason—unconscious suppression, perhaps—is often vague. But the purpose of a memoir for these artists is not total recall, or historical accuracy, but as Henry James put it, "to evoke the image and repaint the scene," although past and present may be confused (or fused) in the same scene, which James said, "glimmers out of a thin golden haze."[3]

The picture painted by the memoirist, then, is part memory, part imagination—often arousing speculation in both the writer and the reader as to which is which. Hellman's purpose was never to write historical biography; she said that she did not want to be the "book-keeper" of her life. Time and again she will preface her materials with such comment as, "I have no clear memories of those days, those years, not of myself where and when, not of other people. I know only that . . ." etc. This is not simply an excuse for inaccuracy: it implies also that what is worth remembering, will be, and that the self-portrait of the writer may be painted in what he chooses to remember.

But Stendhal and James were novelists, and Yeats a poet. Their memoirs are discursive, rambling philosophically between remembered events. They do not limit themselves to tight construction—to any line of "plot" or "character"—but let their wit and imagination roam freely over the past and present. Lillian Hellman, however, is a playwright: a maker of tightly constructed theater pieces, and the best of her memoirs are tales told by a playwright—with plot, character, and carefully paced suspense. Her biography provides a narrative line on which to hang the separate, loosely related episodes; and if some of these owe their mechanical structure to the well-made play and the film script, they owe their thematic, or symbolic structure (when it is there) to a combination of sources—including nineteenth-century American fiction, psychoanalysis, and Christianity.

Hellman's style has often been called elliptical, as indeed it is. She may withhold information at one time, to release it later for dramatic effect; or she may leave us with an unanswered question: "What could they have been talking about?" or a tentative suggestion of an answer. But more often, she leaves the reader with a sense of a mysterious undercurrent of meaning. Some critics have called her style "portentous" (suggesting that it is also pretentious) while others have called it "mysteriously exciting." When the mysterious undercurrent is successful, a "figure in the carpet" (as Henry James called it) gradually emerges. The reader finds that the meaning of events, the motivations of characters, the selection of a setting, all coalesce in a pattern that illuminates the whole.

But "mystery" in Hellman's work serves many purposes, from the subtle to the obvious. Her teaching of Herman Melville to college students must have taught her some of the uses of ambiguity: she seems to believe as Melville did, that ambiguity often presents a truer version of our perceptions than could clarity or sharp distinction. Melville, like other writers, often attempted to understand himself and his characters in the light of myth and ritual, and came up with pre-Freudian psychoanalytic insights, and pre-Jungian archetypal images. Hellman is influenced by her knowledge of the methods of literary symbolism and by her own predilection toward the religious mythic interpretations of experience, and not least, by her own experience of psychoanalysis, with strong religious associations.

The language of the memoirs is what Hellman would call "pretend cool." It is casual, slangy, objective, humorous, self-deprecatory. But these qualities are often deceptive. Sometimes they are masked, restrained expressions of intense and often irrational angers, fears, conflicts. No one knew the destructive danger of these emotions better than Hellman. In the memoirs she often mentions her debt to Dr. Gregory Zilboorg, the psychoanalyst who helped her understand and live with this part of herself. It was to him that she dedicated *Another Part of the*

Forest. Some of the family ghosts that she laid to rest in that play and *The Little Foxes* rise again in the memoirs.

Zilboorg was a prolific and distinguished writer, whose *A History of Medical Psychology* (with George Henry) is still a definitive text. At one period in his life he had also been a drama critic, and had translated Andreyev's *He Who Gets Slapped.* But one of Zilboorg's major interests lay in exploring the relationship between psychoanalysis and religion. *Mind, Medicine, and Man* and the posthumously published *Psychoanalysis and Religion* are collections of his essays on the subject. In these he tried to reconcile the two disciplines. Psychoanalysis and religion, he said, were two different, equally necessary "systems" and by no means incompatible. They had been considered mutually exclusive—chiefly because of Freud's atheism (Freud had called religion an illusion) and the psychological determinism of many of his disciples. Zilboorg thought that Christian doctrine and ritual could be helpful both to the analyst and his patient. He himself had been born a Russian Jew, but became a devout Roman Catholic.

In 1964, when she was in Israel reporting on the Pope's visit to that country, Hellman was reminded of Zilboorg by a Dominican priest who knew Zilboorg's work. Her response to that memory and to the face of the priest echoes through all the memoirs:

The fervent words, the intense face, took me back a long way, to the time when I was seven or eight years old in New Orleans and wandered one Sunday morning into a church whose denomination I don't remember, and possibly never knew, and was so moved by the sermon I didn't understand that I ran from the church crying to be good and never sinful, and fell down the steps and went on home, screaming, to have my knee fixed, knowing, as a child often senses the future, that I would all my life be stirred and comforted and discomforted [sic] by people of strong belief, and that I had better take myself along on home whenever that happened.[4]

One lesson, reflected in the memoirs, that Hellman must have learned from Zilboorg was his often repeated idea that love was essential to both religion and psychoanalysis: "[Religion] sees in love the means for ultimate salvation; [psychoanalysis] the means for ultimate health." But wherever Hellman got her "religious streak," as her friend John Hersey called it[5]—from her mother or the black women in her life or Zilboorg—it runs through the memoirs from the first chapter of *An Unfinished Woman* to the last chapter of *Pentimento*, and surfaces again in *Scoundrel Time*.

Nevertheless, these memoirs, obviously, are not religious, symbolic, or psychoanalytic documents. Some of them are simply anecdotal, freely associated recollections; others are, as I have said, dramatic tales drawn from a life, but not attempting a full chronology of that life, nor exclusively dedicated to biographical revelation. Hellman asks us to read a book about someone named Lillian Hellman, but to keep the character in the book and the author of the book separate. The narrator of the memoirs is also a *persona* or mask for the author, not necessarily a literal replica. The unity imposed on the work by this continuing *persona* never becomes completely clear to the reader—Hellman tells the truth but tells it slant (as Emily Dickinson would say). She consciously creates a legend and is as jealous of her privacy as she is conscious of the legend.

It is beyond the scope of this book—and the ability and intention of its author—to attempt a psychoanalysis of Lillian Hellman. Such presumptuousness always results in what Hellman called "Woolworth Freud." She has told us a great deal about herself in the memoirs, and I leave it to the reader to go beyond what is written there to find the "real" Lillian Hellman. She, herself, might say to the reader—with justice—"That is none of your business!"

The persona, the legend, is the same in all the books,

but each book is unique and deserves its own analysis. The most important difference between the two long books is in their thematic emphasis. *An Unfinished Woman* questions and explores the occasions and rites of initiation, the expiation of guilts, the meaning of suffering and survival—all of these in the context of a deepening insight into self. *Pentimento* seems to be thematically unified around the shapes of love: exploration takes the form of what Richard Poirier has called "emotional range-finding."[6] In the portrait chapters of *Pentimento*, Hellman ponders the nature of her deepest relationships to others. Of course, the two books combine or interchange themes at times: the last two chapters of *Pentimento* raise questions about suffering, guilt, and survival posed earlier in *An Unfinished Woman*. But this is an appropriate ending for the second book and brings the wheel full circle.

6

An Unfinished Woman

When asked about the writing of *An Unfinished Woman*, Hellman said,

It was *faute de mieux*, that book. I decided I didn't want to write for the theater, so what was I to do? I didn't want to do an autobiography—that would have been too pretentious for me. I had a lot of magazine pieces I'd done that hadn't been reprinted and I started to rewrite them. But I didn't like them. I thought, maybe now I can do better with the same memories.[1]

And she did. Some of the sections originating in magazine articles will be indicated below, but what Hellman selects from them has usually been transformed.

The organization of *An Unfinished Woman*, from chapter one through thirteen, is chronological. The last three chapters are portraits. The chronological chapters are arranged in pairs: each pair consists of a short introductory essay, followed by the actual story to be told. (In *Pentimento* Hellman avoids splitting the portraits into numbered chapters, but each one still opens with an introductory "exposition.") Hellman's childhood in New Orleans provides the material for chapters one-two; three-four take us through her early days in New York and her first job there; five-six cover her brief marriage, Hollywood, and first acquaintance with Dorothy Parker, Hemingway, Dashiell Hammett; seven-eight take her to Europe, and Spain during the revolution (1937). (Chap-

ter seven of *An Unfinished Woman* is further developed
as the "Julia" episode in *Pentimento*.) Chapter nine is
transitional, leading from the Spanish experience through
her own "turning toward radicalism." Chapters ten-eleven
cover her adventures in Russia in 1944-45; and twelve-
thirteen take her back to Russia in 1966-67. Chapters
fourteen, fifteen, and sixteen are the portraits of Dorothy
Parker, Helen (Hellman's friend and cook-housekeeper),
and Dashiell Hammett.

The chronological sections (1-13) fall into three
general periods: the southern childhood and adolescence;
young womanhood in New York and Hollywood—finding
herself emotionally and vocationally—and the European
adventures in Spain and Russia, spanning both past and
present—1937-1967. The sequence of these chapters is
obviously from youth to age; from the exploration of
beginnings and initiations to the later questioning of the
meanings of survival. But each initiation is a test, and
the passing of that test—no matter how early or how
tentative—is itself a "survival."

Typically, in the paired chapters of the memoirs, the
first provides background and speculation about the
meaning of a given period in Hellman's life: then the
"test" or event follows in the longer chapter. Chapter one
of *An Unfinished Woman* is a straightforward account of
her feelings toward her parents and others in the family,
including insights into her childhood, acquired much
later, after psychoanalysis. The actual escapades that made
for initiation and survival take place in chapter two.

Hellman always loved her father's family, especially
the two New Orleans aunts, Hannah and Jenny. Her
father was lively and charming, as were his sisters. Her
mother was quietly withdrawn, eccentric, hurt in many
ways by a dominating mother and a philandering husband, and deeply frightened by the "dangerously botched"
birth of her only child. She turned for solace to religion

—not caring which sect, just happy in a church. The mother's passivity and strange fears were irritating to the daughter, who was to spend a lifetime expiating her childhood guilt for that irritability, and for transferring love due her mother to the black wet-nurse, Sophronia, "the first and most certain love of my life."

Hellman's attitude toward her mother's wealthy family was complicated. On one hand she hated their money-based values, and their ill-gotten gains at the expense of the southern poor, black and white. But this was compounded with self-hatred when she saw in herself some of those same values and a need for the symbols of wealth and the life style it can buy. We have already seen the difficulties this family involvement made for Hellman in the writing of *The Little Foxes*. In *An Unfinished Woman* she says that "after *The Little Foxes* was written and put away, this conflict was to grow less important, as indeed the picture of my mother's family was to grow dim and fade away." The ghost of the wronged mother was temporarily laid to rest, as we have seen, in the characters of Birdie in *The Little Foxes* and Lavinia in *Another Part of the Forest*. But the same dybbuk is invoked and exorcised again in *An Unfinished Woman* in the sketch of the long-suffering, gentle mother, and Hellman's final statement, "My mother was dead for five years before I knew I loved her very much." That knowledge would have come in 1940, about the time that Hellman began her analysis with Zilboorg.

Hellman's childhood, she tells us, was torn by other conflicts and other guilts, many of which had to do with being an only child, demanding total love, and being insecure at the impossibility of having it; using her power over her parents to punish them, and ultimately herself. The most severe conscious life-long conflict, dominating her edgy relationships with others, took the form, even in childhood she says, of "the stubborn, relentless, driving desire to be alone as it came into conflict with the desire not to be alone when I wanted not to be." She realized early that for what she calls a "nature" like hers the way would not be easy. This self-knowledge came when, as a child, she made for herself a retreat in the great fig tree on the grounds of her aunt's boarding house in New Orleans. The narrative—or drama—begins in chapter two, with a description of Lillian in the tree.

On her annual six-month visit to New Orleans, from the time she was about eight until she was sixteen, Lillian would often skip school, climb the fig tree with her lunch and books and fishing pole, and spend the day there reading and spying on the passers-by below. Her flossy school dress and patent leather slippers hung on a twig to keep them neat until her return to civilization. Many American readers—women as well as men—have done something like this as a child, with the same ritualization of privacy and growth, even to the excitement of fishing in a muddy gutter for whatever life might be there. Some archetypal form of this experience appears throughout literature in memoirs and fiction. For Hellman it marked the beginning of a lifelong need for balance between the crowds and company of the city and the solitary one-to-one relationship of a human being with the natural world. The little feminine Huck Finn in the tree foreshadows the woman who lived with Dashiell Hammett on a farm with a pond in Pleasantville, New York; and later, the woman who divided her year between New York City and an island off Cape Cod. The fig-tree sequence in *An Unfinished Woman* is not completely serious in tone; it has its funny aspects.

The next New Orleans episode begins also as comedy: after a puppy-love affair and some experience with adult pecadilloes—namely, her father's—the fourteen-year-old Lillian runs away from home. But what follows is a tale of terror, narrated in the detached voice of a bemused adult. The young girl takes a nightmare journey through adolescence toward a religious and sexual initiation. She must find her way not only through the city but through hurts and jealousies and attachments that she does not understand.

The episode begins when Lillian's father scolds her angrily, in front of her aunts' boarders. Her first reaction to the scolding is prophetic: "My mother left the room when my father grew angry with me. . . . I sat on the couch, astonished at the pain in my head. I tried to get up from the couch, but one ankle turned and I sat down again, knowing for the first time the rampage that could be caused in me by anger." Lillian's mother tries to comfort her, but a piece of angel cake is no palliative for the imagined loss of a father's love. Lillian tramps off down St. Charles Avenue—a runaway with a few dollars in a little red purse. Her first adventure comes when she passes a mansion with a smaller version of itself—a doll's house—on its back lawn. A policeman approaches, and to escape him she hides in the doll's house. There she curls up among the miniatures of ornate furniture—a big little girl, like Alice down the rabbit hole.

From the symbolic doll's house, a step forward perhaps, from the womb, the young Lillian finds her next hiding place in a church—the St. Louis Cathedral. There she composed the prayer which she says was to become an obsession during the next five years: "God forgive me, Papa forgive me, Mama forgive me, Sophronia, Jenny, Hannah and all others, through this time and that time, in life and in death."

And from the church her flight takes her to the red-light district. Here she is frightened by some terrifying versions of adult sexuality—whores who shout at her and an old "flasher" who exposes himself. She buys food, and falls asleep with it behind some bushes, only to wake in hysteria when she sees two hungry rats staring at her. She runs back to the church, pounds on the door screaming, but no one comes. The night ends in the ladies' room at the railroad station. Lillian is suffering her first menstrual cramps. She throws away her soiled underwear, and her face in the mirror tells her, with a certain adolescent bathos, "I had gotten older."

She is finally rescued, as she was always to be symbolically rescued, by her surrogate mother, Sophronia. By mentioning Sophronia's name, Lillian has been taken in for the night in a boarding house in the black district. There she sleeps soundly, and wakes to find Sophronia and her father at her bedside. Her father finally apologizes for the scolding, but makes her feel guilty when he adds, "You should not have made me say it." And this evokes her penitential prayer, "God forgive me, Papa forgive me, Mama forgive me, Sophronia, Jenny. . . ." When her father hears what she is saying, he asks—and it's a significant question—"Where do we start your training as the first Jewish nun on Prytania Street?" It has already started, of course.

Lillian tells her father at the end of this chapter that she is "changing life." She has experienced not only intimations of adulthood but also a new insight into the power and the problems of an only child. And equally important, the escapade gave Hellman a "useful and dangerous" lifelong theory of survival: "If you are willing to take the punishment, you are halfway through the battle. That the issue may be trivial, the battle ugly, is another point."

If this were fiction, the symbolic pattern might make the tale too pat, too allegorical. Lillian is almost a female counterpart of Nathaniel Hawthorne's Robin, the young initiate in "My Kinsman, Major Molineux." But we cannot quarrel with Hellman's memory—or dreams—and certainly not with her craftsmanship. It is a great yarn, wittily told, with much more charm than this outline of the "pattern" would suggest. Indeed, it is not until we reach the Russian diaries, the chronicle of another journey a half century later, that we find again such symbolic literary structure.

The rebelliousness against authority that led the child Lillian through the streets of New Orleans, grew more intense in her late teens and is with her still—still making trouble for herself and other people, in spite of Sophronia's advice, "Don't go through life making trouble for people," and Hellman's own efforts to control it. Some of her anger was channeled into the plays, where it is often given a moral or political base. That moral indignation is also in the memoirs, but in *An Unfinished Woman* and *Pentimento*, Hellman faces the fact that moral indignation may at times be only a mask for personal pique, for irritability at an insult or an invasion of privacy. Often—not always—the old prayer for forgiveness is implied, even as she smashes a chair or slaps a face.

The saving grace from either diatribe or sentimentality is the wry, often rueful humor with which Hellman looks at herself. This is the tone of the chapters that take us through her first job, her brief marriage, the Hollywood experience, and the trips to Europe in the 1930s. We learn very little here or in *Pentimento* about her intellectual development as a writer; but her vocational progress in that direction began with her job in publishing.

Life at Horace Liveright's was notable chiefly, as I have said, for the variety of its parties, which contributed to Hellman's social and sexual education. (Her encounters with authors and manuscripts were interesting but incidental.) It is in the context of the Liveright situation that she uses the term "pretend cool" to describe the attitude of her generation toward sex. She had no patience with the prurient curiosity of some of the older "flaming youth" about her own generation, nor with the weepy romantic sentimentality of some of the "lady writers."

But her own cool was all pretend. At nineteen, just before taking the Liveright job, she had had a brief "affair" (the quotation marks are hers) with a young man who seemed to be using her to make his best friend jealous. "The few months it lasted," she says, "did not mean much to me, but I have often asked myself whether I underestimated the damage that so loveless an arrangement made on [sic] my future."

Some of the anecdotes about life at Liveright's are hilarious, but underneath it all is the serious fact that she became pregnant and went through a stoic, lonely abortion (to the admiration of her colleagues). A half year later she married the man involved, Arthur Kober. Neither an affair nor marriage, nor romantic love was ever to be a happy experience for her. The long association with Hammett had some bad times; it was an indispensable fact of her life for thirty-one years, but hardly "happy" or passionately "romantic." There were connotations in her father's joking reference to the "Jewish nun on Prytania Street" that would be echoed later in references to Hellman—by Hellman and others—as a "Puritan" or "Calvinist." The terms applied not only to her "religious streak" but also to a shyness or uneasiness about sex, her protestations to the contrary notwithstanding.[2] But Hellman's inhibitions were more of a nuisance to her than an obsession: she had too many other fish to fry. Romantic love could be—as it was in the plays—a silly, potentially destructive force, best ignored.

Hellman remembered the years of her marriage and her introduction to Hollywood as foggy, tedious, uncertain. It was not until she met Hammett, was divorced, and began to write in earnest that her life took a real direction. The chapters (5-6) in *An Unfinished Woman* on this period begin with Hollywood, then flash forward and backward in time, wherever associations lead. The 1929 visit to Germany receives only slight mention. References to later European trips serve, here, only to pinpoint her meetings with the temperamental, flamboyant older generation of writers who clustered around Gerald and Sara Murphy, their hosts and patrons.

Hellman treats us to some fine gossipy anecdotes about feuds between Hemingway and Fitzgerald, Hammett and Hemingway, Dorothy Parker and Hemingway, Dorothy Parker and Hammett. But she never felt a part of this group; they were too ego-involved, too hypocritical.

It was witty, all of it, but I remember feeling awkward: my generation was perhaps all round duller and certainly less talented, but loyalty, or the rhetoric of it, had come back into fashion with the depression, and these . . . remarkable people . . . came from another world and time.

Some of the most important events of Hellman's personal "world and time" at this period are postponed until *Pentimento*—especially her beginning success as a playwright and the story of "Julia." In *An Unfinished Woman*, the European trips of 1934 to 1944 and after, are concerned with Hellman's growth in relationship to events in Spain and Russia. She writes as a sympathetic outsider in Spain in 1937, and in Russia in 1944-1945. But on her return to Russia in 1967, the world that interests her most is her own; the "nature" of the aging visitor, not the country visited. Her initiations; her survivals— what have they meant?

The Spanish adventure takes the form of a diary; daily entries made in 1937 are remembered, parenthetically, in 1968, but the action of the narrative takes place in 1937. Upon her arrival in Spain, Hellman was briefed on the political intricacies of the revolution, told the progress of the war so far, the atrocities, the numbers of casualties, but this is not, she says, how she learns things, and not the way she tells them to us. Her learning took place in encounters with human beings as they endured the bombings, the hunger, and all the losses of war.

But in spite of many vivid, stirring moments, the essay is marred by suggestions of mystery that never take shape into a pattern. In the intricate design of this "carpet," there is no underlying "figure," or I haven't seen it. Hellman remembers the human dramas, but she tries too consciously to use the techniques of theatrical drama to present them to the reader. She will introduce a character or a group in one diary entry, pose a question about them, and leave the reader cliff-hanging for the answer until a later entry. Sometimes there is no answer: a mystery or premonition may be suggested when characters are introduced but may never be resolved or defined.

Of course, some of the memorable portraits are not mysterious: the hungry people—peasants, city people, guests in expensive hotels—all famished. In Hellman's experience, they are willing to share what they have and grateful for the few things others would share with them. She met engaged, dedicated writers such as Gustav Regler, Otto Simon, and, of course, Hemingway with his apparent enjoyment of the "fireworks"—the bombing of Madrid—and his reluctant macho approval of Hellman when she braved the bombardment in order to make a radio broadcast.

But the reader remains taunted by the fuzzy, ominous characterizations. Who—or what—is that strange couple —the man in black and his companion, the "nun *fanée*?" (Hellman meets them at intervals in Valencia; then seeks them out before she leaves.) What is all that talk with this couple about religion, leading up to a final sexual shocker? Are these Jamesian decadent—if not incestuous —Europeans, near relatives of Teck (himself partly out of James) in *Watch on the Rhine*? Or—oh, no—are they a parable of Franco and the Church? And what about the young Frenchman named Pascal whose sickness and death conclude the chapter? Who *is* the father that he will not see—the waiter? And does he refuse the last rites because, in his delirium, he thinks he is in Spain and the church there is corrupt?

Maybe the 1938 diaries were just too far away for Hellman herself to remember what they "meant." The overtones of mystery and the techniques of melodrama cannot keep them from looking like literary patchwork. The patches are pasted, however, against a background of the pervasive themes of initiation and survival. The Spanish war enforced Hellman's knowledge of the reality and the imminence of death. She carried with her still in 1968, a *memento mori* in the form of some ornaments taken from the wreckage of a bombed-out Spanish home. And then, from Pascal and from the young wounded soldiers in the International Brigade, she learned—and was to relearn from her friend "Julia" and from Hammett—that imprisonment, suffering, death itself are not too much for some people to pay in the service of an ideal. And that such a martyrdom has always been, in mystical or religious terms, its own "survival" or implicit resurrection.

Hellman is groping toward this knowledge in the Spanish interlude just as she is groping her way toward her own kind of radicalism. She knew that she had become seriously politicized late. Hammett had influenced her, of course, but one source of the tension between them was her inability to align herself with any specific revolutionary cause. "Rebels," she explains, "seldom make good revolutionaries, perhaps because organized action, even union with other people, is not possible for them."

The trip to Russia in 1944 was apparently not the product of radical political convictions. Hellman had just collaborated on the rather innocuously pro-Russian film, *North Star*; two of her plays were in rehearsal in Moscow, and both Washington and Ambassador Litvinov thought that she would make a good cultural emissary. Her official, but strictly civilian status was to give her entry into high diplomatic circles as well as to the fighting front.

The prelude to the Russian diary is a vivid, sometimes funny, chronicle of the harrowing two-week flight to Moscow. Hellman was the only passenger on the Russian two-engine plane that took off from Alaska to fly across Siberia. She was treated as the guest of honor—as far as that was possible—and her "escort" and translator was a nineteen-year-old Russian boy who spoke almost no English and called her "Miss Hell." The plane was unheated, the trip bitterly cold, and Hellman arrived in Moscow with not only her usual sprained ankle, but a bad case of pneumonia—among other ailments. The wartime deprivation and suffering of the Russians, however, impressed her more than her own, and this chapter (9) ends on a familiar note: Hellman sees the greatness of the human spirit in what it is capable of surviving. A young Russian soldier who had been shot in the face tried to smile at her through his mutilation—"It was in the next few hours that I felt a kind of exaltation I had never felt before."

The Russian chapters do not lean entirely on the diary form as did the Spanish chapters, although some paragraphs do have dateline headings. Hellman never stays very long with the actual time period of the diary, but slides forward into the present as she writes, often comparing what she remembers now to what the diaries recorded then. 1944-1945 is remembered in 1966-1967 (chapters 12-13), but both are seen in retrospect from 1968. The unifying movement is between retrospection and introspection, and as the narrative proceeds, introspection becomes the dominant mode. The years of 1944-1945 are seen in retrospect; those from 1966 move increasingly inward; their subject is less the past than it is the present, less the outward event than the inner life of the memoirist.

The visit to Russia in 1944-1945 had been described by Miss Hellman in an article in *Collier's* magazine, "I Meet the Front Line Russians" (March 1945). That contemporary report and this one in *An Unfinished Woman* are almost (with the exception of a few passages) entirely different. The *Collier's* article begins with a glum description of the five-day journey to the front, but then turns into a cheerful narrative about two girls (Hellman and her translator) on a great lark to the Russian lines. They are entertained by the gallant soldiers, who are sick of fighting and cheered by the presence and the admiration of the two young ladies. The article was slanted for the slick magazine in which it appeared, and presented a friendly, optimistic view of our wartime Russian ally.[3]

The friendship with Russia is still there, in *An Unfinished Woman*, but the picture has changed drastically. Hellman stayed at the ambassador's mansion, but spent much of her time those first weeks in Moscow at the Hotel Metropole, "a grubby joint, but lively" and inhabited mostly by foreign journalists and businessmen. The escapades of the hotel's inhabitants make up a series of "comedy dramas," as Hellman calls them, whose very triviality provides relief from the hungry winter outside.

The tone of the visit to the front is now somber. The cheerful girl is preoccupied by her fear of the journey, which finally yields to a kind of resignation when she is on the train and "in other hands." The Russians are kind; they appear as characters in a drama, with clearly differentiated personalities. But over them all—Hellman and the soldiers—hangs the specter of the German occupation, brought home to her by the dreadful remains at the ovens in the concentration camp at Maidenek. This horror diminishes all other fears. Hellman joins the Russians in their anger and disgust at the Nazi deserters—

former Storm Troopers—who tried to grovel or lie their way into Russian protection. This later version of the 1944 journey is more angrily anti-Nazi than it is cheerfully pro-Russian.

The chapters on the return to Russia in 1966 and again in 1967 incorporate reminiscences of previous years. Events in Russia in 1966 take Hellman back to events of 1944; and these, in turn, lead forward to memories of life on the farm at Pleasantville, of Hammett, and of the House Un-American Activities Committee hearings in 1952, that brought the loss of the farm and a change of fortune for her and for him. These times and memories seem to be freely associated, but they have an agonizing impact upon Hellman. The images, again, form variations on the theme of survival—on what it means to have lived through pain and punishment and loss. To face these remembrances with self-insight is to raise the inevitable questions of one's responsibility for the past, whether guilt or credit. And to look at that past in the context of a long lifetime, one continuum in which past, present, and future make a whole, is to face also the future—to face age and change. This is what happens in these last two chapters of the memoir as narrative, before Hellman leaves it for the portrait form.

She remembers that as the plane landed in Moscow, in 1966, she found herself crying, and wondering why. "What fragment at the bottom of the pot was the kettle-spoon scraping that it had not reached before?" She knows that the first level of disturbance is the knowledge that she is aging; that the woman who made the plane trip across Siberia in 1944 would never have the strength to do that again. But this kind of self-pity is not in character for her, and she laughs herself out of it, momentarily at least, when she hears the unidiomatic English of the Russian stewardess's announcement of the landing: ". . . . We have come to the end of the road and we must take our parting. . . ." Hellman suggests to the stewardess that she find a less mournful sentence. But the stewardess resents the correction, and her angry face becomes to Hellman the face of a big bullying girl in New Orleans who used to hit her when she was six. Hellman rejects that image with, "I said to myself, to hell with this memory nonsense," and goes forward to meet Raya, her old friend and interpreter of twenty-two years before.

But this memory nonsense will not go to hell—will not be suppressed—just at a word. The threatening face of the stewardess introduces a long series of images of injury, loss, and survival, all finally summarized in the ironic truth of the landing speech, "we must now take our parting," however that may be interpreted. The images flow through Hellman's dreams, waking her at night, disturbing and crippling her daytime life. They occur in her meetings with others—Raya, Tanya, Captain K: long-time Russian friends who have also suffered losses, imprisonment, or mutilation—real and metaphorical— and have witnessed the same and death, for friends and lovers.

Is it Hellman the memoirist or Hellman the novelist manqué who in a gloomy hotel in Moscow finds herself digging up her own "frozen roots"? And who, on that same boozy sleepless night, knocks over a large china figure of a Greek athlete and crawls around the floor trying to find his broken hand? Only to dream then of hers and Hammett's injuries and losses; and to remember the injury she may have done—but had to do—to her father. One incident takes her back twenty years to a memory of Gregory Zilboorg's telling her that her father was senile and must be hospitalized. "He [her father] blamed me for his being in the hospital and thus I lost my father, as he lost his mind, for two years before his death."

The theme of the strong man—father, husband, lover, friend—brought low by injury or age or weakness is reflected in Hellman's own psychic wounds and moves throughout this chapter to the end. Her good friend, Captain K, the Russian soldier whom she had met in 1945 when he was "just out of the hospital after a bad leg wound," greets her in Moscow in 1966. His leg wound was serious, but worse for him was the loss, during combat, of the thesis on American literature that had been his lifelong interest. Hellman tries to help by discussing American writers with him and promising to send him books. Their talk lingers on male novelists— Hemingway, Faulkner, Mailer. One wonders at the coincidence that all three writers were intrigued with the theme of mutilated or impotent strength. And Hellman and the captain also discuss the great film director, Serge Eisenstein, whom Hellman called "one of the most forceful and brilliant men I have ever met"—and whom she still admired after she learned of his weaknesses.

When Hellman meets Captain K again in 1967, they are like two old wounded soldiers. This time they talk about her and the problems she does not really want to talk about—her aging, her sense of mistakes and loss. The captain asks about Zilboorg, and Hellman replies vaguely that she supposed the psychoanalysis helped. Her old cantakerousness is still there, even when she tells him the truth: "I don't like the theater any more and yet it is what I do best. I have cut myself away from it, don't go much, don't learn, don't even want to. And I am getting old and I can't understand how that happened to me."

The last entry in the 1967 diary recounts a visit to the hospital bed of the Russian poet, Olga Bergholz. Hellman is uneasy and irritated until she discovers that she has been reminded of another writer, Dorothy Parker, also lying ill at the time in America. And she goes back to the hotel to write Dottie a letter to cheer her up—she was to die six weeks later. The comic letter that Hellman wrote that night in Moscow was found among Dorothy Parker's few papers and is printed in full in her portrait, the first of three to conclude *An Unfinished Woman*.

"Dorothy Parker"

Like Parker's own work, the portrait is a mixture of wit and pathos. The friendship of Dottie and "Lilly" spanned a period of thirty-six years. It began with dislike, but ripened into understanding and acceptance, on both sides, of each other's quirks—of which there were many. They never agreed on some subjects, especially men, but they were nourished by each other's company and enjoyed each other's sense of humor.

In a newspaper interview, Hellman said that she could never have done that portrait if Parker had been living. "She'd have been pained. We had an elaborately polite relationship—I don't think we said an unpleasant thing in all the years."[4] Parker is usually remembered as the author of sophisticated, polished, and quotable verse, and, as a person, for her gaiety, her mischievous humor, and sharp repartee.

Hellman does nothing to damage that image in the portrait, but there were other truths about Parker, and Hellman presents them with tact and affection. Saddest was the self-destructive quality of some of Parker's clowning: Hellman says she "wanted the put-down from everybody." Then there was her drinking, some early suicide attempts, and chronic disorganization. Toward the end, Parker misplaced—or hid from herself—some large uncashed checks and was convinced that she was poor. But even this delusion comes off as a sort of gallantry in Hellman's eulogy: "She never had much, but what she had she didn't care about, and that was very hat-over-the-windmill stuff in a sick lady of seventy-four."

Parker is a character in the *dramatis personae* of *An Unfinished Woman*, and the image we have seen of her before this, in early chapters, may be more light-hearted, but it is not inconsistent with the final one. In the last years, when Parker was writing little and drinking much, Hellman found her company depressing, saw less of her, then blamed herself for neglecting a brave, still wisecracking invalid. But Parker never doubted Lilly's friendship, and made her the executor of her small estate. Hellman's tribute captures the contradictions in Parker's personality: her need for both success and failure, for love and rejection, admiration and scorn. Dorothy Parker summed up her own character in the much-quoted lines:

Three be the things I shall have till I die:
Laughter and hope and a sock in the eye.

"Helen"

Helen Jackson, Miss Hellman's friend and cook for twenty-odd years, is the subject of the penultimate portrait. If it had been placed last—as the "ultimate" portrait —"Helen" would have closed the circle from Hellman's New Orleans childhood to the present—1969, the time of writing the memoir. For this chapter concerns not only Helen, now dead for three months, but Sophronia, who had died thirty years before. As the images of the two women merge in the writer's mind, the time-gap between them closes.

In actuality, the two black women were individual personalities, but as symbols of a cultural phenomenon of the American south, and of forces in Hellman's life, they flow together in this dreamlike narrative. Only an American southerner close to Hellman's age could understand the subtle intermingling of love and hate between and among southern blacks and whites, especially in this stormy period of integration and black liberation.

The essay is a form of the dramatic tale, constructed in scenes like a film script. It begins with a dreamlike reverie, leading to a dream sequence in which the characters of Helen and Sophronia blend, then separate, as first one, then the other, dominates the action. There is a long flashback to Hellman's childhood, with Sophronia as the setter of standards, but the protagonist throughout the film script is really Helen, that "far-out Christian lady." Her generosity, her refusal to hate—or to acknowledge that she does—constitutes her own kind of pride and activism. This truth about Helen's character comes home only slowly to Hellman, the antagonist in the drama.

The process of discovery starts where it often does for Hellman, in recollection of her love of the sea and her childlike pleasure in the life of ponds and streams and the shore's edge, whether in New Orleans or a half century later at Martha's Vineyard. One need not know the Freudian or Jungian interpretations of water imagery to watch Hellman always linking it with initiation, survival, and insight—birth, death, and symbolic rebirth. In the beautiful opening reverie she acknowledges that digging about on the shore is like digging in one's unconscious, in dreams, for what might lie there, to find on awakening "the answer to a long-forgotten problem."

One stormy night in Cambridge, Massachusetts, when Hellman was teaching at Harvard, she was awakened by the crash of a ceiling light to the floor. Still half asleep, she stared at the shattered lamp on the floor and remembered poking about on the beach and finding a mangled watch there. (A Daliesque image if ever there was one.) It had belonged to Helen, who had concealed from Hellman the fact that Hellman's dog had brought the watch to the beach. "She didn't want to tell me that my dog, who loved her but didn't love me, could have done anything for which he could be blamed." The meaning of the recollection is suddenly clear: "Of course . . . they were one person to you, these two black women you loved more than you ever loved any other women: Sophronia from childhood, Helen so many years later. . . ."

Hellman sees a difference in her relationship to the two, however. Sophronia was always the protector, the tolerant loving mother and strict judgmental father in one.

Helen was the loyal generous friend and equal, whose combination of love and judgment often angered Hellman. There was guilt toward Sophronia—Hellman had not gone to her funeral. But then she had not known when Sophronia died, and her sin of omission was inadvertent—but to Hellman guilt is always too complicated to be expiated by simple cause-and-effect reasoning. Sophronia would have expected her at the funeral and she should have been there. But the guilt to be expiated in the present narrative is that arising from her anger toward Helen. It also involves inadvertent "omission," a failure of insight, like that of the narrator in some of Henry James's fiction, who fails to comprehend the import of the behavior of others until too late. (Daisy Miller "would have appreciated one's esteem.")

There are complex reasons in the essay for the failure of insight and for misunderstanding on both sides. A liberal white is impatient with a conservative black, whose values are Christian and human rather than racial or political. As an angry white liberal, it is hard for Hellman to accept Helen's loyalty to some white people, even to herself. Helen claims that (as a good Christian) she has never hated. But Hellman tries to convince her that this is not true; she has hated, and in a way hates Hellman, her white employer. To her dismay, Hellman succeeds in arousing Helen's anger and rebellion—but not overtly against white people: only against the "slavery" of working for a demanding, unpredictable, erratic "northern" employer. Helen says she was a cook in the south; now she's a slave. Then it is Hellman's turn to rage. She calls Helen a liar, and stomps off to Katonah, New York, and Hammett. Then as usual, Hammett reminds her that she will be sorry for her anger: she realizes that there are some things it is too late for her and Helen to talk about, goes home, and they are reconciled.

In 1963, Hellman covered the freedom march of two

hundred thousand blacks on Washington under the leadership of Martin Luther King. Her report appeared in the
Ladies' Home Journal under the title, "Sophronia's Grandson goes to Washington."[5] (Some of that material has
been incorporated in this portrait of Helen, including a
long flashback to childhood and Sophronia.) But Sophronia's grandson, Orin, never showed up in Washington,
and when, in *An Unfinished Woman*, he is finally brought
to see Hellman in New York, he turns out to be a drug
addict—what Helen calls "a no-good punkie-junkie."
Helen does what she can to help Orin handle withdrawal,
and then sends him on his way. He gives no sign of any
intention to reform.

But Helen's anger is aimed not at the society that
could destroy a young man—as it had her own daughter
—but at the "big city" and the universal human weakness that has always yielded to temptation there. The
young uprooted black from the rural south has been destroyed by the urban north—just like the country boy
from New Hampshire in the melodrama *The Old Home-
stead*. The romantic pastoral is still alive and well in
Helen's consciousness. To Hellman she says, "South got
its points, no matter what you think. Even if just trees."
And, of course, with her own need for "trees"—or the
shore—Hellman must accept this, even if the sentiment
plays havoc with her liberal politics.[6]

Helen befriended other young blacks whom Hellman
had met in Washington and elsewhere. After Helen's
death, one of the young men, George, comes to see Hellman and tells her of Helen's generosity to himself and
others. This becomes the dramatic closing scene of a
screenplay. Printed in that form, the script might look
like this:

GEORGE: . . . Then she gave me one hundred dollars. Eighty-
five for me, she said, or wherever I wanted to give it.
Fifteen for Orin when I found him.

HELLMAN: *Orin? Orin?*

GEORGE: He's still hanging around. She always gave him a little money. But he ain't going to get this fifteen, 'cause I ain't going to find him. She was some far-out lady, Mrs. Jackson. Some far-out Christian lady.

HELLMAN: Sure was.

GEORGE: I hope you feel better. Next time I'm here, I'll come to see you. (exit)

HELLMAN: (to herself) But he never has come to see me again. (She looks off in the distance. Camera moves in tight on her haunted face. Ocean music from first scene up and over. Deep, slow pull–away shot of her figure as she bends down to pick up something on the beach. Fadeout).

"Dashiell Hammett"

The final essay, the portrait of Dashiell Hammett, had been written in 1965 as the introduction to *The Big Knockover*, a collection of Hammett's short stories. Before that, it had been published in *The New York Review of Books*. Hammett, as a presence, is well known to the reader of *An Unfinished Woman* by the time we reach this portrait. Nothing in it comes as a surprise, but as the essay swings between events of his life, and his illness and death, it also sums up the relationship between these two close but separate individualists.

Hammett once said that any biography she wrote of him would turn out to be "the history of Lillian Hellman with an occasional reference to a friend called Hammett." Actually, the portrait is somewhat more than that, but its subject is a relationship rather than a man. Hellman is her old loving/irritable self, able to tolerate just so much intimacy. And she is still the pupil, learning about herself and her craft from this tough disciplinarian and teacher. Hammett was a radical, not only politically, but in the sense that he had to go to the root of things. Throughout the memoirs we watch him help Lillian cut through her self-deceptions, even the well-meaning ones. Under his eyes she could never get away with undeserved self-righteousness.

The essay begins—more or less—with Hammett's illness before his death, then flashes back to their first meeting and the early years, highlighting remembered events in between (with no attempt to "keep books" of them all), and ends with the final illness. The first years were happy and creative, then became sad when his drinking got out of control; then more stable in 1948 when he stopped drinking altogether. It is during this period, from 1948 through the McCarthy years and his imprisonment in 1951, that Hammett emerges in her portrait as a figure of incorruptible integrity; a stubborn hero and patriot. He fought in two wars out of conviction; and found a kind of personal fulfillment in the army —just as some of Hellman's male characters do in the plays. Even his jail term fulfilled a need for him—he remembered the challenge of it, forgetting the deprivation and the illness.

The portrait of Hammett as a public figure, as the idealist, the disciplined writer, then recluse and eclectic reader, the invalid and beloved friend, is multi-dimensional and moving—but not as deeply so as the sections on Helen and Sophronia; or the portrait of "Julia" to emerge in *Pentimento*. Those essays are cries from the soul. "Oh, Sophronia, it's you I want back always. . . ." There is a sense of helpless emotional entanglement with the images of these women—they speak of need, pain, dependence. The essay on Hammett is more rational: it calls up the image of him as the generous good companion, the bulwark, teacher, sometime lover, almost husband. He never liked Helen—or Parker for that matter— as Hellman's father never liked Sophronia: a rival is a rival, acknowledged or not.

The thought of Hammett comes back to Hellman in

conscious recollection as "the most interesting man I've
ever met. I laugh at what he did say, amuse myself with
what he might say, and even this many years later, speak
to him, often angry that he still interferes with me, still
dictates the rules." The hot-headed student remembers the
cool teacher. But the image of the strong dark mother
moves in and out of dreams, day and night, with the
tides of consciousness throughout a lifetime.

7

Pentimento

The title of *Pentimento* is a term from painting: it alludes to the fact that as paint on canvas ages, an earlier painting or parts of one may show through. The artist has "repented" of his first effort and painted over it at a later time. In Hellman's words,

> Perhaps it would be well to say that the old conception, replaced by a later choice, is a way of seeing and seeing again.
>
> That is all I mean about the people in this book. The paint has aged now and I wanted to see what was there for me once, what is there for me now.

Like Henry James, she wanted to "evoke the image and repaint the scene" in past and present time. But in a recent interview, Hellman acknowledged her awareness of fictional or theatrical form in the portraits: "I wouldn't have chosen the people I chose without a feeling for fiction, some belief that what I was writing about was interesting or dramatic."[1]

The memoir form, of course, has supplied Hellman with the leeway for commentary and speculation that could not take place on the realistic stage, in a well-made play. She can be more cavalier with time and the sequence of events—moving backward and forward with associations; interrupting an action at a crucial point for suspense, as well as commentary. But these essays are still such stuff as plays (or movies) are made on. Four are

129

portraits: "Bethe," "Willy," "Julia," and "Arthur W. A. Cowan." The chapter on theater is the exception to the fictional or play form in that it consists of a series of brief "pictures, portraits, mementoes" related to Hellman's plays. The last long essay, "Turtle," is also dramatic, and in it Hellman returns explicitly to the theme of injury and survival. She concludes with a brief, short-story epilogue, "Pentimento," which takes us back to Hammett's death and Helen's.

The essay "Helen," in *An Unfinished Woman*, was the strongest link between that book and *Pentimento*. Its structure is that of a screen play, and its theme, questioning as it did the ways of love in the ways of Helen, illustrated Richard Poirier's concept of "emotional range-finding." Throughout *Pentimento* we watch Hellman trying to define her relationships, in the past and the present, to the people and events in the portraits. Such "range-finding" is predicated on an inquiry into the nature of love. The old anger and rebellion are still there, of course, but they now clearly represent the other faces of love—jealousy and the fear of losing love, coupled with a fear of love itself. Hellman's deepest lessons about love were learned from women—Sophronia and Helen, Hannah and Jenny (her New Orleans aunts), and now, in addition to the others, but not supplanting them, Bethe and "Julia."

"Bethe," like all the portraits, has two strands of plot—the story of Bethe, and the story of Lillian. The Bethe plot is a tale of adult love played against a backdrop of poverty and violence. But the education of Lillian by Bethe and her lover, and by Lillian's aunts, Hannah and Jenny, constitutes the major plot and unifying action or purpose of this "play." Lillian learns about two kinds of love: Eros, or sexual love, with its powerful influence on personality, from Bethe; and agape, or charitable Christian love, with its lesson in humility, from her aunts. The portrait opens with a retrospective prologue,

comparable to the brief introductory chapters before the
major essays in *An Unfinished Woman*. The narrative
proper begins with Hellman's memory of Bethe as a "tall,
handsome woman in her late thirties." She had been
brought to this country from Germany by wealthy cousins,
the Bowmans, who were also Hellman's distant cousins.
The Bowmans hoped that an arranged marriage with
Bethe might reform their profligate son, Styrie. But
Styrie soon abandoned his wife and went back to his old
habits; by way of gambling and unpaid debts, he became
the object of a Mafia contract. His violent fate at their
hands is understated—as is violence throughout the tale.
The understatement only adds to the shock: "Styrie was
found clinging to the fire escape with his right hand
because his left hand was lying on the ground."

But Styrie is no hero, and his final disappearance is
only the preface to Bethe's liaison with a mafioso named
Arneggio, who is destined to be butchered—literally—in
a gang war. Before the murder, however, the teen-age
Lillian, on her six-month visit to New Orleans, seeks out
Bethe, whom she finds mysterious and fascinating. During a lunch with Bethe in an Italian restaurant, Lillian
becomes aware of the love between her and Arneggio,
feels excluded and jealous, and storms out of the restaurant in a temper, typical of the adolescent runaway in
An Unfinished Woman.

Lillian's family enter the Bethe plot, by virtue of
their disapproval of Bethe's "common-law marriage," as
they call it, and by her aunts' fears for Lillian's safety.
Their fears are justified when, on the day after the murder
of Arneggio, the police catch Lillian, who is looking for
Bethe, at the site of the murder. The child and her aunts
are summoned to the police station and questioned. When
the police insist on an explanation from Lillian of her
presence at the scene of the murder she can only answer,
in a state of trembling panic, "I don't know. I read about
Mr. Arneggio last night. Love, I think, but I'm not sure."

The aunts persuade Lillian to stay away from Bethe, and she interprets this to mean that the family have rejected their cousin—have turned their backs on Bethe in time of trouble. To Lillian this is immoral—un–Christian.

Years later, after her divorce, and at the start of her liaison with Hammett, Lillian returns to visit her aunts, still nursing her resentment at their supposed rejection of Bethe, and defensive, now, at the probability that they will reject her too because of her own "common-law marriage."

She tells her aunts:

"I know that you will not approve of my living with a man I am not married to, but that's the way it's going to be."

"How do you know that," said Jenny, "how do you know the difference between fear and approve?"

"Because you deserted, sorry, you gave Bethe up, when she loved a way you didn't like."

But this twenty-five year old Lillian is mistaken on two counts: the real hangups about "the way Bethe loved" are not her aunts' but her own; and the shallow, unforgiving moral code is not theirs but hers. The aunts are hurt by her accusations, and reveal that they have always secretly befriended Bethe; had sacrificed to give her financial help during all the trouble. But they had kept their loyalty and charity to themselves. Here, as elsewhere, Hellman half-mocks her own persistent religiosity and "the high-class moral theory stage, from which I have never completely emerged." She has learned her lesson in agape from Hannah and Jenny, and that high-class morality of hers has taken a blow in the process.

The lessons about eros, however, are harder to learn, more complicated and ambiguous. Hellman had long felt that she somehow owed her relationship with Hammett to her knowledge of Bethe's love for Arneggio. But she is never sure whether that was a good thing or not. The closing scene of "Bethe" suggests that conflicts about love and sex that plagued Lillian at fifteen, still torment her at twenty-five.

After their revelation, the aunts take Lillian to see Bethe in her shack on the edge of town. The next day Lillian feels that she must return alone to talk to Bethe. But as she approaches the site of the cabin, she panics, turns and runs, suddenly coming to a swamp. "I heard things jump in the swamp and I remember thinking I must be sick without feeling sick, feverish without fever." When at last she finds a path out of the swamp, it leads directly to Bethe's house. In the yard stands Bethe, naked, hanging clothes on the line. Lillian pauses to admire the proportions of Bethe's figure, and Bethe, hearing the sound of the "wet, ugly, soil" of the swamp beneath Lillian, tries to cover herself with her hands.

The episode is a mixture of ugliness and beauty, revulsion and attraction. If there is a consistent pattern of symbolism in the essay as a whole, I have missed it; but this adventure is certainly recorded in the manner of Hawthorne. Bethe is a Hawthornesque Eve, after the fall —a sort of Hester Prynne, blossoming in a clearing at the edge of the dangerous swamp of sexuality. Lillian cries out, "It was you who did it! I would not have found it without you. Now what good is it, tell me that?" The reader can only guess what "it" is—presumably love between adults—and at the meaning of what follows. Bethe says nothing, but takes Lillian indoors, and gives her a cup of coffee—which Lillian promptly throws up. But she is not sick, she tells Bethe, "Just the opposite. It was that day in the restaurant, you and Arneggio—" but Bethe silences Lillian with a hand over her mouth.

Bethe seems to be happy enough with the man she now lives with. Hellman never sees her again, but recalls in the last paragraph—as the curtain falls, so to speak— an episode with Hammett when she tried to tell him that "Bethe had a lot to do with him and me." He doesn't understand, or doesn't want to, and in a fit of temper, she drives off to the beach at Montauk, Long Island, in the snow, coming back with a case of the grippe.

All this association of Bethe and Hammett with sickness—or fever—is never clarified completely, but it need not be. Whatever Lillian learned from Bethe would always prove to be upsetting. The forbidden fruit was indigestible.

And what she learned from Hannah and Jenny would always be disquieting, would always remind her of her own self-righteousness. The "first Jewish nun on Prytania Street" is still muttering her penitential prayer, having now reached the phrase, "Jenny, Hannah, and all others forgive me. . . ."

"Willy"

In the portrait of Willy the young Lillian is still trying to fathom adult relationships and to define her own nature. She is less successful here than in "Bethe." The teen-aged Lillian is the same one we've seen before— funny, jealous, prurient, romantic. But her older sister, Lillian a decade later, is incredible.

The territory explored by the fourteen-year-old in "Willy" begins with a closet full of family skeletons— mainly the wealthy Newhouse ones. Willy is Lillian's great-uncle, who is married to her mother's Frenchified aunt, Lily; he is the adventurer who involved the family in the United Fruit Company scandals, including the slaughter of natives in Central America. Ultimately he is caught smuggling weapons into the region to put down a native rebellion. But Willy has such charm and vitality that the teen-aged Lillian thinks of him as glamorous and picaresque, in spite of the opinions of her father and the Hellman aunts that he is a reprobate.

The portrait is rich with suspense and humor as young Lillian collects one gem after another of shocking information about Uncle Willy and his family. She learns that Willy has a Cajun girlfriend in the bayou; he has borrowed money from his wife and never returned it; his wife—Aunt Lily—takes morphine supplied to her by the mulatto chauffeur, who is also her lover. The son, Honey, is well on his way toward the "loony bin" for repeated rape. (But even Honey has enough sense to recognize, eventually, that his mother and her lover became characters in *Toys in the Attic*.)

Lillian has first-hand experience with Honey's sexual compulsions, and avoids rape—somehow typically—by sneezing. But most of her knowledge about the goings-on in Willy's family comes from her friend, the old ex-slave, Caroline Ducky, who lives in the attic and does "fine sewing." Her character is sharp, earthy, funny; she sees through all her white people, serving as a chorus, commenting on the action, and punctuating her comments with her favorite—and often appropriate—expletive, "shit."

Caroline Ducky likes Willy and befriends him in his war with the rest of the family, although she tells Lillian, "He ain't no man of God," and crosses herself. This, in a way, becomes Lillian's own attitude, here and later. When Willy invites her—at fourteen—to go with him on a hunting and fishing trip to the bayou, and when, on the way, he buys her boots and other supplies, including twenty-four handkerchiefs, she is ecstatic and falls in love with him. The ecstasy continues during most of the adventure, but turns to rage when she discovers that the Cajun mistress is very real and very intimate with Willy. After nursing her hurt at rejection, and furious at herself for being jealous, Lillian runs out of the bayou (as she did out of the restaurant and the swamp in "Bethe") and hitches a ride back to the city.

The Willy plot of this tale is beautifully done: Hellman draws unforgettable contrasts between Willy's two "families," the New Orleans decadents in their immaculate, pseudo-elegant house, and the Cajun hunters and fishermen in that rambling, filthy shack in the bayou. The bayou itself excites with its danger and seductive beauty. But the Lillian plot—her pilgrim's progress toward maturity—lacks a clear direction.

Lillian's love for Willy is perfectly convincing as an adolescent crush (or the stirrings of "perberty" as Hellman once called it), but here Hellman takes it seriously. Commenting in her own voice she says:

I was not ever to fall in love very often, but certainly this was the first time and I would like to think I learned from it. But the mixture of ecstasy as it clashed with criticism of myself and the man was to be repeated all my life, and the only thing that made the feeling for Uncle Willy different was the pain of that first recognition: not of love, but of the struggles caused by love; the blindness of a young girl trying to make simple sexual desire into something more complex, more poetic, more unreachable.

And years later, when the young girl is a young woman, Hellman seems to be telling us that Lillian is still trying to make "simple sexual desire" into something complex and unreachable. Or is it just the opposite? Is she trying to interpret complex feelings about Uncle Willy—her need to defend him against her father's family—in terms of sexual desire? The reader can't be sure. In any case, when Lillian has presumably grown up and is living with Hammett—who has tried to make her admit her disapproval of Willy's past—she returns to Hannah's and Jenny's house in New Orleans. She meets Willy, who now seems old, fat, and sick, and is living in a fantasy world of non-existent wealth. He is warm and generous toward her as always, and when she discovers that he is broke and down on his luck, she agrees to go with him to Central America on a romantic expedition, not unlike the original trip to the bayou.

Willy is not painted here as attractive, and it seems unlikely, to this reader at least, that Lillian would be swept away when he touched her hand and said, "Anyway, it's time you and I finished what we started. Come on." But she is, and all that stops her is her aunts' disgust and Hammett's remark, when she calls to tell him of her plans, that she need not call him when she returns. "I'm not crazy about women who sleep with murderers." The stubborn, rebellious Lillian we have known before would have gone with Willy just because of such an ultimatum. But this time her feelings are too mixed, and she flies back to Los Angeles. But she gets even by not calling Dash. (He finds out that she is there and calls her and there is a reconciliation.)

Ambiguity and conflict are one thing; silliness is another. Hellman says she would like to think she learned from the Willy affair, but for the reader, the evidence is against her. The literary failure here may lie in her technique of "half-mocking" herself and others. When she tried it in the plays, audiences often missed the point —as in the character of Alexandra in *The Little Foxes.* When Hellman's view is clear, the characters are clear: we make no mistake about the adolescent Lillian and the young Uncle Willy. But they are the "pentimento," the underlying images which come through so strongly that they obliterate the more recent portrait; and that one— of an adult Lillian and an aging Willy—becomes hazy, and a bit smudged.

"Julia"

Hellman is as certain of her relationship to Julia, the "beloved friend" of the next portrait, as she is uncertain of that between herself and great-uncle Willy. In "Julia" there is no muddle, no ambivalence or guesswork. Here Hellman's touch is sure, and she is candid in the way that our liberated times allow her to be. The "Lillian" and "Julia" strands of plot are now inextricably interwoven with the "Lillian-Julia" relationship; the image of Julia as a person and an influence stirs at the root of feeling—

somewhere beneath consciousness—as do those of Sophronia, Helen, Hannah, and Jenny; more deeply than that of
Bethe or the male subjects of the portraits in *Pentimento*.

The incident around which "Julia" is constructed
occurred in 1937, when Hellman smuggled Julia's $50,000
across the German border, to ransom antifascists. The
episode is interrupted at a crucial moment in the action
by a long flashback into Hellman's childhood, and a forward flash to the 1970s. Then the tale of the Berlin adventure is resumed and concluded. I have told the facts
of the story in the biographical preface, above. The essence of "Julia," however, is not in that plot line, but in
the Lillian-Julia relationship, seen then and seen now, by
the speaker, "Lillian," whose image this time becomes
Hellman's own.

The friendship began in New York, when both girls
were about twelve, and Lillian's year was divided between New Orleans and New York. Julia was the daughter
of a wealthy family and would come into a fortune of her
own. To Lillian, Julia was always the intellectual superior,
mentor, and teacher; later to become a model, like Hammett, of the committed radical whom Hellman could never
be. Julia was also the more sophisticated of the two girls,
acknowledging with restraint and tact whatever was sexual
in the young Lillian's adoration. As Hellman says, the
love she had for Julia was "too strong and too complicated to be defined as only the sexual yearnings of one
girl for another. And yet certainly that was there." As
the two grew up and followed separate careers, they cor-
responded and saw each other now and then. In 1933-1934
when Julia was studying medicine in Vienna and had
been accepted as a student by Freud, Lillian was living
with Dashiell Hammett and was working on *The Children's Hour*. In correspondence Lillian asked Julia what
she thought of the title of that play, and was hurt that
Julia forgot to answer the question and continued in her
letters to warn against the terrors of Nazism, and the

coming holocaust. That message did not really get through to Lillian until she had seen Julia's own torture and death at the hands of the Nazis.

Julia's martyrdom made her another symbol of the paradoxical affirmation of life in the face of death, the "survival" of the courageous spirit, in spite of bodily mutilation, that Hellman so often celebrates in the memoirs. Julia's example, moreover, had called forth the best in Lillian—the delivery of the money demanded a nerve and courage she never knew she had. Even after death, Julia forced adulthood on her friend. Lillian had to act alone, in place of the family that disclaimed the dead, as they had the living, Julia.

And then there was the question of Julia's illegitimate child, another gesture toward life in the face of imminent death. Julia had called the child Lilly; but had never named the father, and the child was never found. But an ironic web of relationships leads Hellman to the angry realization of the father's identity and of still another terrible injustice done her friend. In a recent interview Hellman said that she had changed the names and places in "Julia" to avoid a lawsuit from Julia's family— still living. "I was really saying they had never wanted to find her baby."[2]

Hellman's anger in "Julia" is, for the most part, that of an adult. It is directed at real evil and injustice—is not just a function of purely personal jealousy or injury. She throws one typical Hellman tantrum when she slaps the face of a friend's drunken brother, for making an off-color remark about her relationship with Julia. But we discover gradually, as Lillian does, that the scandal-mongering "friend" is about to marry the father of Julia's child.

Anger, in this essay, is all that makes the suffering bearable for both Hellman and the reader. Julia was the only person who appreciated the value of Lillian's anger as a motivating force; as readers we see in it the alternative

to Lillian's dissolution—the preservative of her sanity.
When Lillian tries to tell Julia's family about her death
and is turned away from the house; when she bends over
the slashed face of the dead friend; and when she brings
the unclaimed body home for cremation instead of a
hero's funeral—Hellman's anger becomes the banner of
her own survival.

"Julia" is the high point of *Pentimento*. All its elements—plot, character, human and physical ambience—
work together to produce exciting drama, and an exciting,
if rather conventionally constructed, film. It may be
instructive, however, to read the comments of the actresses
who play Lillian and Julia.

Jane Fonda: "It's about the relationship between
two women. It's not neurotic or sexually aberrant, it's
just about two friends who care about each other tre-
mendously, who are interested in each other's growth.
There isn't any gossip or jealousy.

"The fact is that it's about a woman who is a real
heroine. It is very important to make movies about women
who grow and become ideological human beings and
totally committed people. We have to begin to put that
image into the mass culture."

Vanessa Redgrave: "Julia is very much like the title
of the book, she is an obscured character whom you can
just catch through the varnish and smoke, but you only
perceive outlines and contours. The story is really about
Lillian Hellman and how she felt about her friend. . . .
It is not remotely a political film. It is about the friendship between two women. It is not about events. The question of why tens of thousands like Julia were defeated is
not even dealt with."[3]

"Arthur W. A. Cowan"

The Broadway theater, which to Hellman had represented
hard work and struggle as she developed an instinctive

talent, seemed remote at the time of the writing of *Pentimento*. The chapter called "Theater" is a collection of
anecdotes, gossip, "chatter of failure and success," as
Hellman puts it. Most of the relevant or important material has been presented above in connection with the
plays or the biography. But the "Theater" chapter serves
as a bridge between the years of "Julia," the late thirties,
and those of the portrait of Arthur W. A. Cowan, the
sixties.

Cowan was a wealthy lawyer and longtime friend of
Hellman. Both his life and death were something of a
mystery—he created conflicting images of himself, and
the truth never quite came through to his friends. In the
retrospect of the memoirs, Hellman sees him as a kind of
sad curiosity, under all his flair and mystery—a good
potential character for a play like *The Autumn Garden*.

Arthur lives high and gives generously, even to liberal causes, although his own politics typify the worst in
American conservatism. When he flaunts his opinionated
bigotry at his liberal friends they find him "unbearable,"
but they know that he is also insecure and sensitive. He
is driven to test people's responses to him—his own type
of "range-finding." At one point, when Arthur fancies
that he has been rejected by Lillian—whom he courts on
and off—he retaliates by accusing her of caring only for
his money. This is a sore point for her—the accusation
that she could be bought. She gives way to one of her
rages, "without control, murderous," and strikes out
verbally at Arthur's sensitive areas—his looks, his aging,
his sexual prowess—and he is crushed. It is not until
much later, near the end of his life, that she watches him
go to pieces in unprovoked, unreasonable rage aimed at
no one in particular. "Something had gone wrong with
Arthur, now forever." She was no longer angry; would
never "pay him the compliment of anger" again.

If Hellman saw any similarity between her own rages
and Cowan's she does not say so; we have no hint that

she ever identifies with him. Both before and after his crackup she considered him a "man of unnecessary things," constantly driven to cover his inadequacies with a passion for luxurious novelty—new cars, new houses, new women. But Lillian is to be reminded by Helen (her black sibylline superego) that she is too unsympathetic to Arthur. Helen has accepted a gift of money and a too-small but expensive coat from Cowan, for *his* sake. She tells Lillian, "He means no harm. You never understood that." It is Helen, too, who senses that Cowan's death is imminent: "He's doing what we all must do, come soon, come late, getting ready for the summons, and you ought to put out a hand."

Hellman says she had heard "that kind of talk before" and does not want to listen, but she has to. For Dash is dying in the house—Arthur Cowan would live to settle his estate—and Helen herself was to answer the summons before long.

"Turtle"

The two final chapters, "Turtle" and "Pentimento," bring together the two major themes of the memoirs, survival and love. In *An Unfinished Woman* and in earlier chapters of this book, Hellman had continually questioned the meanings of those terms. Now they become almost synonymous. The simple human conclusion Hellman comes to is that while all our instincts of self-preservation, and all our longings propel us toward a belief in survival after death for ourselves and others, the only experience we have of such "resurrection" is that of the living—the remembrance of the dead by those who loved them. Both these chapters continue with questioning, floundering, ambivalence, sidetracking, but this is where we come out in the end, although Hellman does not say so directly. She almost never lectures; she dramatizes.

"Turtle" is the macabre, bloody—rather than "black"

—comedy, of a snapping turtle that stubbornly survived its own "death." The event goes back in time to Pleasantville, on the farm, when Hammett and Hellman try to kill a turtle that has injured one of the poodles. But even after the turtle's head has been almost severed—is hanging by a strip of skin—the reflexes keep functioning, and overnight the turtle leaves a trail of blood from the stove, on which it was supposed to be cooked, to the path leading to the lake from which it came. Lillian feels that the turtle has earned its life, and deserves a decent burial out of respect for its struggle, rather than to be cooked and eaten. Hammett resists, as always, what he considers childish superstition; he is himself an ex-Catholic and does not want to be badgered about the significance of the turtle's death, either by Lillian or by Helen, the cook, who is a Catholic convert.

Hammett's opinion becomes, in the essay, a vehicle for Hellman's "half-mockery" of herself and of her earnest but jejune philosophical questions: "What is life? Stuff like that." Hammett refuses to be a party to a funeral for a turtle he had planned to make into soup, and Lillian, with the help of a bottle of whiskey, buries the snapper herself. But some animal digs it up, and Hammett seems to have the last word when he reburies the bones under a wooden sign reading, "My first turtle is buried here. Miss Religious L.H."

This is the last word in the essay, but the real last word is Hellman's "first word" in a prologue to "Turtle," sounding a familiar motif. She has gone swimming from a boat in the sound at Martha's Vineyard. The tide separates her from her boat, and she thinks she is helplessly drifting out to sea—until she washes against a piling of a large pier. As she clings to the piling, she recalls a conversation with Hammett four days after the death of the turtle.

"You understood each other," she said. "He was a survivor and so are you. But what about me?" Hammett did not want to answer, but finally said, "I don't know, maybe you are, maybe not. What good is my opinion?" (Probably he means that no one can judge the significance of a survival except the survivor.) To the reader, Hellman adds, "Holding to the piling, I was having a conversation with a man who had been dead five years about a turtle who had been dead for twenty-six." Neither of them is dead to Hellman. Both survived, if nowhere else, in the memoirs.

So, also, with Helen, the subject of the portrait by that title in *An Unfinished Woman*—now seen again and "repainted" in the final chapter called "Pentimento." And, as usual, the essay is also a look—and a look again—at Lillian. The chapter begins immediately after the death of Hammett, when Hellman and Helen have moved to Cambridge, where the writer is to be teaching at Harvard. Hammett was supposed to have come with them, and to have stayed at a nearby nursing home. His death has been so recent, his presence so immediate, that Hellman finds herself each night walking to the nursing home, where Hammett should have been. Helen is worried about her, and she and a talented student, Jimsie, whom Helen has befriended, keep an eye on Lillian, sometimes following her on her nightly walks.

The subplot of this drama—or screenplay—has to do with the friendship between Helen and Jimsie, and with Jimsie's career. But the major plot, from the opening scene to the final curtain or fadeout, is the relationship of Lillian Hellman to "her dead"—to echo the protagonist of Henry James's tale, "The Altar of the Dead." Everybody in the book, except Jimsie, she says, is dead. "I don't want to write about Jimsie; that isn't the point here and he wouldn't like it."

But Jimsie helps her make her final point in the essay. The sequence begins when she goes to look at the nursing home for one last time and finds that Jimsie has followed her. She gazes at the building, apparently trying to come to terms with her feelings, and says aloud the word, "pentimento." When Jimsie asks what she means the only reply he receives is a scolding, "Don't follow me again, Jimsie, I don't like it."

Then Helen dies. Time passes, and Jimsie, who a few years before had taken Helen's body to South Carolina for burial, contacts Hellman in New York. They talk first about his life and his values—those of a confused, resigned, ex-radical of the 1960s student movement. They talk about Helen, and Jimsie calls her "that great, big, fine lady, doing her best in the world." Helen had once given him a coat. When he told her he could not take "presents from a working lady" she had slapped his face. Hellman said,

"You once told me you didn't understand about like or dislike."

He said, "I loved Helen."

"Too bad you never told her so. Too late now."

"I told it to her," he said, "The night I looked up your word, pentimento."

This is more than just a too-neat way to conclude the book. Jimsie understands that in life, love may not have a second chance to express itself. The only second chance is in the "pentimento" of the memory of those who survive. We remember or repaint what we want to, never mind the reality. Helen understood that, too. She had tried to talk to Hellman about death and about Hammett: "You go stand in front of that place because you think you can bring him back. Maybe he don't want to come back, and maybe you don't. . . ." she breaks off. Hellman adds, "It was a long time before I knew what she had been about to say. . . ." This must have been that Lillian actually—unconsciously—preferred the dim picture from the past, the "pentimento," to the more real and recent image of Dash.

At the end of the portrait of Hammett, Hellman had

said that she did not want to end her book on an elegiac
note. And for all the talk of death and aging in the
memoirs they are not sad, or morbid, or even nostalgic.
Hellman's devotion is to life—to questioning what it
means, if anything, and what we must be, or do, or endure in order to say we have "survived."

And for all her bad temper, *An Unfinished Woman*
and *Pentimento* are not consistently angry books: anger
is intrinsic to survival, in her terms, but so also is love.
She is not talking about "romance"—that out-of-date
term is for the "lady writers" of her generation. She
means human communication and acceptance; faulty,
partial they may be, but they give life its hope and sense
of adventure.

8

Scoundrel Time

Compared to the other memoirs, *Scoundrel Time* (1976), is a minor literary performance that elicited a major political controversy. The book is a slight one, only 155 pages, of which thirty-four are introduction by Garry Wills. The narrative itself is brief, with remembered side-lights and flashbacks. Hellman said that it had originally been part of *An Unfinished Woman*, and then "of a much longer book I've been working on for some time," but her editor persuaded her to publish it separately[1]—a wise decision.

The "time" of the title, of course, was the period of the late forties and early fifties when a "Red scare" resulted in the investigations by, among other bodies, the House Un-American Activities Committee. After enduring what were sometimes inquisitorial hearings, many people who were suspected of being communists or fellow travelers were blacklisted or cited for contempt of Congress, which could result in a prison sentence. The "scoundrels" of the title resembled the characters of Hellman's plays: they included not only the active villains, the "despoilers," like Senator McCarthy himself, but those whom Hellman accused of being *his* fellow-travellers—the "bystanders" who supported the "witch-hunt" by failing to attack McCarthy or to defend or rescue those like herself whose reputations and fortunes had been damaged. In fact,

Hellman is harder on these than she is on the senator and the various committees.

The elliptical and often ambiguous style of the other memoirs was, in those books, a legitimate medium for describing the author's personal reactions to life. Most of the characters in those books were dead; names and identities could be changed and shifted to protect the living. Moreover, those memoirs were intended as artifact, not history; accuracy was not the point. But many of the people accused in *Scoundrel Time* of being bystanders to villainy are still alive, and Hellman attacked them by name. They fought—and are still fighting—back. Their charges are based on alleged inaccuracies and omissions in Hellman's facts, and on her stance as the lonely truth-speaker.

As a literary performance, the book has a certain understated charm. It is discursive and anecdotal, less tightly constructed than the memoir chapters I have called dramatic tales. The tone is less that of anger than of disappointment and weariness that Hellman's "old, respected friends" could have been parties to injustice. But she still constructs a series of dramatic confrontations— somewhat episodic now, and sliding forward and backward in time—to build toward the climax, her appearance before the House Un-American Activities Committee in May of 1952. And in spite of her sad or wry disillusionment, the old cantankerous, hot-tempered Lillian is still the protagonist—the Southern kid now grown up, who took her values from Sophronia, including "my own liking for black people." Sophronia "was an angry woman and she gave me anger, an uncomfortable, dangerous, and often useful gift." Even in the famous letter to the Committee Hellman echoed Sophronia's plea to her not to go through life making trouble for people.

Ah, but then the irony! The first dramatic confrontation, resulting in a flareup of the famous temper, came with the serving of the summons to appear before the

Committee—served by "an over-respectable looking black man, a Sunday deacon." He politely handed Miss Hellman the envelope; she opened it and read the subpoena. "I said, 'Smart to choose a black man for this job. You like it?' and slammed the door." A white Southerner—some white Southerners—might understand her sense of betrayal. But one can only hope that this particular clerk, doing his job, understood that there was nothing racist or personal in this white-lady's rudeness. However.

After the summons, Hellman leads us through further confrontations, some friendly, some not; some spiced with anger or scorn, or humor. She had conferred about her case with lawyer friends and they recommended Joseph Rauh, a distinguished liberal attorney, who had been Chairman of the Executive Committee of Americans for Democratic Action since 1947. Rauh agreed to support her position that she was willing to tell the Committee whatever they wanted to know about her own activities, but was not willing to discuss the activities of anyone else. She and Rauh drafted the letter to the Committee, stating that she did not wish to take the Fifth Amendment, but understood that she might have to do so rather than to name other people, and "bring bad trouble" to them.

Five days before the hearing she went to Washington and holed up alone in a hotel without telling Hammett or her lawyers where she was. The next day she went shopping to build her morale, then called Hammett. During the following days she killed time—went to the museum, did more shopping, and bought an expensive designer dress and appropriate accessories for her "day in court." Through her descriptions of the sleepless nights, retrospective fears, worries, and conflicts, up to the last minute before the hearing, Hellman feeds the reader's anticipation of the courtroom scene.

Rauh was happy when the press crowded into the room. The letter had been refused in writing by the Com-

mittee the day before the hearing: witnesses could not
stipulate the terms under which they would testify. Hellman knew that she would have to take the Fifth Amendment as others had, or testify in full. The questioning
began with her past in Hollywood, and included the
accusation by Martin Berkeley (see biography, above)
that she had attended a Communist Party meeting in his
home in 1937. At this point in the questioning, Hellman
asked to have her letter to the Committee reconsidered.
The chairman, for clarification, ordered the letter read—
aloud—into the record (as well as the letter of refusal
from the Committee). Joseph Rauh was prepared with
mimeographed copies of Hellman's letter on hand, which
he passed out to the press. As the questioning continued,
and she was forced to take the Fifth on some questions,
the members of the press were reading the letter. It was
then that, according to Hellman, a voice from the press
gallery said aloud, "Thank God somebody finally had the
guts to do it."

Hellman said that this was probably the best minute
of her life. It was the high point in her account of the
hearing. She keeps it from sounding too self-congratula-
tory by her customary self-deprecation. "Many people
have said they liked what I did, but I don't much, and if
I hadn't worried about rats in jail, and such. . . ." In
any case, the Committee gave up the questioning and she
was excused from further attendance. Publication of the
letter made her a heroine to many people—indeed, the
following week, when she spoke the narration for Marc
Blitzstein's opera, *Regina*, based on *The Little Foxes*, she
was greeted with "thunderous applause" and a standing
ovation.

This is the essential narrative of *Scoundrel Time*.
It is surrounded by related memories. The hearing was
followed by the sad departure from the farm, told with a
retrospective account—not always kind—of Hellman's

acquaintance with Henry Wallace, the Progressive Party's presidential candidate, for whom she had campaigned. Then the action moves forward to 1953 when she went to Rome to do a movie for Alexander Korda. (Although she was blacklisted, it was possible for her to work outside of Hollywood.) After the movie failed to materialize, Hellman was shadowed by an American agent of the CIA. To her, that was adding insult to recent injury, and convinced her beyond doubt that there was a close connection between the national fear of communism in the fifties, on which a McCarthy could thrive, and the same fear that in later times would lead to CIA surveillance of private citizens and would be related to Watergate, "dirty tricks," and the Vietnam war.

The logic of these connections is not, however, universally acknowledged, or made clear in *Scoundrel Time*. Hellman has always insisted that politics and history are not her game; her commitments, apparently, have always been dependent upon personal experience and loyalties— to "Julia," Hammett, Raya Kopelev (her Russian guide) —rather than upon ideology or comprehensive knowledge of historical fact. Hellman's leftist leanings reflected not only her admiration of "radicals, domestic and foreign," but also her awareness of economic injustice—sharpened by her own guilt about the big money she made during the Depression from *The Children's Hour* and her screenwriting. But she left the broader aspects of history and politics to the specialists, like those who wrote her introductions: Garry Wills to the American edition of *Scoundrel Time*, and James Cameron to the English edition.

Hellman may be neither historian nor political scientist, nor logician, but her book and Wills' inflammatory introduction brought into focus a deep and irreconcilable conflict in American views of history. The conflict is not simply between the right and the left, but between factions of the intellectuals on the left. It goes back to the 1930s

when news began to leak through the iron curtain of the
crimes of the Stalinist regime in Russia—the purges, the
mock trials, the mass imprisonments. Many Marxist and
Leninist intellectuals in America abandoned the pro-
Communist position when it became clear that Stalin,
like Hitler, posed a real threat to world freedom.

Other intellectuals, however, considered that threat
to be much over-rated. They held that the Western
military-industrial establishment was the real destroyer of
liberty; that in America, the effort of this establishment
to perpetuate itself has led to unjust wars abroad and
capitalistic abuses of individual freedom at home. In the
battle over *Scoundrel Time* this view was supported by
the revisionist historians, who held with Garry Wills
(himself an ex-hardline-conservative) that it was American aggression under Truman, rather than Russian aggression under Stalin, that, by way of the Cold War,
McCarthyism, and Korea, had led to Nixon and Vietnam.
Hellman's own support of this position in *Scoundrel
Time* is done through assumptions, suggestions, and allusions to her own experience rather than through the
citation of facts. These were plentifully available in the
publications of her own Committee for Public Justice,
and might have strengthened her position.

But Hellman has always been a bit dogmatic in her
value judgements—especially if she has been personally
offended—and sometimes is carried away by the opportunity to air an old grudge. So she let fly in *Scoundrel
Time*—sometimes masking her anger under the tone, as
I have said, of sorrowful disillusionment with old friends
who belonged to the intellectual anticommunist left. These
friends included the writers and editors of most of the
literary journals, such as *Partisan Review* and *Commentary*, who, Hellman said, had not published articles attacking McCarthy or defending those people who were
attacked by him; Hollywood writers like Clifford Odets
and Elia Kazan who became "friendly witnesses"; anti-

communist intellectual leaders and critics, like Diana and Lionel Trilling.

These, and many others, were the targets of her fire, but Hellman so scattered her shot that her book seemed to some critics to be snobbish and antisemitic, or at least, in the words of *The Economist* "offensively patrician."[2]

Simply, then and now, I feel betrayed by the nonsense I had believed. I had no right to think that American intellectuals were people who would fight for anything if so doing would injure them; they have very little history that would lead to that conclusion. Many of them found in the sins of Stalin Communism—and there were plenty of sins and plenty that for a long time I mistakenly denied—the excuse to join those who should have been their hereditary enemies. Perhaps that, in part, was the penalty of nineteenth-century immigration. The children of timid immigrants are often remarkable people: energetic, intelligent, hardworking; and often they make it so good that they are determined to keep it at any cost.

When *Scoundrel Time* first came out in April of 1976 the reviews (with some exceptions) were ecstatic, and the book sailed through the spring and summer on the best-seller list for twenty-three weeks. But by the fall, Nathan Glazer had answered in *Commentary*,[3] William Phillips, in and for the *Partisan Review*.[4] Diana Trilling had had a book rejected by Little, Brown and Company because of her attack on one of its authors (Hellman)[5] and Irving Howe had answered Hellman in *Dissent*.[6] That winter the *London Times Literary Supplement* entered the fray with Richard Mayne's critique of the British edition, followed in subsequent weeks by letters pro and con.[7]

But the salvo in which war was really declared, was fired in *The New York Times* of October 3 with a review by Hilton Kramer commenting on the current interest in the period of the House Un-American Activities Committee hearings, as seen in two new movies (*The Front*

and *Hollywood on Trial*) and *Scoundrel Time*. Kramer
attacked Hellman's position and that of the revisionist
historians.

In the next two issues of the Sunday *Times*, sixteen
letters and two more columns of commentary on the
subject appeared. Opinion was divided much as I have
described the two positions above. On the whole, Hellman
came out very well; the opposition to Kramer, accusing
him of distorting history, wrote more and longer letters.
The quarrel has kept Hellman and her views in the spot-
light, and will no doubt add to public interest in any
additional memoirs to come. But her counter-attackers in
the *Scoundrel Time* debate have denied her allegations
and seriously challenged some of her facts, her veracity,
and the "persona" of herself that emerges from this book.
The debate, pro and con, still continues—from liberal
magazines, to the right-wing *National Review*, with a
scathing attack by William F. Buckley Jr.;[8] from serious
literary and aesthetic journals, to *Esquire*, with a perceptive discussion by Alfred Kazin;[9] it has even extended to
television interviews[10] and news commentary.

The argument against Hellman was perhaps best
summarized by Sidney Hook in the British magazine,
Encounter.[11] Professor Hook pointed out some of her
mistakes in fact and argued that she and her proponents
were either ignorant of the past or lacking in "historical
memory" of the political crimes of Stalinist Communism
—and were banking on a similar lapse of memory in
Hellman's readers. (This was the argument picked up by
Eric Sevareid in his news commentary of April 1, 1977,
reporting on her speech about her political past in her
presentation of Oscar Awards a few days before.)

Hellman's implicit assumption that to be anti-Communist meant to be pro-McCarthy was particularly in-
furiating to people like Diana Trilling. When her book,
We Must March My Darlings was finally published in
the summer of 1977, the passages which persuaded Little,

Brown and Company to turn it down seemed mild, indeed. But Trilling added several pages of notes contradicting Hellman and pointing out mistakes and fallacies in her arguments.[12]

Hellman's defenders on the whole, have not addressed themselves—as her attackers have—to the actual text of *Scoundrel Time*. Some have leaned heavily on argument *ad hominem*: i.e. her character and behavior; others have talked to the political issues raised by the book. Thomas R. Edwards, for example, in his review of Diana Trilling's book, defended Hellman's general position as a liberal and especially "the commitment to pride in self and loyalty to others that made Lillian Hellman's response to persecution so humanly admirable. . ."[13] Revisionist historians, however, have given strong support to Hellman's contention that the intellectuals who were anti-communist were partly responsible for the Cold War and the mentality that would ultimately sacrifice democratic liberties to government surveillance.[14]

But Hellman herself has not answered her opponents in any cogent, credible way. She claims that she was writing her personal story, not history. Some of her hostile critics have called the book "self-serving;" the character of "Lillian" too heroic, too put-upon and almost martyred, considering the comparative extent of her financial losses and persecution. But the readers who made the book a best-seller thought it was a modest understatement of heroism; that the portrait she presents is of a woman who, in evil times, stuck to her own values against odds and under pressure, and won. These values were based on a personal code of justice, decency, and loyalty to ones friends.

Just as she would not name her friends to the Committee, so Hellman did not decline to write an introduction for a friend's book that challenged her own ideological views. The book is Lev Kopelev's *To Be Preserved Forever* (Lippincott, 1977). The author is the husband of Raya, Hellman's Russian interpreter, guide, and friend of thirty-odd years. Kopelev, a distinguished scholar and writer, is a former doctrinaire Stalinist who spent ten years in Russian prison camps on various trumped-up charges. But his book is a confession that he had been deluded by Stalinist Communism and only the long imprisonment could have made him see the truth:

I came to understand that my fate, which had seemed so senselessly, so undeservedly cruel, was actually fortunate and just. It was just because I did deserve to be punished—for the many years I had zealously participated in plundering the peasants, worshipping Stalin, lying and deceiving myself in the name of "historical necessity," and teaching others to believe in lies and to bow before scoundrels.[15]

Thus Kopelev gives confirmation to the judgment of Hellman's opponents, the American anti-Communist left. Still, he was a friend—or the husband of a friend—and she introduced the book with a wary, somewhat sentimental recollection of Raya and Lev. She concluded with the footnote, "I have written these notes before Kopelev's book came from the printer. I am thus in no position to comment on it. But perhaps that is just as well. I set out to show my respect for the man."[16]

Such a value system as Hellman's, whether in the plays or the memoirs, with its clearcut criteria of good and evil, has a reassuring emotional appeal; it makes us nostalgic for a child's world (where the worst crime is to tattle on your friends) and for the make-believe world of fiction and drama, of despoilers and bystanders, where such a system flourishes. But the adult realm of politics and history demands complexities of knowledge and fact, in which value judgments are painfully arrived at. We must do more than ask Sophronia.

Lillian Hellman's insight is sharpest when it is most personal and specific. If some of her plays seem dated now it is probably because of their "well-made," realistic mode and their two-dimensional, good-or-evil character-izations. But three plays (and perhaps others) have had current repertory revivals—*The Autumn Garden*, *Toys in the Attic*, and *The Children's Hour*. These are the less structured ones, more concerned with psychology than plot, and with moral ambiguity rather than moral defini-tion.

As a memoirist, Hellman was able to present her materials dramatically, without the limitations imposed by the stage. The memoir form allowed, too, for subtlety in the exploration of character; for unanswered questions, and for a certain mysterious quality that evoked a re-sponse from readers who knew that mystery for their own.

The personal, the ambiguous, were not appropriate, however, to the politics of *Scoundrel Time*, and Hellman has taken some punishment for that mistake. But she formulated her philosophy of survival when she was four-teen: "If you are willing to take the punishment, you are halfway through the battle."

Lillian Hellman is still producing, still battling, still surviving, still performing. Whatever we may think of her politics or temperament, we must rejoice in the en-ergy, ingenuity, and skill of the performance.

Notes

I. HELLMAN IN HER TIME: A BIOGRAPHICAL PREFACE

1. Rex Reed, *Valentines and Vitriol*, (New York: Delacorte Press, 1977) p. 105.
2. Eric Bentley (ed), *Thirty Years of Treason, Excerpts from Hearings before the House Committee on Un-American Activities 1938-1968*, (New York: The Viking Press, 1971) p. 533.
3. Richard Moody, *Lillian Hellman, Playwright* (New York: Pegasus, 1972) p. 140.
4. Lillian Hellman, *The North Star: A Motion Picture about Some Russian People* (New York: The Viking Press, 1943).
5. Walter Goodman, *The Committee* (New York: Farrar, Straus & Giroux, 1968), p. 187.
6. Typical of this view is that of Nathan Glazer, one of the earliest attackers of *Scoundrel Time*: "I thought then—and I believe now—that the defense of freedom required one to expose the Communist organizers of this meeting, required one to demonstrate the obscenity of speaking of world peace under the auspices of a movement whose leaders ran a huge system of slave camps for dissenters, who extirpated even the most modest efforts at independence of mind, who just about then were executing the leading Jewish poets and writers of Russia (even though these poets and writers had served them well). What was Lillian Hellman doing in

that company?" "An Answer to Lillian Hellman," *Commentary*, 61, (June, 1976) p. 37.

7. Sen. McCarthy (R. Wisc.) made his maiden flight from obscurity to notoriety on the strength of a speech he made in 1950 alleging that the State Department was full of Communists (the number varied between 205 and 57 and "a lot") and that this fact was known to the Secretary of State. The charge—never proved—set off a series of investigations which threatened the reputations and livelihoods of thousands, in and out of government service, and ultimately succeeded in inhibiting two presidents, both of whom despised McCarthy.

8. Walter Goodman, *The Committee* (New York: Farrar, Straus & Giroux, 1968) p. 219.

9. Dr. Jerome Wiesner, "In Celebration of Lillian Hellman: Origins of the CPJ," *CPJ Newsletter* (Spring, 1976) p. 4.

10. Pat Watters and Stephen Gillers, (ed.) *Investigating the FBI*, (Garden City, N.Y.: Doubleday and Company, Inc., 1973)

     Norman Dorsen and Stephen Gillers, (ed.) *None of Your Business: Government Secrecy in America*, (New York: The Viking Press, 1974).

1. HELLMAN'S DRAMATIC MODE— "THE THEATRE IS A TRICK . . ."

1. Thomas Lask, "A Theater Event Called 'I'," *New York Times*, 4 February, 1977, p. C-3. For additional material on Theatricalist drama see John Gassner, *Directions in Modern Theatre and Drama: An Expanded Edition of Form and Idea in Modern Theatre* (New York: Holt, Rinehart, Winston, 1965) and Richard Gilman, *The Making of Modern Drama* (New York: Farrar, Straus & Giroux, 1974).

2. John Russell Taylor, *The Rise and Fall of the Well-Made Play* (New York: Hill and Wang, 1967) pp. 12, 15.

2. SIGNPOSTS

1. Burns Mantle (ed.), *The Best Plays of 1934-35* (New York: Dodd, Mead & Co., 1935). The statistics above have been compiled, not quoted, from this source.

2. For a fuller listing of plays on homosexuality in the 1920s and 30s see W. David Sievers, *Freud on Broadway* (New York: Hermitage House, 1955) pp. 93-95, 216-219.

3. Manfred Triesch, *The Lillian Hellman Collection at the University of Texas* (Austin, Texas: 1966) A-ld, quoted in Appendix, p. 102. (Hereafter cited as *Hellman Collection-University of Texas*).

4. Brooks Atkinson, "The Play: *The Children's Hour,*" *New York Times* (21 November, 1934) p. 23.

5. Eric Bentley, "Lillian Hellman's Indignation" in *The Dramatic Event: An American Chronicle* (New York: Horizon Press, 1953) pp. 49-52.

6. Christine Doudna, "A Still Unfinished Woman," *Rolling Stone* (24 February, 1977), p. 55.

7. Sam Smiley, *The Drama of Attack* (Columbia: University of Missouri Press, 1972) p. 29.

8. M. Triesch, *Hellman Collection-University of Texas* (Austin: 1966) A- 2b, p. 20.

3. THE DESPOILERS

1. These are described in *Pentimento*; the first eight are available in M. Triesch, *Hellman Collection-University of Texas* (Austin: 1966) A-3c, d, e, f, g, h, i, j, pp. 25-27.

2. Lillian Hellman, "Back of Those Foxes," *New York Times* (26 February, 1939) Sec. 10, p. 1.

3. John Phillips and Anne Hollander, "Lillian Hellman" in *Writers at Work: The 'Paris Review' Interviews,* third series, Intro. Alfred Kazin (New York: The Viking Press, 1967) p. 121.

4. Lillian Hellman, *Pentimento* (New York: Little Brown and Co., 1973) p. 148.

5. George Jean Nathan, "Dour Octopus," *Newsweek*, Vol. 13 (27 February, 1939) p. 36.

6. Elizabeth Hardwick, *"The Little Foxes* Revived," *New York Review of Books*, vol. 9 (21 December, 1967) pp. 4-5.

7. Edmund Wilson, "An Open Letter to Mike Nichols," *New York Review of Books*, vol. 9 (4 January, 1968) p. 32.

8. Brooks Atkinson, "The Play: *Another Part of the Forest,"* *New York Times* (21 November, 1946) p. 42:2.

9. Lillian Hellman, "Author Jabs the Critic," *New York Times* (15 December, 1946) sec. 2, p. 3.

10. M. Triesch, *Hellman Collection-University of Texas* (Austin: 1966) p. 40.

11. In the first printing of *Eugene O'Neill and the Tragic Tension* (New Brunswick, New Jersey: Rutgers University Press, 1958), I mistakenly attributed Ezra Mannon's death to the withholding of medicine—as in Horace's—rather than a substitution of poison for the medicine, which takes place in the O'Neill play. Even the two stricken daughters standing by, Lavinia and Alexandra, are similar.

12. Wolcott Gibbs, "This Is It," *The New Yorker*, vol. 17 (12 April, 1941), p. 32.

13. Margaret Harriman, "Miss Lily of New Orleans: Lillian Hellman" in *Take Them Up Tenderly* (New York: Alfred A. Knopf, 1945) p. 104.

4. THE BYSTANDERS

1. M. Triesch, *Hellman Collection-University of Texas* (Austin: 1966) pp. 114-116.

2. Margaret Marshall, "Drama," *The Nation*, vol. 158 (Apr. 22, 1944) p. 495.

3. John Gassner, *Theatre at the Crossroads* (New York: Holt, Rinehart, Winston, 1960) p. 136.

4. John Mason Brown, "A New Miss Hellman," *The Saturday Review*, Vol. 34 (31 March, 1951) p. 27.

5. Harry Gilroy, "Lillian Hellman Drama Foregoes A Villain," *New York Times* (25 February, 1951) sec. 2, p. 1.

6. Ibid.
7. Harold Clurman, "Lillian Hellman's Garden," *The New Republic*, 124 (26 March, 1951) p. 22.
8. Ibid.
9. I shall give these only brief mention here, but for additional comment and bibliography the student should consult the relevant chapters in Richard Moody, *Lillian Hellman, Playwright* (New York: Pegasus, 1972) and Manfred Triesch, *Hellman Collection-University of Texas* (Austin: 1966).
10. Anton Chekhov, *The Selected Letters of Anton Chekhov*, ed. Lillian Hellman, Trans. Sidonie Lederer (New York: Farrar, Straus & Co., 1955).
11. Burt Blechman, *How Much?: A Novel by B. Halpern as told to Burt Blechman.* (New York: I. Obalensky, 1961).
12. Jacob H. Adler, "Miss Hellman's Two Sisters," *Educational Theatre Journal*, 15 (May, 1963) pp. 112, 117.
13. Richard Moody, *Lillian Hellman, Playwright* (New York: Pegasus, 1972) p. 306.
14. Richard G. Stern, "Lillian Hellman on her Plays," *Contact*, Vol. 3 (1959) p. 117.
15. Alan S. Downer, *Recent American Drama* (Minneapolis: University of Minnesota Press, 1961) p. 42.

5. Form and Theme in the Memoirs— "Through This Time and That Time . . ."

1. Lacey Fosburgh, "Why More Top Novelists Don't Go to Hollywood," *New York Times*, (21 November, 1976) p. 13.
2. Stendhal (Marie-Henri Beyle) *The Life of Henry Brulard*, trans. Jean Stewart and B.C.J.G. Knight (London: The Merlin Press, 1958).

   W. B. Yeats, *The Autobiography of William Butler Yeats* (New York: Macmillan, 1966).

   Henry James, *A Small Boy and Others* (New York: Charles Scribner's Sons, 1913).

   ————, *Notes of a Son and Brother* (New York: Charles Scribner's Sons, 1914).

3. Henry James, *A Small Boy and Others* (New York: Charles Scribner's Sons, 1913) p. 3.

4. Lillian Hellman, "The Land that Holds the Legend of our Lives," *Ladies' Home Journal*, Vol. 81, (Apr. 1964) p. 57.

5. Hersey said that Hellman had "a hidden religious streak but an open hatred of piety." (John Hersey, "Lillian Hellman," *The New Republic*, 175 [18 September, 1976] p. 25).

6. Richard Poirier, "*Pentimento: A Book of Portraits by Lillian Hellman*," *The Washington Post*, Book Review Section (16 September, 1973) p. 4.

6. AN UNFINISHED WOMAN

1. Nora Ephron, "Lillian Hellman Walking, Cooking, Writing, Talking," *New York Times Book Review* (23 September, 1973) p. 2.

2. Two of Hellman's earliest publications ridicule "modern" (1933) overemphasis on sexual expression and freedom. (Lillian Hellman, "I Call Her Mama Now," *American Spectator*, vol. I (September 1933) p. 2, and "Perberty in Los Angeles," *American Spectator*, vol. II (Jan. 1934) p. 4.

3. Lillian Hellman, "I Meet the Front Line Russians," *Colliers*, vol. 11 (31 March, 1945) p. 11, 68-69.

4. N. Ephron, "Lillian Hellman Walking, etc." *New York Times Book Review* (23 September, 1972) p. 2.

5. Lillian Hellman, "Sophronia's Grandson Goes to Washington," *Ladies' Home Journal*, 80 (December, 1963) pp. 78-80.

6. In *Pentimento* the old black woman, Caroline Ducky, remarks of Hellman's mother, "Your Ma's changed. City no good for country folk, your Ma and me."

7. PENTIMENTO

1. Christine Doudna, "A Still Unfinished Woman," *Rolling Stone*, Issue 233 (24 February, 1977) p. 53.

2. Ibid., p. 54.
3. Judith Weinraub, "Two Feisty Feminists Filming Hellman's 'Pentimento'," *New York Times* (31 October, 1976) p. 17.

8. SCOUNDREL TIME

1. John F. Baker, "Lillian Hellman," *Publisher's Weekly*, vol. 209 (26 April, 1976) p. 6.
2. "Being Too Comfortable," *The Economist*, 261 (20 November, 1976) p. 140.
3. Nathan Glazer, "An Answer to Lillian Hellman," *Commentary*, 61 (June, 1976) pp. 36-39.
4. William Phillips, "What Happened in the Fifties," *Partisan Review*, 43, No. 3 (1976) pp. 337-340.
5. *New York Times* (24 September, 1976) pp. 1, 45.
6. Irving Howe, "Lillian Hellman and the McCarthy Years," *Dissent*, (Fall 1976) pp. 378-382.
7. Richard Mayne, "Ishmael and the Inquisitors," *Times Literary Supplement*, 12 November 1976, p. 1413. Letters from Diana Trilling and others, 3 December, p. 1516; 10 December, 1560; 17 December, p. 1586.
8. William F. Buckley, Jr., "Who is the Ugliest of them All?" *National Review*, 29 (21 January, 1977) pp. 101-106.
9. Alfred Kazin, "The Legend of Lillian Hellman," *Esquire*, 88 (August, 1977) pp. 28, 30, 34.
10. "Who's Who" Edition I, Show 9, March 8, 1977.
11. Sidney Hook, "Lillian Hellman's Scoundrel Time," *Encounter*, vol. 48 (February, 1977) pp. 82-91.
12. Diana Trilling, *We Must March My Darlings*, (New York and London: Harcourt, Brace, Jovanovich, 1977) 45-50.
13. Thomas R. Edwards, "A Provocative Moral Voice," *The New York Times Book Review* (29 May, 1977) p. 17.
14. Richard A. Falk, "*Scoundrel Time*: Mobilizing the Intelligentsia for the Cold War" *Performing Arts Journal*, vol. 1 (Winter, 1977) pp. 97-102.

Richard Gillam, "Intellectuals and Power," *The Center Magazine*, vol. 10 (May/June, 1977) pp. 27-28.

15. Lev Kopelev, *To Be Preserved Forever* (Philadelphia and New York: J. B. Lippincott Company, 1977) pp. 260-261.

16. Ibid. "Foreword" (unpaginated).

Bibliography

WORKS BY LILLIAN HELLMAN

1. Books

The Collected Plays. Boston-Toronto: Little, Brown and Co., 1972. The definitive text of the plays. Contents: "The Children's Hour," "Days to Come," "The Little Foxes," "Watch on the Rhine," "The Searching Wind," "Another Part of the Forest," "Montserrat," "The Autumn Garden," "The Lark," "Candide," "Toys in the Attic," "My Mother, My Father, and Me."

Four Plays. New York: Random House, 1942. Contents: Introduction by Lillian Hellman, "The Children's Hour," "Days to Come," "The Little Foxes," and "Watch on the Rhine."

Six Plays. New York: Random House, 1960. Contents: Introduction by Lillian Hellman, "Another Part of the Forest," "The Autumn Garden," "The Children's Hour," "Days to Come," "The Little Foxes," and "Watch on the Rhine."

The Children's Hour. New York: Knopf, 1934 and London: Hamish Hamilton, 1937.

Days to Come. New York and London: Knopf, 1936.

The Little Foxes. New York: Random House, and London: Hamish Hamilton, 1939.

Watch on the Rhine. New York: Random House, 1941, and London: English Theatre Guild, 1946.

The Searching Wind. New York: Viking Press, 1944.

Another Part of the Forest. New York: Viking Press, 1947.

Montserrat, adaptation of a play by Emmanuel Roblès. New
York: Dramatists Play Service, 1950.

The Autumn Garden. Boston: Little, Brown and Co., 1951.

The Lark, adaptation of a play by Jean Anouilh. New York:
Random House, 1955.

Candide, music by Leonard Bernstein, lyrics by Richard
Wilbur, John LaTouche, and Dorothy Parker, adaptation of the novel by Voltaire. New York: Random House,
1957.

Toys in the Attic. New York: Random House, 1960.

My Mother, My Father and Me, adaptation of the novel *How
Much?* by Burt Blechman. New York: Random House,
1963.

*The North Star: A Motion Picture about Some Russian Peo-
ple*. New York: Viking Press, 1943.

An Unfinished Woman: A Memoir. Boston-Toronto: Little,
Brown and Co., 1969.

Pentimento: A Book of Portraits. Boston-Toronto: Little,
Brown and Co., 1973.

Scoundrel Time with introduction by Garry Wills. Boston-
Toronto: Little Brown and Co., 1976. English edition,
Introduction by James Cameron, Commentary by Garry
Wills. London: Macmillan, 1976.

The Letters of Anton Chekhov, edited and with an introduction by Lillian Hellman. Translated by Sidonie Lederer.
New York: Farrar, Straus, 1955.

*The Big Knockover: Stories and Short Novels by Dashiell
Hammett*. Introduction by Lillian Hellman. New York:
Random House, 1966. As *The Dashiell Hammett Story
Omnibus*. London: Cassell, 1966.

2. *Articles*

"Author Jabs the Critic." *New York Times* (15 December
1946) 2, p. 3.

"Back of those Foxes." *New York Times* (26 February 1939)
10, p. 1.

"A Day in Spain." *New Republic*, 94 (13 April 1938) p. 140.

"I Call Her Mama Now." *American Spectator*, I (September
1933) p. 2.

"I Meet the Front Line Russians." *Colliers*, 11 (31 March 1945) pp. 11, 68-69.

"Interlude in Budapest." *Holiday*, 42 (November 1967) pp. 60-61.

"The Land that Holds the Legend of our Lives." *Ladies' Home Journal* 81 (April 1964) pp. 56-7, 122-24.

"Perberty in Los Angeles." *American Spectator*, II (January 1934) p. 4.

"Reports on Yugoslavia." *New York Star* (4 November, p. 13; 5 November, p. 9; 7 November, p. 8; 8 November, p. 1, 9; 9 November, p. 6; 10 November, p. 11, 1948).

"Scotch on the Rocks." *The New York Review of Books*, 1 (17 October 1963) p. 6.

"Sophronia's Grandson Goes to Washington." *Ladies' Home Journal*, 80 (December 1963) pp. 78-80.

"Plain Speaking with Mrs. Carter." *Rolling Stone* (18 November 1976) pp. 43-45.

"The Time of the Foxes." *New York Times* (22 October 1967) 2, p. 1.

Works about Lillian Hellman

1. Books

Adler, Jacob H. *Lillian Hellman*. Southern Writers Series No. 4. Austin, Texas: Steck-Vaughn Co., 1969.

Holmin, Lorena Ross. *The Dramatic Works of Lillian Hellman*. Uppsala: Almqvist & Wiksell, 1973.

Moody, Richard. *Lillian Hellman, Playwright*. New York: Pegasus, 1972.

Triesch, Manfred. *The Lillian Hellman Collection at the University of Texas*. Austin: The University of Texas Press, 1966. Descriptive bibliography.

2. Other Critical and Biographical Writings

Adler, Jacob H. "Miss Hellman's Two Sisters." *Educational Theatre Journal*, 15 (May 1963) pp. 110-117.

Atkinson, Brooks. "The Play: *The Children's Hour*." *New York Times* (21 November 1934) p. 23.

Baker, John F. "Lillian Hellman." *Publisher's Weekly*, 209 (26 April 1976) pp. 6-7.

Bentley, Eric. "Lillian Hellman's Indignation." *The Dramatic Event: An American Chronicle.* New York: Horizon Press, 1953.

——— (ed.) *Thirty Years of Treason, Excerpts from Hearings before the House Committee on Un-American Activities, 1938-1968.* New York: The Viking Press, 1971.

Buckley, William F., Jr. "Who is the Ugliest of them All?" *National Review*, 29 (21 January 1977) pp. 101-106.

Downer, Alan S. *Recent American Drama.* Minneapolis: University of Minnesota Press, 1961.

Doudna, Christine. "A Still Unfinished Woman." *Rolling Stone* (24 February 1977) pp. 53-56.

Edwards, Thomas R. "A Provocative Moral Voice." *The New York Times Book Review* (29 May 1977) pp. 1, 17.

Ephron, Nora. "Lillian Hellman Walking, Cooking, Writing, Talking." *The New York Times Book Review* (23 September 1973) pp. 2, 51.

Falk, Richard A. "*Scoundrel Time*: Mobilizing the Intelligentsia for the Cold War." *Performing Arts Journal*, 1 (Winter 1977) pp. 97-102.

Feldheim, Marvin. "*The Autumn Garden*: Mechanics and Dialectics." *Modern Drama*, 3 (September 1960) pp. 191-195.

Gassner, John. *Theatre at the Crossroads.* New York: Holt, Rinehart, Winston, 1960.

Glazer, Nathan. "An Answer to Lillian Hellman." *Commentary*, 61 (June 1976) pp. 36-39.

Goldstein, Malcolm. *The Political Stage: American Drama and Theater in the Great Depression.* New York: Oxford University Press, 1974.

Harriman, Margaret Case. "Miss Lily of New Orleans: Lillian Hellman." *Take Them Up Tenderly.* New York: Alfred A. Knopf, 1945.

Howe, Irving. "Lillian Hellman and the McCarthy Years." *Dissent* (Fall 1976) pp. 378-382.

Kazin, Alfred. "The Legend of Lillian Hellman." *Esquire*, 88 (August 1977) pp. 28, 30, 34.

Mantle, Burns (ed). *The Best Plays of 1934-35*. New York: Dodd, Mead and Co., 1935. (Other volumes appropriate to dates of Hellman's plays are also useful and are cited in footnotes.)

Meehan, Thomas. "Q: Miss Hellman, What's Wrong with Broadway? A: It's a Bore." *Esquire*, 58 (December 1962) pp. 140, 142, 235-236.

Moyers, Bill. "Lillian Hellman; The Great Playwright Candidly Reflects on a Long, Rich Life," The Center for Cassette Studies 36648-1974.

Phillips, John and Hollander, Anne. "Lillian Hellman" in *Writers at Work: The Paris Review Interviews*, Third Series. Introduction by Alfred Kazin. New York: The Viking Press, 1967.

Phillips, William. "What Happened in the Fifties." *Partisan Review*, 43 (1976) pp. 337-340.

Poirier, Richard. *"Pentimento: A Book of Portraits* by Lillian Hellman." *The Washington Post* Book Review Section (16 September 1973) pp. 1, 4, 5.

Reed, Rex. *Valentines and Vitriol*. New York: Delacorte Press, 1977.

Sievers, W. David. *Freud on Broadway*. New York: Hermitage House, 1955.

Smiley, Sam. *The Drama of Attack*. Columbia: University of Missouri Press, 1972.

Stern, Richard G. "Lillian Hellman on her Plays." *Contact*, 3 (1959) pp. 113-119.

Trilling, Diana. *We Must March my Darlings*. New York and London: Harcourt, Brace, Jovanovich, 1977.

Weales, Gerald. *American Drama Since World War II*. New York: Harcourt, Brace and World, Inc., 1962.

Weinraub, Judith. "Two Feisty Feminists Filming Hellman's 'Pentimento.'" *New York Times* (31 October 1976) p. 17.

MODERN LITERATURE MONOGRAPHS

In the same series (continued from page ii)